F. (Franz) Swediaur

The philosophical Dictionary

Or, The Opinions of modern Philosophers on metaphysical, moral, and political

Subjects - Vol. I

F. (Franz) Swediaur

The philosophical Dictionary
Or, The Opinions of modern Philosophers on metaphysical, moral, and political Subjects - Vol. I

ISBN/EAN: 9783337069797

Printed in Europe, USA, Canada, Australia, Japan

Cover: Foto ©ninafisch / pixelio.de

More available books at **www.hansebooks.com**

THE PHILOSOPHICAL DICTIONARY:

OR, THE OPINIONS OF MODERN PHILOSOPHERS ON METAPHYSICAL, MORAL, AND POLITICAL SUBJECTS.

IN FOUR VOLUMES.

VOL. I.

LONDON:
PRINTED FOR G. G. J. AND J. ROBINSON;
AND
FOR C. ELLIOT, EDINBURGH.
M,DCC,LXXXVI.

PREFACE.

THE following Work is compiled from the writings of the most eminent philosophers in Europe. It was undertaken originally with no other view but to serve as a Common-place Book for private use. If the publication of it can add to the amusement of travellers who carry few books with them, or satisfy the curiosity of those who cannot purchase many books, or have little time to read them, it will answer every purpose the editor could expect.

There are some articles in it which have been the subject of controversy amongst ancient as well as modern philosophers: on these subjects, the arguments on both sides of the question are, in general, extracted for the satisfaction of the reader. If the work meet the approbation of the Public, the defects of it may be amended in a Supplement or future Edition.

A love of truth, and warm wishes for its diffusion, under respectable authorities, were the sole objects of the editor in this publication.

LONDON,
January 1786.

F. S*******R, M. D.

Entered in Stationers Hall.

CONTENTS

OF THE

FIRST VOLUME.

	Page
ABSURDITY laughs at folly	13
ADMIRATION and Acquaintance incompatible	14
ADULTERY, and its punishment	15
ADVICE	17
On the same subject	18
AMBITION	24
ATTACHMENT (our) and esteem for others depend on the analogy of their ideas to our own	25

Contents.

	Page
ANIMALS (the origin of the inferiority of to man)	28
ANIMALS (the reason of)	31
ARTS and Sciences (free governments alone favourable to the rise of)	33
ASSASINATION of Princes	34
ASSENT derived from testimony and experience	35
ASSENT to be regulated by the ground of probability	37
ASSOCIATION of ideas	40
ASSOCIATION of ideas (a general view of Hartley's doctrine of)	41
ASSURANCE	48
ATHEISM	50
On the same subject	51
On the same subject	54
ATHEISM and superstition	55
ATHEISTS and Theists (the disputes between) verbal	56
AVARICE	58
On the same subject	59
BANKRUPTCY (national)	61
BEASTS	66
BEAUTY and BEAUTIFUL	69

	Page
BEING (a cogitative) has existed from eternity	70
BELIEF	74
On the same subject	76
On the same subject	78
BELIEF or DISBELIEF	82
BENEFICENCE	84
BENEFICENCE and gratitude	85
BIGOTRY (religious)	86
BLACKNESS (the effects of)	87
CALVINISTIC Divinity	91
CAUSE and effect	94
CAUSE (existence of a first)	95
CERES ELEUSINA (mysteries of)	97
On the same subject	101
CERTAINTY	104
CHAIN of events	105
CHANCE and Causes	107
CHARACTER	109
CHARACTERS (national)	110
CHARACTER (dignity of)	111
CHARLES I. (punishment of)	115
CHASTITY (the merit of) derived from its utility	117
CHILDREN (the different capacities of)	119
CHRISTIAN religion, its progress and establishment in the Roman empire	121

CHRI-

Contents.

	Page
CHRISTIANITY, not adapted to make a constitutional part in any system of legislation.	124
CIVIL commotions	127
CLIMATES (the difference of men in different)	128
CLIMATE (the influence of) on mankind	132
CLIMATE (the influence of)	133
COMMERCE favourable to civilization and peace	134
CONSCIENCE	135
On the same subject	139
CONSCIENCE (liberty of)	143
CONTEMPT	144
CONTROVERSY	145
CONTROVERSIES (religious)	ib.
CONVERSATION	150
On the same subject	ib.
CORN (exportation of)	152
COUNTRY	154
CORRUPTION (religious and political)	156
COURTEZANS	158
CREATION	160
CREDULITY and authority	162
CRIMES (degrees of)	163
CRIMES (evidence of)	164
CRIMES and punishments (the proportion between)	166

CROWN.

                                                        Page
CROWN (influence of the) in the British Parliament - - 167
CUSTOMS (the origin of barbarous and ridiculous) in various ages and nations 168

DARKNESS (Locke's opinion concerning) considered - - - 173
DEITY - - - 178
On the same subject - - 182
DEITY (idea and belief of) not innate 183
DEITY (worship of) - - 184
DELICACY of taste and of passion - 185
DELIRIUMS - - 188
DELUGE - - - 190
DESTINY - - - 192
DISCRETION - - - 194
DIVISIBILITY of matter - - 195
DIVORCE and repudiation - 197
DOTAGE - - 199
DREAMS - - - 200
DRESS (female) - - - 202
DURATION - - - 203

ECCLESIASTICAL power and its influence 206

Ec-

	Page
ECCLESIASTICAL (the advantage of uniting the civil and) powers	220
ECONOMY	ib.
EDUCATION	222
On the fame fubject	223
On the fame fubject	225
On the fame fubject	227
EDUCATION (a comparative view of ancient and modern)	229
EDUCATION (attention to the) of the common people, incumbent upon the public	240
EMPIRE (caufes of the decadency of)	253
ENGLAND (conftitution of)	258
ENGLISH conftitution (abufes in the)	261
ENNUI,	263
ENTHUSIASM	265
EQUALITY	267
On the fame fubject	268
On the fame fubject	269
On the fame fubject	ib.
ESTABLISHMENTS for the religious inftruction of the people	272
EVIDENCE	284
EVIDENCE (hiftorical)	285
EVIL (the origin of)	286
EVIL (natural and moral)	289
EXPERIENCE (difcovery of)	300

Ex-

	Page
EXPERIENCE (the foundation of all conclusions from)	303
EXTERNAL objects (the existence of) only probable	309
FABULOUS stories (difficulty of detecting)	311
FACT (matters of) not demonstratively certain	312
FACT (nature of our reasonings concerning matters of)	313
FAITH	314
On the same subject	318
FAITH and reason	ib.
FAME	319
FAME (origin of the love of)	320
FANATICISM	321
FANATICISM (the punishment of)	323
FILIAL affection	324
FINAL causes	325
FLATTERY	327
FRIENDSHIP	328
On the same subject	329
FUTURE punishments	334
FUTURE rewards and punishments	335
FUTURE state	336

G.

	Page
GALLANTRY	338
GENIUS	340
GOD	342
On the same subject	348
GOOD (the prevalence of) over evil	352
GOVERNMENT (the difference between a free and a despotic)	353
GOVERNMENT (resistance to)	354
On the same subject	358
GOVERNMENT (civil)	363
GOVERNMENT	364
On the same subject	367
GOVERNMENT (principles of)	ib.

THE
PHILOSOPHICAL
DICTIONARY.

A.

ABSURDITY LAUGHS AT FOLLY.

THE Duke of Lorrain gave a grand entertainment to his whole court. The supper was served up in a vestibule, which opened on a parterre. In the midst of the supper a lady thought she saw a spider: she was seized with fear, screamed out, left the table, fled into the garden, and fell down on the grass. At the moment of her fall she heard somebody near her; this was the Duke's prime minister. " O, " Sir," said she, " you give me spirits; how " much am I obliged to you! I was afraid I "had been guilty of impertinence." "O, Madam! who could stay there?" replied the minister.—"But tell me, was it a very large one?" "Dear Sir, it was quite frightful." "Did it fly near me?" added he. "What do you mean? The spider fly?" "How!" returned he, "is it only for a spider that you make all this to do? Go, Madam, you are very weak; I thought it had been a bat." This fact is the history of all mankind; whatever we have that is ridiculous, we always conceal from ourselves, we only perceive it in others. In this world it is always absurdity that laughs at folly. HELVETIUS.

ADMIRATION AND ACQUAINTANCE INCOMPATIBLE.

"NO man," said the Prince de Condé, "is a hero," to his *valet de chambre*. It is certain, that admiration and acquaintance are altogether incompatible towards any mortal creature. Sleep and love convinced even Alexander himself that he was not a god: but I suppose, that such as attended him daily could easily, from the numberless weaknesses to which he was subject, have given him many still more convincing proofs of his humanity. HUME.

ADUL-

ADULTERY, AND ITS PUNISHMENT.

ADULTERY is a crime which, politically considered, owes its existence to two causes, viz. Pernicious laws, and the powerful attraction between the sexes. This attraction is similar in many circumstances to gravity, the spring of motion in the universe. Like this, it is diminished by distance; one regulates the motion of the body, the other that of the soul. But they differ in one respect: the force of gravity decreases in proportion to the obstacles that oppose it; the other gathers strength and vigour as the obstacles increase.——Adultery proceeds from an abuse of that necessity which is constant and universal in human nature; a necessity anterior to the formation of society: whereas, all other crimes tend to the destruction of society, and arise from momentary passions, and not from a natural necessity. It is the opinion of those who have studied history and mankind, that this necessity is constantly in the same degree in the same climate. If this be true, useless or rather pernicious must all laws and customs be which tend to diminish the sum total of the effects of this passion; such laws would only burden one part of the society with the additional necessities of the other: but, on the contrary, wise are the laws which, following the natural course of the river, divide the stream into a number of equal branches,

preventing thus both sterility and inundation.——
Conjugal fidelity is always greater in proportion
as marriages are more numerous and less difficult.
But when the interest or pride of families, or paternal authority, not the inclination of the parties,
unite the sexes, gallantry soon breaks the slender
ties, in spite of common moralists, who exclaim
against the effect, whilst they pardon the cause.
———The act of adultery is a crime so instantaneous, so mysterious, and so concealed by the veil
which the laws themselves have woven, a veil necessary indeed, but so transparent as to heighten
rather than conceal the charms of the object; the
opportunities so frequent, and the danger of discovery so easily avoided; that it were much easier
for the laws to prevent this crime, than to punish
it when committed.———To every crime which
from its nature must frequently remain unpunished, the punishment is an incentive. Such is
the nature of the human mind, that difficulties,
if not insurmountable, nor too great for our natural indolence, embellish the object, and spur us
on to the pursuit; they are so many barriers that
confine the imagination to the object, and oblige
us to consider it in every point of view. In this
agitation the mind naturally inclines and fixes itself to the most agreeable part, studiously avoiding
every idea that might create disgust. BECCARIA.

ADVICE.

IS a man to be turned aside from an imprudent and dangerous action, and does humanity undertake to give him advice in the affair? It operates on his vanity; it shows him the truth, but in expressions the least offensive, and at the same time softens the most severe parts of it by tone and gesture.——Severity speaks bluntly: malignity in a manner the most mortifying.

Pride commands imperiously; it is deaf to all reply; it will be obeyed without hesitation.

Reason examines with the man the sagacity of his actions, hears his reply, and submits to the judgment of those it concerns.

Amity, full of tenderness for his friend, contradicts him with regret: if he be not able to persuade, he has recourse to prayers and tears, and conjures him by the sacred bond that unites their happiness, not to expose himself to so dangerous an action.

Love takes another tone; and to combat the resolution of her admirer, alleges no other arguments than her pleasure and her love; if those fail, she at last condescends to reason, for reason is always the last resource of love.——One may, therefore, discover the sort of character or passion our advisers are possessed with, by the manner in which the advice is given. But has deceit a peculiar language? No; the knave borrows sometimes

times that of friendship, and is to be discovered by the difference there is between the sentiments he affects, and those he ought to have.

Different passions and different characters have different languages. HELVETIUS.

ON THE SAME SUBJECT.

EVERY man whom we consult always believes that his counsel is dictated by friendship. He says so; most men believe him on his word, and their blind confidence often leads them into error. It would, however, be very easy to undeceive ourselves in this particular; for we love but few people, and would advise all the world. From whence does this madness of giving advice derive its source? From our vanity. Most men have the folly to believe themselves wise, and much more so than their neighbours; and therefore they are pleased with every thing that confirms this opinion. Whoever consults us, is agreeable to us; for this is a confession of an inferiority which flatters our vanity. Besides, what opportunities does our being consulted give us to display our maxims, our ideas, and our sentiments, to talk much of ourselves, and to our own advantage! Thus there is nobody who does not take advantage of it. More employed about the interest of our vanity than about the interest of the person who comes to consult us, he commonly

leaves

leaves us without being instructed or enlightened; and our counsels have been our own panegyric. Thus our advice is almost constantly dictated by vanity, and hence we would correct all the world.

In the case of ignorance, there is no doubt but advice may be very useful: a physician, a counsellor, a philosopher, and a politician, may each in their separate professions give excellent advice. In every other case it is useless, and often very ridiculous; because people in general always propose themselves for a model.——Let an ambitious man consult a person of moderate passions, and propose to him his views and projects: Abandon them, the latter will say; do not expose yourself to dangers and vexations without number, but amuse yourself in tranquillity and peace. To this the ambitious man will reply, If I had still my choice to make, I might follow your advice; but my passions are fixed, my character formed, and my habits settled: I would make the best of them, so as to promote my own happiness; and upon this point I would consult you. In vain would he add, that the character being once formed, it is impossible to change it; that the pleasures of a man of moderate desires are insipid to one filled with ambition: whatever he alleged, the man of moderate passions would constantly repeat, Be not ambitious. The physician may as well say to his patient,

tient, Sir, do not have a fever.——Old men constantly use the same language. When a young man consults them in regard to the conduct he ought to observe: Fly, say they, plays, operas, balls, the assemblies of women, and every frivolous amusement; imitate us, and employ yourself entirely about making your fortune. But the young man will reply, I am still fond of pleasure, I love women to distraction; how then shall I renounce them? You must be sensible that at my age this pleasure is an appetite. Whatever he can say, an old man will never comprehend that the enjoyment of a woman is so necessary to the happiness of a young man. Every sensation which we do not experience, we cannot allow to exist: The old man no longer seeks pleasure, and pleasure no longer seeks him: the objects with which he was incessantly employed in his youth, insensibly retire from his sight. Whoever considers the ardour with which men propose themselves for models, may imagine that he sees a number of persons swimming upon a great lake, and being carried by different currents, lift up their heads above the water, crying to each other, It is me you must follow, and there you must land. Held fast by chains of brass, fixed to a rock, the wise man contemplates their folly, crying, Do you not see, that drawn by different currents, you cannot land at the same place? To advise a man to

say

say this, or to do that, is commonly nothing more than, I would act in that manner, or I would speak thus. The passage in Moliere, *You are a goldsmith, Master Josse,*—applied to the pride of setting ourselves up for an example, is more general than is imagined. There is not a blockhead but would take upon himself to direct the conduct of the man of the greatest genius. The chief of the Natches, every morning at the rising of Aurora, walks out of his cabbin, and marks out for the sun, his brother, the course he is to take.——But, say you, the man who is consulted may doubtless be under an illusion, and attribute to friendship what is only the effect of vanity. But how can this illusion pass upon him who consults him? Why is not he enlightened by his own interest? It is because he readily believes that others take an interest in his concerns, which they really do not; because most men are weak, and not being able to conduct themselves, they have occasion for others to mark out their conduct; and it is very easy, as observation proves, to communicate to such a person the high opinion the adviser has of himself. This is not the case with a man of sense: if he consults, it is because he is ignorant of a particular matter; he knows that in every other case, and especially in what relates to his own happiness, he ought to consult none but his own judgment. In fact, if the propriety of advice depends

pends upon an exact knowledge of the circumstances in which those whom we advise are placed, to whom can a man apply better than to himself? Who knows whether, on the character being formed, and the habits fixed, each person is not able to conduct himself as well as possible, even though he should appear a fool? Every body knows the answer of a famous oculist: A countryman went to consult him, and found him sitting at table, eating and drinking heartily: " What must I do for my eyes?" said the peasant. " You must abstain from wine," replied the oculist. " But it seems to me," returned the peasant, walking up nearer to him, " that your eyes are not much better than mine, " and yet you drink." " Truly," replied the oculist, " that is because I am fonder of drinking " than of being cured." How many men are there like this oculist, whose happiness depends on passions that must plunge them in the greatest misery; and yet, however, if I may venture to say so, would be fools, did they endeavour to be more wise! There are men, and experience has shown that they are pretty numerous, who are so miserable, they can no otherwise be happy than by performing actions that lead to the grave. If, as Pascal says, habit is a second, and perhaps a first nature, it must be acknowledged that a bad habit once confirmed, will last as long as life. But it

may

may be anfwered, There are alfo men who, for want of wife advice, daily commit the groffeft faults; and good advice doubtlefs might make them efcape their misfortunes. To which it is replied, that they would commit more confiderable ftill, if they gave themfelves up inconfiderately to the counfels of others. Whoever blindly follows them muft obferve a conduct full of inconfiftences, commonly more fatal than the excefs even of the paffions.——Inconfiderate advice precipitates us too often into the abyfs of misfortune. Hence we ought often to call to mind this faying of Socrates : " May I," fays that philofopher, " always be on my guard againft my mafters and " my friends, conftantly preferve my foul in a " tranquil ftate, and obey none but reafon, the " beft of counfellors!" Whoever hears reafon, is not only deaf to bad counfel, but alfo weighs in the balance of doubt the advice even of thofe men who are refpectable by their age, their dignity, and their merit, yet confider themfelves as of too much importance, and, like the hero of Cervantes, have a corner of folly to which they would bring every thing.——If advice be ever ufeful, it is when it puts us in a condition to judge better for ourfelves: if it be prudent to afk it, it is only fo when it is afked of thofe wife men who, knowing the value and fcarcity of good counfel, are very frugal in giving it. In fact, in order to give fuch as will be of use, it requires the greatest care to dive into the character of the man. What knowledge is necessary for the adviser to have of his taste, his inclinations, the sensations by which he is animated, and the feelings by which he is affected? What skill to foresee the faults he would commit, and the circumstances in which he may be placed by fortune; and to judge in consequence of this, whether the fault he would correct, would not be changed into a virtue in the station in which he will probably be placed? These are the difficulties which render the wise so reserved on the article of giving advice. Thus it is only of those, who scarce ever give any, that we ought to demand it. All other counsels may be justly suspected. HELVETIUS.

AMBITION.

Those great objects of self-interest, of which the loss or acquisition quite changes the rank of the person, are the objects of the passion properly called Ambition; a passion which, when it keeps within the bounds of prudence and justice, is always admired in the world, and has even sometimes a certain irregular greatness which dazzles the imagination when it passes the limits of both these virtues, and is not only unjust but extravagant. Hence the general admiration for heroes and conquerors, and even for statesmen, whose projects have been very daring and extensive, tho' altogether devoid of justice; such as those of the Cardinals of Richelieu and of Retz. The objects of avarice and ambition differ only in their greatness. A miser is as furious about a halfpenny, as the man of ambition about the conquest of a kingdom.   A. SMITH.

Our ATTACHMENT AND ESTEEM FOR OTHERS DEPEND ON THE ANALOGY OF THEIR IDEAS TO OUR OWN.

EVERY idea offered to us, has always some regard to our stations, passions, or opinions. Now, in all these several cases we value an idea in proportion to its use. The pilot, the physician, and the engineer, will have more regard for a shipwright, a botanist, and mechanic, than a bookseller, a goldsmith, and a mason will have for the same persons; they always preferring to them the novelist, the designer, and the architect.—With regard to ideas proper for opposing or countenancing our passions or our taste, we shall doubtless account those the most valuable which most flatter those passions or tastes. A woman of an amorous complexion will place a greater value on a romance than on a metaphysical treatise: A person of the character of Charles XII. will prefer

fer the history of Alexander to every other work: and, certainly, the miser will perceive understanding only in those who shall inform him where to place his money at the highest interest. On the analogy of ideas is founded also the strong attraction between persons of genius; that attraction which as it were forces them to seek the acquaintance of each other, notwithstanding the danger that often attends their intercourse from their common thirst of fame: hence that sure way of judging of a person's temper and understanding by his choice of books and friends. The fool has only fools for his companions: every connexion of friendship, when not founded on an interest of *decency, love, protection, avarice, ambition, or some other similar motive,* always supposes between men some resemblance of ideas or sentiments. It is this that brings together persons of very different conditions: on this account it was that Augustus, Mæcenas, Scipio, Julian, Richelieu, and Condé, lived familiarly with men of genius; and hence the well known proverb, the truth of which is confirmed by its frequent use, *Show me your company, and I will show you the man.*—Thus the analogy or conformity of ideas is to be considered as the attractive and repulsive force which separates men or draws them nearer to one another. The desire of esteem is common to all men; though some, to the pleasure of being

ing admired, will add the merit of contemning admiration: but this contempt is not real, the person admired never thinking the admirer stupid. Now if all men are fond of esteem, every one knowing from experience that his ideas will appear estimable or contemptible to others only as they agree or clash with their own; the consequence is, that, swayed by vanity, every one cannot help esteeming in others a conformity of ideas, which assure him of their esteem; and hating in them an opposition of ideas, as a certain indication of their hatred, or at least of their contempt, which is to be considered as a corrective of hatred. —How can we forbear having the highest ideas of ourselves? Every man changes his opinions as soon as he believes that those opinions are false. Every one therefore believes that he thinks justly, and consequently much better than those whose ideas are contrary to his own. Now, if there are not two men who think exactly alike, it must necessarily follow, that each in particular believes that his sentiments are more just than those entertained by all the rest of mankind. The Duchess de la Ferte said one day to Madam de Stahl, " I must confess, my dear friend, that I find no- " body always in the right but myself." Let us hear the Talopins, the Bonzes, the Bramins, the Guebres, the Imans, and the Marabouts, when they preach against each other in the assembly of the multitude, does not each of them say, like the Duchess de la Ferte, Ye people, I assure you that I alone am always in the right? Each then believes that he has a superior understanding; and the fools are not the persons who are the least sensible of it.—Our esteem is so dependent on this conformity of ideas, that nobody can attentively examine himself without perceiving that in all the minutes of a day he does not afford the same person exactly the same degree of esteem. Thus we see the reason why people form themselves into different societies: there is scarcely a man so stupid, but if he pays a certain attention to the choice of his company, may spend his life amidst a concert of praises uttered by sincere admirers; while there is not a man of sense who, if he promiscuously joins indifferent companies, will not be successively treated as a fool and a wise man, as agreeable and tiresome, as stupid and a man of genius. HELVETIUS.

The Origin of the Inferiority of Animals to Man.

1. ALL the feet of animals terminate either in horn, as those of the ox and the deer; or in nails, as those of the dog and the wolf; or in claws, as those of the lion and the cat. Now this different organisation of the feet of animals from that of our hands,

hands, deprives them, as Mr Buffon afferts, not only of all claim to the fenfe of the touch, but alfo of the dexterity requifite in handling an inftrument, in order to make any of the difcoveries which fuppofe the ufe of hands.—2. The life of animals, in general, being of a fhorter duration than that of man, neither permits them to make fo many obfervations, nor confequently to acquire fo many ideas.—3. Animals being better armed and better clothed by nature than the human fpecies, have fewer wants, and confequently ought to have lefs invention. If the voracious animals are more cunning than others; it is becaufe hunger, ever inventive, infpires them with the art of forming ftratagems to furprife their prey.—4. The animals compofe only a fociety that flies from man; who by the affiftance of weapons made by himfelf, is become formidable to the ftrongeft among them. —Befides, man is the moft fruitful animal upon earth: He is born and lives in every climate; while many of the other animals, as the lion, the elephant, and the rhinoceros, are found only in a certain latitude: And the more a fpecies of animals capable of making obfervations is multiplied, the more ideas and genius it poffeffes.—But fome may afk, why monkeys, whofe paws are nearly as dexterous as our hands, do not make a progrefs equal to that of man? Becaufe they are inferior to him in feveral refpects; becaufe men are more

mul-

multiplied on the earth; becaufe, among the different fpecies of monkeys, there are but few whofe ftrength can be compared to that of man; becaufe the monkeys being frugivorous, have fewer wants, and therefore lefs invention than man; becaufe their life is fhorter, and they form only a fugitive fociety with regard to man, and fuch animals as the tyger, the lion, &c.; and, finally, becaufe the organical difpofition of their body, keeps them, like children, in perpetual motion, even after their defires are fatisfied. Monkeys are not fufceptible of laffitude; which ought to be confidered as one of the principles of the perfection of the human mind.—By combining all thefe differences between the nature of man and beaft, we may underftand why fenfibility and memory, though faculties common to man and other animals, are in the latter only fterile faculties.—If nature, inftead of hands and flexible fingers, had terminated our wrift with the foot of a horfe, mankind would doubtlefs have been totally deftitute of art, habitation, and defence againft other animals. Wholly employed in the care of procuring food, and avoiding the beafts of prey, they would have ftill continued wandering in the forefts like fugitive flocks. It is therefore evident, that according to this hypothefis the police would never have been carried in any fociety to that degree of perfection to which it is now arrived. There is

not

not a nation now exifting, but, with regard to the action of the mind, muft have continued very inferior to certain favage nations, who have not two hundred different ideas, nor two hundred words to exprefs thofe ideas; and whofe language muft confequently be reduced, like that of animals, to five or fix different founds or cries, if we take from it the words bow, arrow, nets, &c. which fuppofe the ufe of hands. From whence I conclude, that without a certain exterior organifation, fenfibility and memory in us would prove two fterile faculties. HELVETIUS.

THE REASON OF ANIMALS.

IT feems evident, that animals as well as men learn many things from experience, and infer that the fame events will follow, from the fame caufes. By this principle they become acquainted with the more obvious properties of external objects, and gradually, from their birth, treafure up a knowledge of the nature of fire, water, earth, ftones, heights, depths, &c. and of the effects which refult from their operation. The ignorance and inexperience of the young are here plainly diftinguifhable from the cunning and fagacity of the old, who have learned, by long obfervation, to avoid what hurts them, and to purfue what gives eafe and pleafure. A horfe accuftomed to the field

field will not attempt what exceeds his force or ability. An old greyhound will truſt the more fatiguing part of the chace to the younger, and will place himſelf ſo as to meet the hare in her doubles; this ſagacity is founded on obſervation and experience.——This is ſtill more evident from the effects of diſcipline and education on animals; who, by the proper application of rewards and puniſhments, may be taught any courſe of action moſt contrary to their natural inſtincts and propenſities. Is it not experience which renders a dog apprehenſive of pain, when you menace him, or lift up the whip to beat him? Is it not experience which makes him anſwer to his name? It is cuſtom alone which engages animals, from every object that ſtrikes their ſenſes, to infer its uſual attendant, and carries their imagination from the appearance of one to expect the other.——But though animals learn much of their knowledge from obſervation, they derive alſo much from the original hand of nature; which greatly exceeds their ſhare of capacity on ordinary occaſions, and in which they improve little or nothing by the longeſt practice and experience. Theſe we call *inſtincts*.

HUME.

FREE

Free Governments alone favourable to the Rise of the Arts and Sciences.

Though a republic fhould be barbarous, it neceffarily, by an infallible operation, gives rife to law, even before mankind have made any confiderable advances in the other fciences. From law arifes fecurity; from fecurity curiofity; and from curiofity knowledge. The latter fteps of this progrefs may be more accidental: but the former are altogether neceffary. A republic without laws can never have any duration. On the contrary, in a monarchical government, law arifes not neceffarily from the forms of government. Monarchy, when abfolute, contains even fomething repugnant to law. Great wifdom and reflection can alone reconcile them. But fuch a degree of wifdom can never be expected, before the great refinements of human reafon. Thefe refinements require curiofity, fecurity, and law. The firft growth, therefore, of the arts and fciences can never be expected in defpotic governments.——There are other caufes which difcourage the rife of the refined arts in defpotic governments; though the want of laws, and the delegation of full powers to every petty magiftrate, feem to be the principal. Eloquence certainly fprings up more naturally in popular governments: emulation, too, in every accomplifhment, must there be more animated and enlivened; and genius and capacity have a fuller scope and career. All these causes render free governments the only proper nursery for the arts and sciences.

HUME.

ASSASSINATION of PRINCES.

The maxim, which forbids assassination in every case whatever, is the result of prudent reflection, and has a tendency to allay the jealousy, and to mitigate the cruelty, of persons who, by violent usurpations which laws cannot restrain, have incurred the resentment of mankind. Even tyrants, it is supposed, are cruel from fear, and become merciful in proportion as they believe themselves secure: it were unwise, therefore, to entertain maxims which keep the powerful in a continual state of distrust and alarm. This prudential morality, however, was entirely unknown in the ancient republics, or could not be observed without surrendering the freedom for which the citizens contended. Amongst them the people were obliged to consider, not what was safe, but what was necessary; and could not always defend themselves against usurpations, neither by legal forms, nor by open war. It was thought allowable, therefore, to employ artifice, surprise, and secret conspiracy, against an usurper. And this was

was so much the case at Rome, that no names were held in greater veneration than those of citizens who had assassinated persons suspected of views dangerous to the commonwealth, or who by any means whatever rendered abortive the projects of adventurers who attempted to arm any party against the legal constitution of their country. The sacrifice of Cæsar to the just indignation of his country, was a striking example of what the arrogant have to fear in trifling with the feelings of a free people; and at the same time a lesson of jealousy and of cruelty to tyrants, or an admonition not to spare in the exercise of their power those whom they have insulted by usurping it.

FERGUSON.

ASSENT DERIVED FROM TESTIMONY AND EXPERIENCE

In things that happen indifferently, as that a bird should fly this or that way, that it should thunder on a man's right or left hand, &c. when any particular matter of fact is vouched by the concurrent testimony of unsuspected witnesses, there our assent is unavoidable. Thus, that there is such a city in Italy as Rome; that about one thousand seven hundred years ago, there lived in it a man called Julius Cæsar; that he was a general, and that he won a battle against another called Pompey.

pey; this, though in the nature of the thing there be nothing for nor againſt it, yet being related by hiſtorians of credit, and contradicted by no one writer, a man cannot avoid believing it; and can as little doubt of it, as he does of the being and actions of his own acquaintance, whereof he himſelf is a witneſs.

Thus far the matter goes on eaſy enough. Probability upon ſuch grounds carries ſo much evidence with it, that it naturally determines the judgment, and leaves us as little liberty to believe or diſbelieve, as a demonſtration does, whether we will know or be ignorant. The difficulty is when teſtimonies contradict common experience, and the reports of hiſtory and witneſſes claſh with the ordinary courſe of nature, or with one another; there it is, where diligence, attention and exactneſs are required, to form a right judgment, and to proportion the aſſent to the different evidence and probability of the thing; which riſes and falls according as thoſe two foundations of credibility, viz. common obſervation in like caſes, and particular teſtimonies in that particular inſtance, favour or contradict it. Theſe are liable to ſo great a variety of contrary obſervations, circumſtances, reports, different qualifications, tempers, deſigns, overſights, &c. of the reporters, that it is impoſſible to reduce into preciſe rules the various degrees wherein men give their assent. This only may be said in general, that as the arguments and proofs for and against, upon due examination, nicely weighing every particular circumstance, shall to any one appear, upon the whole matter, in a greater or less degree to preponderate on either side; so they are fitted to produce in the mind such different entertainments, as we call belief, conjecture, guess, doubt, wavering, distrust, disbelief, &c. LOCKE.

ASSENT TO BE REGULATED BY THE GROUND OF PROBABILITY.

THE grounds of probability, as they are the foundations on which our assent is built, so are they also the measure whereby its several degrees are, or ought to be, regulated: only we are to take notice, that whatever grounds of probability there may be, they yet operate no farther on the mind, which searches after truth, and endeavours to judge right, than they appear; at least in the first judgment or search that the mind makes. I confess, in the opinions men have and firmly stick to in the world, their assent is not always from an actual view of the reasons that at first prevailed with them: it being in many cases almost impossible, and in most very hard, even for those who have very admirable memories, to retain all the proofs which upon a due examination made them embrace that side of the question. It suffices that they have once with care and fairness sifted the matter as far as they could; and that they have searched into all the particulars that they could imagine to give any light to the question, and with the best of their skill cast up the account upon the whole evidence: and thus having once found on which side the probability appeared to them, after as full and exact an inquiry as they can make, they lay up their conclusion in their memories as a truth they had discovered; and for the future they remain satisfied with the testimony of their memories, that this is the opinion, that by the proofs they have once seen of it deserves such a degree of their assent as they afford it.

This is all that the greatest part of men are capable of doing in regulating their opinions and judgment; unless a man will exact of them, either to retain distinctly in their memories all the proofs concerning any probable truth, and that too in the same order and regular deduction of consequences in which they have formerly placed or seen them; which sometimes is enough to fill a large volume on one single question: or else they must require a man, for every opinion that he embraces, every day to examine the proofs: both which are impossible. It is unavoidable, therefore, that the memory be relied on in the case, and

that

that men be perfuaded of feveral opinions, whereof the proofs are not actually in their thoughts; nay, which perhaps they are not able actually to recall. Without this the greateft part of men muft be either very fceptics, or change every moment, and yield themfelves up to whoever, having lately ftudied the queftion, offers them arguments, which, for want of memory, they are not able prefently to anfwer.

I cannot but own, that mens fticking to their paft judgment, and adhering firmly to conclufions formerly made, is often the caufe of great obftinacy in error and miftake. But the fault is not that they rely on their memories for what they have before well judged; but becaufe they judged before they had well examined. May we not find a great number (not to fay the greateft part) of men that think they have formed right judgment of feveral matters; and that for no other reafon, but becaufe they never thought otherwife? who imagine themfelves to have judged right, only becaufe they never queftioned, never examined their own opinion? which is indeed to think they judged right, becaufe they never judged at all: and yet thefe of all men hold their opinion with the greateft ftiffnefs; thofe being generally the moft fierce and firm in their tenets who have leaft examined them. What we once know, we are certain is fo: and we may be fecure, that there are no latent proofs undiscovered, which may overturn our knowledge or bring it in doubt. But in matters of probability, it is not in every case we can be sure that we have all the particulars before us that any way concern the question; and that there is no evidence behind, and yet unseen, which may cast the probability on the other side, and outweigh all that at present seem to preponderate with us. LOCKE.

ASSOCIATION of IDEAS.

THE association of ideas is the cement which unites the fabric of the human intellect; without which, pleasure and pain would be simple and ineffectual sensations. The vulgar, that is, all men who have no general ideas or universal principles, act in consequence of the most immediate and familiar associations: but the more remote and complex only present themselves to the minds of those who are passionately attached to a single object; or to those of greater understanding, who have acquired an habit of rapidly comparing together a number of objects, and of forming a conclusion; and the result, that is, the action in consequence, by these means becomes less dangerous and uncertain. BECCARIA.

A GENERAL VIEW OF HARTLEY'S DOCTRINE OF ASSOCIATION OF IDEAS.

THE mechanical affociation of ideas that has been frequently prefented to the mind at the fame time, was firft noticed by Mr Locke; but he had recourfe to it only to explain thofe fympathies and antipathies which he calls *unnatural*, in oppofition to thofe which, he fays, are born with us; and he refers them to trains of motion in the animal fpirits.

It appeared probable to Hartley, who took the hint firft from Locke, that not only all our intellectual *pleafures* and *pains*, but all the phenomena of *memory, imagination, volition, reafoning,* and every other mental direction and operation, are only different modes and cafes of the affociation of ideas: fo that nothing is requifite to make any man whatever he is, but a fentient principle, with this fingle property (which admits of great variety), and the influence of fuch circumftances as he has actually been expofed to.—— In order to fee the poffibility of Hartley's theory of the mind, we muft obferve, that all the phenomena of the mind muft be reduced to the faculties of *memory, judgment,* the *paffions* and the *will*, to which may be added the power of *mufcular motion*. ——Suppofing the human mind to have acquired a ftock of ideas by means of the external fenfes, and that these ideas have been variously associated together, so that when one of them is present, it will introduce such others as it has the nearest connection with and relation to; nothing more seems necessary to explain the phenomena of *memory*. For we have no power of calling up any idea at pleasure, but only recollect such as have a connection, by means of former associations, with those that are at any time present to the mind. Thus the sight, or the idea, of any particular person, generally suggests the idea of his name, because they have been frequently associated together. If that fail to introduce the name, we are at a loss, and cannot recollect it at all, till some other associated circumstance help us. In naming a number of words or lines in a poem, the end of each preceding word being connected with the beginning of the succeeding one, we can easily repeat them in that order; but we are not able to repeat them backwards, till they have been frequently named in that contrary order. By this means, however, we acquire a facility of doing it, as may be found by the names of numbers from one to twenty. In the wildest flights of fancy, it is probable that no single idea occurs to us but such as had a connection with some other impression or idea previously existing in the mind; and what we call *new thoughts,* are only

only new combinations of old simple ideas, or decompositions of complex ones.

Judgment is nothing more than the perception of the univerfal concurrence or the perfect coincidence of two ideas, or the want of that concurrence and coincidence; as, *that milk is white;* that *twice two is four;* or transferring the idea of truth by affociation from one propofition to another that refembles it.

When we fay that *Alexander conquered Darius*, we mean, that the perfon whom we diftinguifh by the name of Alexander, is the fame with him who conquered Darius; and when we fay that *God is good*, we mean, that the perfon whom we diftinguifh by the name of *God*, appears by his works and conduct to be poffeffed of the fame difpofition that we call *good* or *benevolent* in men. And having attained to the knowledge of *general truths*, the idea or feeling which accompanies the perception of truth, is transferred by affociation to all the particulars which are comprifed under it, and to other propofitions that are analogous to it; having found by experience, that when we have formed fuch conclufions, we have not been deceived.

When we fay that any idea or circumftance excites a particular *paffion*, it is explained by obferving, that certain feelings and emotions have been formerly connected with that particular idea or circumstance, which it has the power of recalling by association. Thus, with respect to the passion of *fear*, it is evident to observation, that a child is unacquainted with any such thing till it has received some hurt; upon which the painful idea, left in the mind by the remembrance of the hurt, becomes associated with the idea of the circumstances in which he received the hurt; and by degrees with that circumstance only which is essential to it, and which he therefore considers as the proper cause of his hurt. If a variety of painful emotions and disagreeable feelings have been associated with the idea of the same circumstance, they will all be excited by it in one general *complex emotion*, the *component* parts of which will not be easily distinguishable; and by their mutual associations they will at length entirely coalesce, so as never to be separately perceived.—— A child has no fear of fire till he has been burnt by it, or of a dog till he has been bit by one, or without having had reason to think that a dog would bite him, and having some notion from things of a similar nature what the bite of a dog is. In like manner, the passion of *love* is generated by the association of agreeable circumstances with the idea of the object which excites it. And all our other passions are only modifications of these general ones of *fear* or *love*, varying with the situation of the object of *fear* or *love*

with

with respect to us, as whether it be near or distant, expected or unexpected, &c.

According to this hypothesis, all our passions are at first *interested*, respecting our own pleasures or pains; and this sufficiently agrees with our observation: and they become *disinterested* when these complex emotions are transferred by association to other persons or things. Thus the child loves his nurse or parent, by connecting with the idea of them the various pleasures which he has received from them, or in their company: but having received the most happiness from them, or with them, when they themselves were cheerful and happy, he begins to desire their happiness; and in time it becomes as much an object with him as his own proper happiness.

The natural progress of a passion may be most distinctly seen in that of *the love of money;* which is acquired so late in life, that every step in the progress may be easily traced. No person is born with the love of money as such. A child is indeed pleased with a piece of coin, as he is with other things, the form or the splendor of which strikes his eye; but this is very different from that emotion which a man who has been accustomed to the use of money, and has known the want of it, feels upon being presented with a guinea or a shilling. This emotion is a very complex one; the component parts of which are distinguishable,

but

but which have all been separately connected with the idea of money and the uses of it. For after a child has received the first species of pleasure from a piece of money, as a mere *play-thing*, he receives additional pleasure from the possession of it, by connecting with the idea of it the idea of the various pleasures and advantages which it is able to procure him. And in time, that complex idea of pleasure, which was originally formed of the various pleasures which it was the means of procuring, is so intimately connected with the idea of money, that it becomes an object of a proper passion; so that men are capable of pursuing it, without ever reflecting on any *use* that it may possibly be of to them.

A *volition* is a modification of the passion of *desire*, exclusive of any tumultuous emotion which the idea of a favourite object not possessed may excite; and it is generally followed by those actions with which that state of mind has been associated, in consequence of those actions having been found by experience to be instrumental in bringing the favourite object into our possession.

At first a child stretches out his hand, and performs the motion of *grasping*, without any particular intention, whenever the palm of his hand is irritated, or by any general stimulus which puts the whole muscular system into motion. But play-things being put into his hand, and it
closing

closing upon them, he learns by degrees to stretch forth his hand, as well as to grasp any thing. At length the action becomes familiar, and is intimately associated with a sight of a favourite object; so that the moment it is perceived, the actions of reaching and grasping immediately and mechanically succeed. Any person who has been accustomed to observe the actions of children, must have frequently seen all the steps of this process; and in a similar manner, it may be conceived that we learn to procure the gratification of all our desires.

There is nothing that has more the appearance of *instinct* than the motions of particular muscles in certain circumstances; and yet there is hardly one of them that Hartley has not in a manner demonstrated to have been originally *automatic;* the muscles being first forced to contract involuntarily, and becoming afterwards associated with the idea of the circumstance, so that the one immediately and mechanically follows the other.—— What can be more instantaneous, and have more the appearance of instinct, than the endeavour of all animals to recover the *equilibrium* of their bodies when they are in danger of falling; yet children have it not, but acquire it gradually and slowly. The same is the case of the action of sucking, and the motion of the eye-lids when any thing approaches the eye. This association, however,

ever, grows so firm in a course of years, that it is hardly possible to counteract it by the most determined resolution when we are grown up; though you may bring any thing ever so near, and ever so suddenly, to the eye of a young child, when it is most perfectly awake, without exciting any motion in the eye-lids.

In fine, we must admire the simplicity of nature, and the provision for the *growth* of *all the passions* and propensities just as they are wanted, and in the degree in which they are wanted through life: All is performed by the general disposition of the mind to conform to its circumstances, and to be modified by them without particular instincts. PRIESTLEY.

ASSURANCE.

WHERE any particular thing, consonant to the constant observation of ourselves and others in the like case, comes attested by the concurrent reports of all that mention it, we receive it as easily, and build as firmly upon it, as if it were certain knowledge; and we reason and act thereupon with as little doubt as if it were perfect demonstration. Thus if all Englishmen, who have occasion to mention it, should affirm that it froze in England the last winter, or that there were swallows seen there in the summer; I think a
man

man could almost as little doubt of it as that seven and four are eleven. The first, therefore, and highest degree of probability, is, when the general consent of all men, in all ages, as far as it can be known, concurs with a man's constant and never-failing experience in like cases, to confirm the truth of any particular matter of fact attested by fair witnesses: such are all the stated constitutions and properties of bodies, and the regular proceedings of causes and effects in the ordinary course of nature. This we call an argument from the nature of things themselves: For what our own and other mens constant observation has found always to be after the same manner, that we with reason conclude to be the effects of steady and regular causes, though they come not within the reach of our knowledge. Thus that fire warmed a man, made lead fluid, and changed the colour or consistency in wood or charcoal; that iron sunk in water, and swam in quicksilver: these and the like propositions about particular facts, being agreeable to our constant experience, as often as we have to do with these matters; and being generally spoken of (when mentioned by others) as things found constantly to be so, and therefore not so much as controverted by any body; we are put past doubt, that a relation affirming any such thing to have been, or any predication that it will happen again in the same manner, is very true. These probabilities rise so near to certainty, that they govern our thoughts as absolutely, and influence all our actions as fully, as the most evident demonstration; and in what concerns us, we make little or no difference between them and certain knowledge. Our belief, thus grounded, rises to assurance.   Locke.

ATHEISM.

Why is a society of Atheists thought impossible? Because it is thought that men under no restraint could never live together; that laws avail nothing against secret crimes; and that there must be an avenging God, punishing in this world or the other those delinquents who have escaped human justice. Though Moses's law did not reach a life to come, did not threaten any punishment after death, and did not leave the primitive Jews the least insight into the immortality of the soul; still the Jews, so far from being Atheists, so far from denying a divine vengeance against wickedness, were the most religious men on the face of the earth.——They not only believed the existence of an eternal God, but they believed him to be ever present among them: they dreaded being punished in themselves, in their wives, in their children, in their posterity
to

to the fourth generation: and this was a very powerful restraint.

But among the Gentiles, several sects had no curb: the Sceptics doubted of every thing; the Epicureans held that the Deity could not concern himself about human affairs, and in reality they did not allow of any Deity; they were persuaded that the soul is not a substance, but a faculty born and perishing with the body; consequently their only check was morality and honour.—— The Roman senators and knights were downright Atheists; as neither to fear or expect any thing from the gods, amounts to a denial of their existence: so that the Roman senate, in Cæsar's and Cicero's time, was in fact an assembly of Atheists.

VOLTAIRE.

On the same Subject.

PLUTARCH thinks unworthy opinions of the Deity more criminal than Atheism. But, with submission to Plutarch, nothing can be more evident, than that it was infinitely better for the Greeks to stand in awe of Ceres, Neptune, and Jupiter, than to be under no manner of awe. The sacredness of oaths is manifest and necessary; and they who hold that perjury will be punished, are certainly more to be trusted than those who think that a false oath will be attended with no ill consequence.

quence.——It is beyond all queſtion, that in a policed city, even a bad religion is better than none.——But fanaticiſm is certainly a thouſand times more dangerous than Atheiſm: there is in Atheiſm no temptation to thoſe ſanguinary procedures, for which fanaticiſm is notorious; if Atheiſm do not ſuppreſs crimes, fanaticiſm incites to the commiſſion of them.——The fanatics committed the maſſacre of St. Bartholomew.—— Hobbes was accounted an Atheiſt; yet he led a quiet harmleſs life, whilſt the fanatics were deluging England, Scotland, and Ireland with blood. ——Spinoſa was not only an Atheiſt, but taught Atheiſm: yet who can ſay he had any hand in the juridical murder of Barneveldt? It was not he who tore the two De Witts to pieces, and broiled and eat their fleſh.——Atheiſts for the moſt part are men of ſtudy, but bold and erroneous in their reaſonings; and, not comprehending the creation, the original of evil, and other difficulties, have recourſe to the hypotheſis of the eternity of things and of neceſſity.——The ſenſualiſt and ambitious have little time for ſpeculation, or to embrace a bad ſyſtem; to compare Lucretius with Socrates is quite out of their way.——It was otherwiſe with the ſenate of Rome, which almoſt totally conſiſted of Atheiſts both in theory and practice, believing neither in a Providence nor a future ſtate. ——It was a meeting of philoſophers, of votaries of pleasure and ambition; all very dangerous sets of men, and who accordingly overturned the republic.——I would not willingly lie at the mercy of an atheistical prince, who might think it his interest to have me pounded in a mortar: I am very certain that would be my fate.——And were I a sovereign, I would not have about me any atheistical courtiers, whose interest it might be to poison me. So necessary is it both for princes and people that their minds be thoroughly imbibed with an idea of a supreme Being, the Creator, Avenger, and Rewarder.——What are the inferences from all this? That Atheism is a most pernicious monster in sovereign princes, and likewise in statesmen, however harmless their life be, because from their cabinet they can make their way to the former. That if it be not so mischievous as fanaticism, it is almost ever destructive of virtue.——I congratulate the present age on there being fewer Atheists now than ever; philosophers having discovered, that there is no vegetable without a germ, no germ without design, and that corn is not produced by putrefaction.——Some unphilosophical geometricians have rejected final causes: but they are admitted by all real philosophers; and, to use the expression of a known author, a catechism makes God known to children, and Newton demonstrates him to the learned.

VOLTAIRE.

On the same Subject.

There is no man of understanding who does not acknowledge an active power in nature. There is, therefore, no Atheist.——He is not an Atheist who says, that motion is God; because, in fact, motion is incomprehensible, as we have no clear idea of it, as it does not manifest itself but by its effects; and, lastly, because by it all things are performed in the universe.——He is not an Atheist who says, on the contrary, that motion is not God; because motion is not a being, but a mode of being.——They are no Atheists who maintain that motion is essential to matter, and regard it as the invisible and motive force that spreads itself through all its parts. Do we not see the stars continually changing their places, and rolling perpetually round their centre? do we not see all bodies destroyed and reproduced incessantly, under different forms? in short, do we not see nature in an eternal fermentation and dissolution? —Who then can deny that motion is, like extension, inherent in bodies, and that motion is not the cause of what is?—In fact, says Mr Hume, if we always give the names of cause and effect to the concomitance of two facts, and conclude, that wherever there are bodies there is motion; we ought then to regard motion as the universal soul of matter, and the divinity that alone penetrates its

sub-

substance. But are the philosophers of this last opinion Atheists? No: they equally acknowledge an unknown force in the universe. Are even those who have no ideas of God Atheists? No; because then all men would be so; because no one has a clear idea of the Divinity; because in this case every obscure idea is equal to none; and, lastly, to acknowledge the incomprehensibility of God, is to say by a different turn of expression, that we have no idea of him.   HELVETIUS.

ATHEISM AND SUPERSTITION.

IF superstition, in every degree of it, be founded in error, and if it counteract the effects of knowledge and goodness, it is a positive and active evil: Whereas, Atheism being the effect merely of ignorance, is rather a misfortune; and its effects are the harmless ones which usually follow upon mere ignorance. The wise and able moralist Plutarch said, it was much better men should even disbelieve and deny the existence of a God, than believe him to be ill-disposed and of an immoral character. All quibbles which have been brought to obviate the consequences of this proposition; the appeals to prudence, expedience, and interest, may do very well in modern politics, and in the schemes of legislators and priests, whose only aim is to keep the people like cattle in those

tracks

tracks where they may be most serviceable to them; but will be despised by every one who apprehends, and judges, and feels like a man.——To see the difference between ignorance and error in all possible cases, take a child totally unacquainted with truth, and take a good old lady who is, as she supposes, just going to heaven loaded with points of faith and principles of religion; and you will have proofs as many as you can wish, as clear and convincing as any mathematical conclusions, of the great and important difference between ignorance and error. Take a savage uncorrupted by European commerce; take a simple savage who, in the compass and variety of his knowledge, is little above a brute; take a religious savage; millions of which we may have in Europe; and in attempting to instruct both, we shall have more convincing proofs of the very important difference between ignorance and error. The former we may easily benefit; the latter we seldom or never can. WILLIAMS.

The Disputes between ATHEISTS and THEISTS verbal.

I ask the Theist, If he does not allow that there is a great and immeasurable, because an incomprehensible, difference between the human and Divine mind? The more pious he is, the more readily

dily will he assent to the affirmative, and the more he will be disposed to magnify the difference: He will even assent that the difference is of a nature which cannot be too much magnified.—I next turn to the Atheist, who, I assert, is only nominally so, and can never possibly be in earnest; and I ask him, Whether, from the coherence and apparent sympathy in all the parts of the world, there be not a certain degree of analogy among all the operations of nature, in every situation, and in every age? Whether the rotting of a turnip, the generation of an animal, and the structure of human thought, be not energies that probably bear some remote analogy to each other?— It is impossible he can deny it; he will readily acknowledge it.—Having obtained this concession, I push him still farther in his retreat; and I ask him, if it be not probable that the principle which first arranged, and still maintains order in the universe, bears not also some remote inconceivable analogy to the other operations of nature, and, among the rest, to the œconomy of mind and thought?——However reluctant, he must give his assent.—Where then, cry I, to both these antagonists, is the subject of your dispute? The Theist allows that the original principle of order bears some remote analogy to it.—Will you quarrel about the degrees, and enter into a controversy which admits not of any precise meaning,

ing, nor consequently of any determination? If you should be so obstinate, I should not be surprised to find you change sides: Whilst the Theist, on the one hand, exaggerates the dissimilarity between the Supreme Being and frail, imperfect, variable, fleeting, and mortal creatures; and the Atheist, on the other, magnifies the analogy among all the operations of nature, in every period, every situation, and every position.——Consider then, where the great point of controversy lies; and if you cannot lay aside your disputes, endeavour at least to cure yourselves of your animosity.

HUME.

AVARICE.

WHEN a miser contents himself with giving nothing, and saving what he has got, and is in other respects guilty of no injustice, he is perhaps of all bad men the least injurious to society; the evil he does is properly nothing more than the omission of the good he might do. If, of all the vices, avarice be the most generally detested, it is the effect of an avidity common to almost all men; it is because men hate those from whom they can expect nothing. The greedy misers rail at sordid misers.

HELVETIUS.

On the same Subject.

The avaricious either desire riches, as the means of procuring pleasure, or as an exemption from the miseries with which poverty is attended. Man, by nature, is sensible of no other pleasures than those of the senses; these pleasures are consequently the only object of his desires. A fondness for luxury is then an artificial passion, necessarily produced by the natural wants either of love or of the pleasures of the table. Indeed, what real pleasure can luxury and magnificence procure the avaricious voluptuary, if he does not consider them as the means of obtaining the favours of love, if they are the objects of his fondness; or of imposing on men, and forcing them, by the uncertain hope of a reward, to remove from him every pain, and to assemble around him every pleasure? With these avaricious voluptuaries, who certainly do not properly deserve to be called covetous, avarice is the immediate effect of the fear of pain and the love of pleasure. But it may be asked, How can this love of pleasure, this fear of pain, be excited in the really avaricious, those wretched misers who never part with their money to purchase pleasure? If they pass their lives in the want of common necessaries, and exaggerate to themselves and others the pleasures annexed to the possession of gold, it is merely to divert their attention from a misfortune which nobody can or ought to pity. There is a surprising contradiction between their conduct and the motives from which they act. They have an incessant desire of pleasure, and always deprive themselves of its enjoyment. This kind of avarice derives its source from an excessive and ridiculous fear of the possibility of indigence, and of the many evils with which it is accompanied. The avaricious are like those afflicted with an hypochondriac melancholy, who live in perpetual agonies, see themselves surrounded with dangers, and are afraid of being crushed by every one that approaches them. This species of the avaricious we commonly find among those who were born in a state of indigence, and have themselves experienced the long train of evils with which it is attended. Their folly is therefore in this respect more pardonable than in men born in a state of affluence, among whom there are seldom found any of the avaricious, except the proud or voluptuous. Avarice increases in old age, as the habit of accumulating wealth is no longer counterbalanced by the desire of enjoying it, which will be strengthened by the mechanical fear of want, wherewith old age is frequently accompanied.

HELVETIUS.

B.

National BANKRUPTCY.

IT will scarcely be asserted, that no bounds ought ever to be set to national debts; and that the public would be no weaker, were twelve or fifteen shillings in the pound, land-tax, mortgaged with the present customs and excises. There is, however, a strange supineness from long custom creeped into all ranks of men with regard to public debts, not unlike what divines so vehemently complain of with regard to their religious doctrines. We all own, that the most sanguine imagination cannot hope either that this or any future ministry will be possessed of such rigid and steady frugality, as to make a considerable progress in the payment of our debts; or that the situation of foreign affairs will, for any long time, allow them leisure and tranquillity for such an undertaking. *What then is to become of us?* Were we ever so good Christians, and ever so resigned to Providence, this, methinks, were a curious question, even considered as a speculative one, and what it might not be altogether impossible to form some conjectural solution of.

The events here will depend little upon the contingencies of battles, negociations, intrigues, and factions. There seems to be a natural progress in things which may guide our reasoning. As it would have required but a moderate share of prudence when we first began this practice of mortgaging, to have foretold, from the nature of men and of ministers, that things would necessarily be carried to the length we see; so now, that they have happily reached it, it may not be difficult to guess at the consequences. It must indeed be one of these two events; either the nation must destroy public credit, or public credit will destroy the nation. It is impossible they can both subsist after the manner they have been hitherto managed in this as well as in some other countries.

It has been computed, that all the creditors of the public, natives and foreigners, amount only to 17000. These make a figure at present on their income; but in case of a public bankruptcy, would in an instant become the lowest, as well as the most wretched, of the people. The dignity and authority of the landed gentry and nobility is much better rooted, and would render the contention very unequal if ever we come to that extremity. One would incline to assign to this event a very near period, such as half a century, had not our fathers prophecies of this kind been found fallacious by the duration of our public credit so much beyond all reasonable expectation.

tion. When the astrologers in France were every year foretelling the death of Henry IV. " These fellows," says he, " must be right at " last." But, however, it is not altogether improbable, that, when the nation become heartily sick of their debts, and are cruelly oppressed by them, some daring projector may arise with visionary schemes for their discharge. And as public credit will begin by that time to be a little frail, the least touch will destroy it, as happened in France during the regency; and in this manner it will *die of the doctor.*

But it is more probable that the breach of national faith will be the necessary effect of wars, defeats, misfortunes, and public calamities; or even, perhaps, of victories and conquests. Let the time come, and surely it will come, when the new funds, created for the exigences of the year, are not subscribed to, and raise not the money projected. Suppose, either that the cash of the nation is exhausted, or that our faith, which has been hitherto so ample, begins to fail us. Suppose that in this distress the nation is threatened with an invasion; a rebellion is suspected, or broken out at home; a squadron cannot be equipped for want of pay, victuals, or repairs; or even a foreign subsidy cannot be advanced. What must a prince or minister do in such an emergence? The right of self-preservation is unalienable

able in every individual, much more in every community. And the folly of our statesmen must be greater than the folly of those who contracted the debt, or, what is more, than the folly of those who trusted or continue to trust this security, if these statesmen have the means of safety in their hands, and do not employ them. The funds created and mortgaged will, by that time, bring in a large yearly revenue, sufficient for the defence and security of the nation. Money is, perhaps, lying in the exchequer, ready for the discharge of the quarterly interest: Necessity calls, fear urges, reason exhorts, compassion alone exclaims. The money will immediately be seized for the current service, under the most solemn protestations, perhaps, of being immediately replaced. But no more is requisite. The whole fabric, already tottering, falls to the ground, and buries thousands in its ruins. And this is called the *natural death* of public credit: for to this period it tends as naturally as an animal body to its dissolution and destruction.—The public is a debtor whom no man can oblige to pay. The only check which the creditors have on her, is the interest of preserving credit; an interest which may easily be overbalanced by a great debt, and by a difficult and extraordinary emergence, even supposing that credit irrecoverable. Not to mention that a present necessity often forces states into

into measures which are, strictly speaking, against their interest.

Those two events supposed above are calamitous, but not the most calamitous. Thousands are hereby sacrificed to the safety of millions. But we are not without danger, that the contrary event may take place, and that millions may be sacrificed for ever to the temporary safety of thousands. Our popular government, perhaps, will render it difficult and dangerous for a minister to venture on so desperate an expedient as that of a voluntary bankruptcy. And though the House of Lords be altogether composed of the proprietors of lands, and the House of Commons chiefly, and consequently neither of them can be supposed to have great property in the funds; yet the connections of the members may be so great with the proprietors, as to render them more tenacious of public faith than prudence, policy, or even justice, strictly speaking, requires. And perhaps our foreign enemies may be so politic as to discover that our safety lies in despair, and may not, therefore, show the danger, open and barefaced, till it be inevitable. The balance of power in Europe, our grandfathers, our fathers, and we, have all esteemed too unequal to be preserved without our attention and assistance. But our children, weary with the struggle, and fettered with incumbrances, may sit down secure, and see their neighbours oppressed and conquered; till at last they themselves and their creditors lie both at the mercy of the conqueror. And this may be demonstrated the *violent death* of our public credit.—These seem to be events which are not very remote, and which reason foresees as clearly almost as she can do any thing that lies in the womb of time.   HUME.

BEASTS.

IS it possible any one should say, or affirm in writing, that beasts are machines void of knowledge and sense, have a sameness in all their operations, neither learning nor perfecting any thing, &c.? How! this bird who makes a semicircular nest when he fixes it against a wall; who, when in an angle, shapes it like a quadrant, and circular when he builds it in a tree; is this having a sameness in its operations? Does this hound, after three months teaching, know no more than when you first took him in hand? Your Canary-bird, does he repeat a tune at first hearing? or rather, is it not some time before you can bring him to it? Is he not often out, and does he not improve by practice?—Is it from my speaking that you allow me sense, memory, and ideas? Well; I am silent; but you see me come home very melancholy, and with eager anxiety look for a paper, open the bureau where I remember to have put it, take it up and read it with apparent joy. You hence infer, that I have felt pain and pleasure, and that I have memory and knowledge.

Make then the like inference concerning this dog, who, having lost his master, runs about every where with melancholy yellings, comes home all in ferment, runs up and down, roves from room to room, till at length he finds his beloved master in his closet, and then expresses his joy in softer cries, gesticulations and fawnings.—This dog, so very superior to man in affection, is seized by some barbarian virtuosos, who nail him down on a table, and dissect him while living, the better to show you the meseraic veins. All the same organs of sensation which are in yourself you perceive in him. Now, machinist, what say you? Has he nerves to be impassible? For shame! charge not nature with such weakness and inconsistency.— But the scholastic doctors ask what the soul of beasts is? This is a question I do not understand. A tree has the faculty of receiving sap into its fibres, of circulating it, of unfolding the buds of its leaves and fruits. Do you now ask me what the soul of a tree is? It has received these properties, as the animal above has received those of sensation, memory, and a certain number of ideas. Who formed all those properties, who has imparted all these faculties? He who causes the
grass

grafs of the field to grow, and the earth to gravitate towards the fun.—The fouls of beafts are fubftantial forms, fays Ariftotle, the Arabian fchool, the Angelic fchool, and the Sorbonne.—The fouls of beafts are material, cry other philofophers; but as little to the purpofe as the former. When called upon to define a material foul, they only perplex the caufe : they muft neceffarily allow it to be fenfitive matter. But from whence does it derive this fenfation ? From a material foul; which muft mean, that it is matter giving fenfation to matter: beyond this circle they have nothing to fay. According to others equally wife, the foul of beafts is a fpiritual effence dying with the body : but where are your proofs? What idea have you of this fpiritual being, which with its fenfation, memory, and its fhare of ideas and combinations, will never be able to know fo much as a child of fix years ? What grounds have you to think that this incorporeal being dies with the body ? But ftill more ftupid are they who affirm this foul to be neither body nor fpirit. By fpirit we can mean only fome thing unknown, which is not body; the foul of beafts, therefore, according to this fyftem, is neither body, nor fomething which is not body.—Whence can fo many contradictory errors arife ? From a cuftom, which has always prevailed among men, of inveftigating the nature of a thing before they knew whether any

fuch

such thing existed. The sucker or clapper of a bellows is likewise called the soul of the bellows. Well, what is the soul? It is only a name I have given to that sucker or clapper, which falls down, lets in air, and, rising again, propels it through a pipe on my working the bellows.—Here is no soul distinct from the machine itself; but who puts the bellows of animals in motion? I have already told you; he who puts the heavenly bodies in motion. The philosopher who said, *est Deus anima brutorum* should have added, *Quod Deus est anima mundi.* VOLTAIRE.

BEAUTY AND BEAUTIFUL.

ASK a negro of Guinea, What is beauty, the supremely beautiful, the το καλον? he will answer you, A greasy black skin, hollow eyes, and a flat nose.

Consult the philosophers, they will tell you some unintelligible jargon for answer; they must have something correspondent to beauty in the abstract.

I once sat next to a philosopher at a tragedy. That is beautiful, said he! How beautiful? said I. Because the author has attained his end. The next day he took a dose of physic, which had a very good effect. That is a beautiful physic, said I, it has attained its end. He perceived that a
me-

medicine is not to be called beautiful, and that the word beauty is applicable only to those things which give a pleasure accompanied with admiration: that tragedy, he said, had excited these two sensations in him, and that was the το-καλον.—We went to England together, and happened to be at the same play, perfectly well translated; but the spectators one and all yawned. He then concluded that beauty is very relative; that what is decent at Japan is indecent at Rome; and what is fashionable at Paris is otherwise at Pekin.

VOLTAIRE.

A COGITATIVE BEING HAS EXISTED FROM ETERNITY.

THERE is no truth more evident, than that something must be from eternity. I never yet heard of any one so unreasonable, or that could suppose so manifest a contradiction, as a time wherein there was perfectly nothing: this being of all absurdities the greatest, to imagine that pure nothing, the perfect negation and absence of all beings, should ever produce any real existence.

If then there must be something eternal, let us see what sort of being it must be. And to that, it is very obvious to reason, that it must necessarily be a cogitative being. For it is as impossible to conceive, that ever bare incogitative matter should

should produce a thinking intelligent being, as that nothing should of itself produce matter. Let us suppose any parcel of matter eternal, great or small, we shall find it, in itself, able to produce nothing. For example, let us suppose the matter of the next pebble we meet with to be eternal, closely united, and the parts firmly at rest together; if there were no other being in the world, must it not eternally remain so, a dead inactive lump? Is it possible to conceive it can add motion to itself, being purely matter, or produce any thing? Matter, then, by its own strength, cannot produce in itself so much as motion: the motion it has must also be from eternity or else be produced and added to matter by some other being more powerful than matter; matter, as is evident, having not power to produce motion in itself. But let us suppose motion eternal too; yet matter, incogitative matter and motion, whatever changes it might produce of figure and bulk, could never produce thought: knowledge will still be as far beyond the power of motion and matter to produce, as matter is beyond the power of nothing or nonentity to produce. And I appeal to every one's own thoughts, whether he cannot as easily perceive matter produced by nothing, as thought to be produced by pure matter, when before there was no such thing as thought, or an intelligent being existing?

Divide

Divide matter into as minute parts as you will (which we are apt to imagine a fort of fpiritualizing or making a thinking thing of it), vary the figure and motion of it as much as you pleafe; a globe, cube, cone, prifm, cylinder, &c. whofe diameters are but 1000000th part of a gry, will operate no otherwife upon other bodies of proportionable bulk than thofe of an inch or foot diameter; and you may as rationally expect to produce fenfe, thought, and knowledge, by putting together, in a certain figure and motion, grofs particles of matter, as by thofe that are the very minuteft that do any where exift. They knock, impel, and refift one another juft as the greater do, and that is all they can do. So that if we will fuppofe nothing firft or eternal, matter can never begin to be: if we fuppofe bare matter without motion eternal, motion can never begin to be: if we fuppofe only matter and motion firft or eternal, thought can never begin to be. For it is impoffible to conceive matter, either with or without motion, could have originally in and from itfelf fenfe, perception, and knowledge; as is evident from hence, that then fenfe, perception, and knowledge, muft be a property eternally infeparable from matter and every particle of it. Not to add, that though our general or fpecific conception of matter makes us fpeak of it as one thing, yet really all matter is not one in-

individual thing, neither is there any such thing existing as one material being, or one single body that we know or can conceive. And therefore, if matter were the eternal first cogitative being, there would not be one eternal infinite cogitative being, but an infinite number of eternal finite cogitative beings, independent one of another, of limited force and distinct thoughts, which could never produce that order, harmony and beauty, which are to be found in nature. Since therefore whatsoever is the first eternal being, must necessarily be cogitative; and whatsoever is first of all things, must necessarily contain in it, and actually have, at least, all the perfections that can ever after exist; nor can it ever give to another any perfection that it hath not, either actually in itself, or at least in a higher degree; it necessarily follows, that the first eternal being cannot be matter.—If therefore it be evident, that something necessarily must exist from eternity, it is also as evident, that that something must necessarily be a cogitative being: for it is as impossible that incogitative matter should produce a cogitative being, as that nothing, or the negation of all beings, should produce a positive being or matter.

LOCKE.

BELIEF.

We believe a thing, becaufe we fee it, we perceive it, or underftand it. It is not poffible for our belief to go further. The credit we give to the teftimoney of another, is quite a different principle from the perfuafion of our own mind; and has been confounded with it only to ferve the purpofes of artful men in impofing on the ignorant. The art of believing what is above our comprehenfion and reafon, and not contrary to it, is a fophifm, with the advantage of a jingle upon words, invented for the fame purpofes. There is juft as much good fenfe and truth and poffibility of believing what is above our underftanding, as in feeing what is beyond our fight, hearing what is out of hearing, or feeling what is totally out of reach. We cannot in truth be faid to believe further than we underftand.—Thofe who pretend to fee myfteries, and to believe them, talk idly; for no man ever did, or ever could, believe a myftery, any more than he could fee what was tranfacted in any invifible world. The complaifance and deference to authority, by which men are led to pretend to believe, is like the fervility of thofe who, though their eyes are imperfect and faulty, always fee as we do, or hear as we hear. This being the cafe, it is not eafy immediately to underftand why men fhould ever have

have been blamed or punished because they could not believe. Believing is an act of the mind, upon considering a fact or proposition; as seeing is an act in consequence of turning the eye on an object. Men are influenced in both these actions exactly alike; by the strength and goodness of their natural organs; by their situation and point of view in which they consider things. Every object, every fact, and every principle, may appear, in some circumstances, different to different persons. Why then, if we punish a man for not discerning truths as we discern them, do we not punish him for not seeing as we see? There is no distinction between these cases, which is founded in truth and common sense; but there is, in the artifices of policy and the wiles of priestcraft. If men be taken early enough, they may be induced to give up the faculties of their minds; but they must use their bodily senses.—It has been said, that a right faith is the consequence of being well and properly disposed. It is very true, that a man may dispose himself; *i. e.* he may warp and bias his mind so as to make any doctrine or principle suit it: But all kinds of predisposition and prearrangement are injuries to the judgment; and it would be as difficult for the mind to determine fairly on a fact or the truth of a principle, when it was so predisposed, as it would be for a judge to determine fairly in a caufe, on one fide of which he was bribed.—Our faith is meritorious only as it is a proof that we ufe our intellectual faculties in the purfuit of truth ; juft as feeing is a proof that we ufe our eyes, or hearing that we ufe our ears. And the common infolence, rage, and cruelty of zealots, on account of faith, is owing to their extreme ignorance, or extreme wickednefs; for they in 'fact muft have the leaft real faith of all mankind. They have taken every thing for granted, without examination or judgment; and have confequently nothing which they truly believe. Their faith is the faith of devils : they believe and tremble under an almighty power which they dread : they believe every thing which is enjoined them, from a fear of damnation ; and have no principle, but what may be common to them with all the evil fpirits in the univerfe.

WILLIAMS.

On the same Subject.

BELIEF, according to fome philofophers, is independent of our intereft. Thefe philofophers are right or wrong according to the idea they attached to the word *Belief*. If they mean by it a clear idea of the matter believed; and that they can, like the geometricians, demonftrate the truth of it; it is certain that no error is believed, that none will stand the examen, that we form no clear idea of it, and that in this sense there are few believers. But if we take the word in the common acceptation, and mean by a believer an adorer of the bull Apis; if the man who, without having a clear idea of what he believes, believes by imitation, who, so to say, believes he believes, and maintains the truth of his belief at the hazard of his life; in this sense there are many believers. The Catholic church boasts continually of its martyrs; but I know not wherefore. Every religion has its own. "He that pretends to a revelation ought to die in the maintenance of what he asserts; that is the only proof he can give of its truth." It is not so with the philosopher: his propositions must be supported by facts and reasonings: whether he die or not in the maintenance of his doctrine, is of little importance: his death would prove only that he was obstinately attached to his opinion; not that it was true.—As for the rest, the belief of fanatics, always founded on imaginary, but powerful interest in heavenly rewards, constantly imposes on the vulgar; and it is to those fanatics that we must attribute the establishment of almost all general opinions.

HELVETIUS.

On the same Subject.

NOTHING is more free than the imagination of man; and though it cannot exceed that original stock of ideas furnished by the internal and external senses, it has unlimited power of mixing, compounding, separating, and dividing these ideas, to all the varieties of fiction and vision. It can feign a train of events with all the appearance of reality, ascribe to them a particular time and place, conceive them as existent, and paint them out to itself with every circumstance that belongs to any historical fact which it believes with the greatest certainty. Wherein, therefore, consists the difference between such a fiction and belief? It lies not merely in any peculiar idea, which is annexed to such a conception as commands our assent, and which is refused to every known fiction. For as the mind has authority over all its ideas, it could voluntarily annex this particular idea to any fiction, and consequently be able to believe whatever it pleases; contrary to what we find by daily experience. We can, in our conception, join the head of a man to the body of a horse; but it is not in our power to believe that such an animal has ever really existed.—It follows, therefore, that the difference between fiction and belief lies in some sentiment or feeling which is annexed to the latter, not to the former, and which

which depends not on the will, nor can be commanded at pleasure. It must be excited by nature, like all other sentiments; and must arise from the particular situation in which the mind is placed at any particular juncture. Whenever any object is presented to the memory or senses, it immediately, by the force of custom, carries the imagination to conceive the object which is usually conjoined to it; and this conception is attended with a feeling or sentiment different from the loose reveries of the fancy. In this consists the whole nature of belief. For as there is no matter of fact which we believe so firmly that we cannot conceive the contrary, there would be no difference between the conception assented to, and that which is rejected, were it not for some sentiment which distinguishes the one from the other. If I see a billiard-ball moving towards another on a smooth table, I can easily conceive it to stop upon contact. This conception implies no contradiction; but still it feels very differently from that conception by which I represent to myself the impulse and the communication of motion from one ball to another.—Were we to attempt a *definition* of this sentiment, we should, perhaps, find it a very difficult, if not an impossible task; in the same manner as if we should endeavour to define the feeling of cold, or passion of anger, to a creature who never had an experience
of

of these sentiments. Belief is the true and proper name of this feeling; and no one is ever at a loss to know the meaning of that term; because every man is every moment conscious of the sentiment represented by it. It may not, however, be improper to attempt a description of this sentiment; in hopes we may, by that means, arrive at some analogies which may afford a perfect explication of it. I say then, that belief is nothing but a more vivid, lively, forcible, steady conception of an object, than what the imagination alone is ever able to attain. This variety of terms, which may seem so unphilosophical, is intended only to express that act of the mind which renders realities, or what is taken for such, more present to us than fictions, causes them to weigh more in the thought, and gives them a superior influence to the passions and imagination. Provided we agree about the thing, it is needless to dispute about the terms. The imagination has the command over all the ideas, and can join and mix and vary them in all the ways possible. It may conceive fictitious objects with all the circumstances of place and time; it may set them in a manner before our eyes in their true colours, just as as they might have existed: but as it is impossible that this faculty of imagination can ever of itself reach *Belief*, which is a term that every one sufficiently understands in common life; and in

phi-

philosophy, we can go no farther than assert, that belief is something felt by the mind, which distinguishes the ideas of judgment from the fictions of the imagination; it gives them more weight and influence; makes them appear of greater importance; enforces them in the mind; and renders them the governing principle of our actions. I hear at present, for instance, a person's voice with whom I am acquainted; and the sound comes as from the next room. This impression of my senses immediately conveys my thought to the person, together with all the surrounding objects. I paint them out to myself as existing at present with the same qualities and relations of which I formerly knew them possessed. These ideas take faster hold of my mind than ideas of an inchanted castle. They are very different to the feeling, and have a much greater influence of every kind, either to give pleasure or pain, joy or sorrow.—The sentiment, therefore, of belief is nothing but a conception more intense and steady than what attends the mere fictions of the imagination; and this manner of conception arises from a customary conjunction of the object with something present to the memory or senses.

HUME.

THE BELIEF OR DISBELIEF

Of any Religion can neither be a virtue nor a Crime in any one using the best Means in his Power for Information.

IF we take a survey of that variety of sects which are scattered over the face of the earth, and who mutually accuse each other of falsehood and error, and ask which is the right; every one of them in their turns will answer *theirs;* we know our sect is in the right, because God hath declared so. " All " of them," says Charron, " pretend that they de- " rive their doctrine, not from men, nor from any " created being, but from God. But to say truth, " without flattery or disguise, there is nothing " in such pretensions: however they may talk, " they owe their religion to human means; wit- " ness the manner in which they first adopt it. " The nation, country, and place where they are " born and bred, determine it. Are we not cir- " cumcised or baptized, made Jews, Turks, or " Christians, before we are men?" Our religion is not the effect of choice, but of accident; and to impute it to us, is unjust: it is to reward or punish us for being born in this or that country. If the method taken by him who is in the right, and by him who is in the wrong, be the same;

what merit or demerit hath the one more than the other? Now, either all religions are good, and agreeable to God; or if there be one which he hath dictated to man, and will punish him for rejecting, he hath certainly distinguished it by manifest signs and tokens as the only true one. These are common to all times and places, and are equally obvious to all mankind. If natural religion be insufficient, it is owing to the obscurity in which it necessarily leaves those sublime truths it professes to teach. It is the business of revelation to exhibit them to the mind in a more clear and sensible manner, to adapt them to the understandings of men, in order that they may be capable of believing them. True faith is assured and confirmed by the understanding; and the best of all religions is undoubtedly the clearest. If there be only one religion in the world which can prevent our suffering eternal damnation, and ensure our title to future happiness; and there be on any part of the earth a single mortal who is sincere, and is not convinced of its evidence; the God of that religion must be a cruel tyrant. Would we seek the truth therefore in sincerity, we must lay no stress on the place and circumstances of our birth, nor on the authority of fathers or teachers; but appeal to the dictates of reason and conscience concerning every thing taught us in our youth. It is to no purpose to bid me subject my reason to the truth of things of

which

which it is incapacitated to judge; the man who would impose on me a falsehood, may bid me do the same. It is necessary therefore I should employ my reason even to know when I ought to submit. ROUSSEAU.

BENEFICENCE.

THE proper exercise of wisdom, and the right use of riches, are not yet subject to legal regulations; and all the pleasing duties of beneficence are in our hands. We shall deservedly forfeit this privilege if we abuse it; or if we make the distinction we are favoured with in society, the occasion of mischief and injury to it. If the labourer thinks himself obliged by his wants, by his connections with his wife and children, and by the fear of bodily punishment, not only to refrain from theft and injustice, but to work hard, and to exercise his prudence and understanding to make his family happy;—what must be the obligations of the rich and wise, if they can not only save their friends and connections from wants and distresses, but extend their hands to numbers around them, and assist those who are not so happy?——Is there any comparison between the necessity and obligation of these duties? Those who would say the former is a duty, because the poor man cannot avoid it; and the latter is not a duty, because the wife and rich may avoid it, do not underſtand the meaning of moral obligation. The wretch who can avoid it, be his talents and rank what they may, does not deſerve the name of man. Every man's abſolute obligations and duties increaſe in proportion to his wiſdom, power, and wealth; and all omiſſions in expreſſions of benevolence, are as criminal and injurious to the world as fraud, theft, or any other villany.

WILLIAMS.

BENEFICENCE AND GRATITUDE.

There is a kind of contract, and the ſtrongeſt of all contracts, between the benefactor and the obliged. It is a ſort of ſociety they form between each other, ſtricter than that which in general unites men; and when the obliged tacitly engages himſelf to gratitude, the benefactor likewiſe is equally engaged to the other to preſerve, ſo long as he does not render himſelf unworthy, the ſame attentions he has already experienced, and to renew his proofs of it every time it is required, or that he has it in his power. Thoſe are not the expreſs conditions, but they are the natural effects of the relations they have ſettled between them. He who for the firſt time refuſes a gratuitous ſervice aſked, gives no right of complaint to him he has refuſed; but he who in a like caſe equally re-

refuses the same favour he had granted before, crosses a hope he had authorised to be conceived, he deceives and baulks the expectation he created. We feel in the refusal something of I don't know how unjust and more cruel than in the other; but it is not less the effect of an independence the heart is fond of, and which it cannot renounce without effort. If I pay a debt, it is a duty I owe: if I bestow a gift, it is a pleasure I procure myself. Thus the pleasure of doing our duty is of those virtue gives birth to; those which proceed immediately from nature are not so elevated.

Rousseau.

Religious BIGOTRY.

A violent contention about external forms and ceremonies of religion, is an indication of ignorance, superstition, and barbarity. It was carried to excess in some of the darker ages of the church; and has always been the characteristic of absurd and illiterate sectaries: But as men have become better acquainted with the Scriptures, and the spirit and genius of Christianity; as they have improved in liberal arts and sciences, in politeness, and a knowledge of the world; they have likewise become more candid and moderate in their religious controversies, and the persecution of reputed heretics. It is indeed painful to every humane

mane and benevolent spectator, to see men furiously abusing and persecuting one another for some trifling difference in their dress, their forms of devotion, their canonical ceremonies, and their theological speculations, without the least regard for the most sacred obligations of Christianity. Whenever therefore we see a man of this temper, that is, an angry bigot, we can entertain no favourable opinion of his head and heart.

* *

The Effects of BLACKNESS.

BLACKNESS is but a *partial darkness;* and therefore it derives some of its powers from being mixed and surrounded with coloured bodies. In its own nature it cannot be considered as a colour. Black bodies, reflecting none, or but a few rays, with regard to sight, are but so many vacant spaces dispersed among the objects we view. When the eye lights on one of these vacuities, after having been kept in some degree of tension by the play of the adjacent colours upon it, it suddenly falls into a relaxation, out of which it as suddenly recovers by a convulsive spring. To illustrate this; let us consider, that when we intend to sit in a chair, and find it much lower than we expected, the shock is very violent; much more violent than could be thought from so slight a fall as the difference between

tween one chair and another can possibly make. If, after descending a flight of steps, we attempt inadvertently, to take another step in the manner of the former ones, the shock is extremely rude and disagreeable; and by no art can we cause such a shock by the same means, when we expect and prepare for it. This is owing to the change being made contrary to expectation, not solely when the mind expects, but likewise when any organ of sense is for some time affected in some one manner, if it be suddenly affected otherwise, there ensues a convulsive motion; such a convulsion as is caused when any thing happens against the expectance of the mind. And though it may appear strange that such a change as produces a relaxation, should immediately produce a sudden convulsion; it is yet most certainly so, and so in all the senses. Every one knows that sleep is a relaxation; and that silence, where nothing keeps the organs of hearing in action, is in general fittest to bring on this relaxation: yet when a sort of murmuring sounds dispose a man to sleep, let these sounds cease suddenly, and the person immediately awakes; that is, the parts are braced up suddenly, and he awakes. In like manner, if a person in broad day-light were falling asleep, to introduce a sudden darkness would prevent his sleep for that time, though silence and darkness in themselves, and not suddenly introduced, are very fa-

favourable to it. From experience we also learn, that on the first inclining towards sleep, we have been suddenly awakened with a most violent start; and that this start was generally preceded by a sort of dream of our falling down a precipice. Whence does this strange notion arise, but from the too sudden relaxation of the body, which by some mechanism in nature restores itself by as quick and vigourous an exertion of the contracting power of the muscles? The dream itself is caused by this relaxation; and it is of too uniform a nature to be attributed to any other cause: the parts relax too suddenly, which is in the nature of falling, and this accident in the body induces this image in the mind. When we are in a confirmed state of health and vigour, as all changes are less sudden then, and less on the extreme, we can seldom complain of this disagreeable sensation.

Though the effects of black be painful originally, we must not think they always continue so. Custom reconciles us to every thing. After we have been used to the sight of black objects, the terror abates, and the smoothness and glossiness, or some agreeable accident of bodies so coloured, softens in some measure the horror and sternness of their original nature; yet the nature of the original impression still continues. Black will always have something melancholy in it, because the sensory will always find the change to it from other colours too violent; or if it occuppy the whole compaſs of the ſight, it will then be darkneſs, and the effcts of darkneſs applicable to it.

BURKE.

C.

C.

CALVINISTIC Divinity.

WHAT strange ideas, says he, would an Indian or a Chinese philosopher have of our holy religion, if they judged by the schemes given of it by our modern free-thinkers, and Pharisaical doctors of all sects? According to the odious and too vulgar systems of these incredulous scoffers, and credulous scriblers, the God of the Jews is a most cruel, unjust, partial, and fantastical being. He created about 6000 years ago a man and a woman, and placed them in a fine garden in Asia, of which there are no remains. This garden was furnished with all sorts of trees, fountains, and flowers. He allowed them the use of all the fruits of this beautiful garden exescept of one, that was planted in the midst thereof, and that had in it a secret virtue of preserving them in continual health, and vigour of body and mind, of exalting their natural powers, and making them wise. The devil entered into the body of a serpent, and solicited the first woman to eat of this forbidden fruit;

fruit; she engaged her husband to do the same. To punish this slight curiosity and natural desire of life and knowledge, God not only threw our first parents out of Paradise, but he condemned all their posterity to temporal misery, and the greatest part of them to eternal pains, though the souls of these innocent children have no more relation to that of Adam than to those of Nero and Mahomet; since, according to the scholastic drivellers, fabulists, and mythologists, all souls are created pure, and infused immediately into mortal bodies as soon as the fœtus is formed. To accomplish the barbarous partial decree of predestination and reprobation, God abandoned all nations to darkness, idolatry, and superstition, without any saving knowledge or salutary graces; unless it was one particular nation, whom he chose as his peculiar people. This chosen nation was, however, the most stupid, ungrateful, rebellious, and perfidious of all nations. After God had thus kept the far greater part of all the human species, during near 4000 years, in a reprobate state, he changed all of a sudden, and took a fancy for other nations beside the Jews. Then he sent his only begotten Son to the world, under a human form, to appease his wrath, satisfy his vindictive justice, and die for the pardon of sin. Very few nations, however, have heard of this gospel; and all the rest, though left in invincible ignorance, are

damned

damned without exception or any possibility of remission. The greatest part of those who have heard of it, have changed only some speculative notions about God, and some external forms in worship: for in all other respects the bulk of Christians have continued as corrupt as the rest of mankind in their morals; yea, so much the more perverse and criminal as their lights were greater. Unless it be a very small select number, all other Christians, like the Pagans, will be for ever damned; the great sacrifice offered up for them will become void and of no effect; God will take delight for ever in their torments and blasphemies; and though he can by one *fiat* change their hearts, yet they will remain for ever unconverted and unconvertible, because he will be for ever unappeased and irreconcilable. It is true, that all this makes God odious; a hater of souls, rather than a lover of them; a cruel vindictive tyrant, an impotent or a wrathful demon, rather than an all-powerful, beneficent father of spirits: yet all this is a mystery. He has secret reasons for his conduct that are impenetrable; and though he appears unjust and barbarous, yet we must believe the contrary, because what is injustice, crime, cruelty, and the blackest malice in us, is in him justice, mercy, and sovereign goodness. Thus the incredulous free-thinkers, the Judaizing Christians, and the fatalistic doctors, have disfigured

and

and dishonoured the sublime mysteries of our holy faith; thus they have confounded the nature of good and evil, transformed the most monstrous passions into divine attributes, and surpassed the Pagans in blasphemy, by ascribing to the Eternal Nature, as perfections, what makes the most horrid crimes amongst men. The grosser Pagans contented themselves with divinizing lust, incest, and adultery; but the predestinarian doctors have divinized cruelty, wrath, fury, vengeance, and all the blackest vices.

Chevalier Ramsay's *Philosophical Principles of Natural and Revealed Religion.*

CAUSE AND EFFECT.

IN the notice that our senses take of the constant vicissitude of things, we cannot but observe that several particulars, both qualities and substances, begin to exist; and that they receive this their existence from the due application and operation of some other being. From this observation we get our *ideas* of *cause* and *effect*. That which produces any simple or complex idea, we denote by the general name *Cause;* and that which is produced, *Effect*. Thus finding, that, in that substance which we call wax, fluidity, (which

is

is a simple idea, that was not in it before), is constantly produced by the application of a certain degree of heat, we call the simple idea of heat, in relation to fluidity in wax, the cause of it, and fluidity the effect. So always finding, that the substance, wood, which is a certain collection of simple ideas so called, by the application of fire, is turned into another substance called ashes, *i. e.* another complex idea, consisting of a collection of simple ideas quite different from that complex idea which we call wood; we consider fire in relation to ashes as cause, and the ashes as effect. So that whatever is considered by us to conduce or operate to the producing any particular simple idea, of collection of simple ideas, whether substance or mode, which did not before exist, hath thereby in our minds the relation of a cause, and is so denominated by us.

LOCKE.

The existence of a First CAUSE.

LIBERTY, as it is understood by many schoolmen, is in fact an absurd chimera. If they will pay the least attention to reason, and not be satisfied with mere words, it will be evident, that whatever exists, or is self-created, is necessary; for if it was not necessary, it would be useless. The

The respectable sect of Stoics thought so; and, what is very singular, this truth may be found in a hundred places of Homer, who makes Jupiter submit to fate.

There exists a something, which must be eternal, as is demonstrated; otherwise we should have an effect without a cause. Thus all the ancients, without a single exception, believed matter to be eternal.

It is not the same of immensity, nor of an almighty power. I cannot see the necessity of all space being filled; and I do not comprehend the reasoning of Clarke, who says, that *whatever necessarily exists in one place, ought necessarily to exist in every place*. Wherefore is it impossible that there should be more than a determined quantity of beings? I can much easier conceive a bounded nature, than an infinite nature.

Upon this article I can only have probabilities, and I can only submit to the strongest. By the universal agreement in every thing which I know of nature, I perceive a design: this design shows that there must be a first cause; that cause is undoubtedly very powerful; but simple philosophy does not teach me to believe that this great artist is infinitely powerful. A house forty feet high proves to me that there must have been an architect; but reason alone cannot convince me that this architect could build a house ten thousand leagues high. Perhaps his powers did not admit of his building one more than forty feet high. My reason alone does not tell me, that in the immensity of space there is but one architect; and if a man was to allege that there were a great many similar architects, I do not see how I could convince him of the contrary.

VOLTAIRE.

The Mysteries of CERES ELEUSINA.

IN the chaos of popular superstition, which would have made almost the whole globe one vast den of ferocious animals, there was a salutary institution, which prevented one part of the human species from degenerating into an entire state of brutality: this consisted of mysteries and expiations. Philosophers endeavoured to bring men back to reason and morality. Those sages made use of superstition itself to correct its enormous abuses.

The mysteries of Zoroaster are no longer known: we know but little of those of Isis: but we cannot doubt that they foretold the grand system of a future state; for Celsus says to Origines, book 8. *" You boast of believing in eternal pu-*
" nishments; and did not all the mystical ministers
" preach them to their initiated?"

God's unity was the principal dogma of all the mysteries. Apuleius has preserved for us the prayer of the priestesses of Isis: "*The celestial powers serve thee; the infernal regions are submitted to thee; the universe revolves in thine hand; thy feet trample upon Tartarus; the planets answer to thy voice; the seasons return to thy order; the elements obey thee.*"

The mystical ceremonies of Ceres were in imitation of those of Isis. Those who had committed crimes, confessed them and expiated them; they fasted, purified themselves, and gave alms. All the ceremonies were held sacred by solemn oaths to make them more venerated. The mysteries were celebrated at night; certain species of tragedies were represented to describe the happiness of the just, and the punishments of the wicked.

Some very learned men have proved, that the sixth book of the Æneid is only a picture of what was practised in those secret and famous representations. The mysteries of Eleusina became the most celebrated. One very remarkable thing is, that they read the beginning of the theogony of Sanchoniathon the Phœnician. This is a proof that Sanchoniathon had preached one supreme God, creator and governor of the world. It was then that this doctrine was unveiled to the initiated, instructed in the belief of Polytheism. Those who participated of the mysteries assembled

bled in the temple of Ceres; and the Hierophanta taught them, that instead of adoring Ceres, leading Triptolemus upon a car drawn by dragons, they should adore that God who nourished men, and permitted Ceres and Triptolemus to render agriculture so honourable.

This is true, that the Hierophanta began by reciting the ancient verses of Orpheus. *Walk in the path of justice; adore the sole master of the universe: he is one, he is singly by himself; to him all beings owe their existence; he acts in them, and by them; he sees all, and never was seen by mortal eyes.*

The greatest discretion was necessary, not to shock the prejudices of the multitude. Bishop Warburton observes after Plutarch, that the young Alcibiades having assisted at these mysteries, insulted the statues of Mercury in a party of pleasure, and that the people in their rage insisted upon Alcibiades's being condemned. Alexander himself having obtained leave in Egypt of the Hierophanta of the mysteries, to acquaint his mother with the secrets of the initiated, at the same time conjured her to burn his letter after reading it, that she might not irritate the Greeks.

Those who have imagined that the mysteries were only infamous debauches, ought to be undeceived by the word which answers to *initiated*; it signifies that they entered on a new life. Not that

that it is to be doubted that in all thefe myfteries, the ground work of which was fo fenfible and ufeful, many cenfurable fuperftitions were introduced. Superftition led to debauchery, which brought on contempt.

But it indubitably appears, that the primary intention of thefe myfteries was to infpire virtue, from the fet form with which the affembly was difmiffed. Amongft the Greeks, the two ancient Phœnician words, *koff omphet*, " *watch* and *be pure*," were pronounced. We may produce an additional proof, that the emperor Nero, who was guilty of his mother's death, could not be admitted to thefe myfteries when he travelled in Greece : the crime was too enormous; and as great an emperor as he was, the initiated would not receive him amongft them. Zozimus alfo fays, that Conftantine could find no Pagan priefts who would purify him or abfolve him of parricide. —According to Tertullian, the ceremony of regeneration was very ridiculous. It was neceffary that the initiated fhould feem to be reborn : this was the fymbol of the new kind of life he was to embrace. He was prefented with a crown, and he trampled upon it. The Hierophanta held the facred knife over his head; the initiated, who feigned to be ftruck with it, fell as if he were dead; after which he appeared to regenerate.

There was (amidft all the fhameful cuftoms,
trifling

trifling ceremonies, and ridiculous doctrines, which the people and priests followed in honour of some imaginary gods, who were despised and detested by the sages) a pure religion, which consisted in acknowledging the existence of a supreme God, his providence and justice.

VOLTAIRE.

On the same Subject.

THE mysteries of *Eleusis* were celebrated twice a-year, at seed-time and harvest; and the festival continued nine days. Each day had its peculiar ceremonies. The *first* was consecrated to the preliminaries of the festival. On the *second*, the initiated or *mystæ* went in a kind of procession to the sea, where reservoirs of salt-water, sacred to Ceres and Proserpine, were set apart for their purification. The *third* was passed in fasting, affliction, and mysterious lamentations, which represented the complaints and groans of Ceres and Proserpine: though something not *of the afflicting kind* seems to have been also represented by the *mystic beds* surrounded with bands of purple, which were employed to convey an idea of the situation of Proserpine on her arrival in the infernal regions. The *fifth* was set apart for a sacrifice, in which the greatest care was observed to avoid touching the genitals of the victim; and the offering was accompanied with myftic dances in a meadow enamelled with flowers, about the fpring of *Callichorus*. The *fixth* day was diftinguifhed by the proceffion of torches, of which there is a reprefentation ftill to be feen on a baffo-relievo difcovered by *Spon* and *Wheler*. In this proceffion, the initiated marched two by two, with a folemn pace, in deep filence, to the Eleufinian temple of Ceres, and were fuppofed to be purified by the odour which exhaled from the torches. The young Iacchus, reprefented with a myrtle crown and a torch in his hand, was carried in pomp from the *Ceramicus* to *Eleufis*. The myftical van, which was an emblem of the feparation of the *initiated* from the *prophane*, the *calathus*, a branch of laurel, a kind of wheel, and the *phallus*, followed the beautiful marble ftatue of the god, and the cries of *Io Bacche* were loudly repeated during the proceffion: Iacchus was invited to take a part in the dances and pleafures of the day, and to be an interceffor with Ceres in favour of the Athenians. In their hymns and invocations, they befeeched the goddefs to procure for thofe who were admitted to the myfteries, an abundance of diverfions and dancing, to grant them the talents of wit and pleafantry, and the power of furpaffing others in jokes and farcafms. The inhabitants of the adjacent places came in crowds to fee this *holy* troop; which, on its arrival at the bridge of

the

the *Cephifus*, they faluted with volleys of fatirical witticifms and buffooneries, which the *initiated* anfwered in the fame ftyle, and retorted with the fame fpirit. Thofe among the *initiated*, who gained the victory in this fingular conflict, were here applauded and adorned with fillets of purple. The *eighth* day was employed in a repetition of the initiation, which was originally occafioned by a particular mark of refpect paid to Æfculapius, who having come to Eleufis to be initiated after the ceremony was over, was favoured with a repetition of the myfteries. This repetition became a conftant practice. The *ninth* and laft day feems to have been diftinguifhed by no other ceremony than the filling of two vafes with water, and pouring out the contents of the one towards the eaft, and of the other towards the weft, and pronouncing, during this act, feveral myfterious words and phrafes, with their eyes alternately turned to the *heavens* and the *earth*, confidered as the common father and mother of all beings. It feems that this ceremony was rather of a doleful and melancholy complexion, and that the libations ufual in the celebration of funeral rites, were employed in this concluding day of the Eleufinian myfteries.

The fecret of thefe myfteries feems to have confifted principally in a particular manner of teaching the doctrine of future rewards and punifhments;

ments; by which the rewards were fuppofed to regard the *initiated* alone, and the punifhments only the *profane*, or thofe who were not initiated. This is confirmed by many authorities; and, among others, by that fhrewd obfervation of Diogenes Laertius: *What? Shall the future ſtate of the robber Paræcion be happier*, becaufe he is initiated, *than that of Epaminondas?* Upon the whole, it does not appear that the unity of the Supreme Being was a part of the fecret doctrine here in queſtion.

DE-ST. CROIX.

CERTAINTY.

HAD you, in Copernicus's time, afked all the world, Did the fun rife, did the fun fet, to-day? they would one and all have anfwered, That is a certainty; we are fully certain of it: thus they were certain, and yet miftaken.—Witchcraft, divinations, and pofſeſſions, were for a long time univerfally accounted the moſt certain things in the world.—What numberlefs crowds have feen all thefe fine things, and have been certain of them! but at prefent fuch certainty begins to lofe its credit.—A mathematical demonſtration is a very different certainty from thefe: they were only probabilities, which, on being fearched into, are found errors; but mathematical certainty is immutable

mutable and eternal.—I exift, I think, I feel pain; is all this as certain as a geometrical truth? Yes. And why? becaufe thefe truths are proved by the fame principle, that a thing cannot at the fame time be and not be.—I cannot at one and the fame time exift and not exift, feel and not feel.—A triangle cannot have and not have a hundred and eighty degrees, the fum of two right angles.—Thus the phyfical certainty of my exiftence and my fenfation, and mathematical certainty, are of a like validity, though differing in kind.—But this is by no means applicable to the certainty founded on appearances, or the unanimous relations of men. VOLTAIRE.

CHAIN OF EVENTS.

IT is an old fuppofition, that all events are linked together by an invincible fatality; this is deftiny, which Homer makes fuperior to Jupiter himfelf.—The fyftem of neceffity and fatality has, according to Leibnitz, been ftruck out by himfelf under the appellation of *fufficient reafon;* but it is in reality of very ancient date, that no effect is without a caufe; and that often the leaft caufe produces the greateft effects, is what the world is not to be taught at this time of day.—My Lord Bolingbroke owns, that the trivial quarrel between the Dutchefs of Marlborough and Mrs Mafham,

put

put him upon making the separate treaty between Queen Anne and Lewis XIV. This treaty brought on the peace of Utrecht. This peace settled Philip V. on the Spanish throne: Philip dispossessed the house of Austria, of Naples, and Sicily. Thus the Spanish prince, who is now king of Naples, evidently owes his sovereignty to Mrs Masham: he would not have had it, perhaps he would not so much as have been born, had the Dutchess of Marlborough behaved with due complaisance towards the Queen of England: his existence at Naples depended on a few follies committed at the court of London. Inquire into the situations of all nations on the globe, and they all derive from a chain of events, apparently quite unconnected with any one thing, and connected with every thing. In this immense machine all is wheel-work, pully, cords, and spring. It is the same in the physical system. A wind, blowing from the south of Africa and the Austral seas, brings with it part of the African atmosphere, which falls down again in rain among the valleys of the Alps; and these rains fructify the lands. Again, our northern wind wafts our vapours among the negroes. Thus we benefit Guinea, and are benefited by it; and this chain reaches from one end of the universe to the other.

VOLTAIRE.

The Distinction between CHANCE and CAUSES.

The beſt general rule to help us in diſtinguiſhing between chance and cauſes, is the following: *What depends upon a few perſons, is in a great meaſure to be aſcribed to chance, or ſecret and unknown cauſes: What ariſes from a great number, may often be accounted for by determinate and known cauſes.*

Two natural reaſons may be aſſigned for this rule: Firſt, if you ſuppoſe a dye to have any bias, however ſmall, to a particular ſide, this bias, though perhaps it may not appear in a few throws, will certainly prevail in a great number, and will caſt the balance entirely to that ſide. In like manner, when any *cauſes* beget a particular inclination or paſſion at a certain time, and among a certain people, though many individuals may eſcape the contagion, and be ruled by paſſions peculiar to to themſelves, yet the multitude will certainly be ſeized by the common affection, and be governed by it in all their actions.—Secondly, Thoſe principles or cauſes which are fitted to operate on a multitude, are always of a groſſer nature, leſs ſubject to accidents, and leſs influenced by whim and private fancy, than thoſe which operate on a few only. The latter are commonly ſo delicate and refined, that the ſmalleſt incident in the health, education, or fortune of a particular person, is sufficient to divert their course, and retard their operation; nor is it possible to reduce them to any general maxims or observations. Their influence at one time will never assure us concerning their influence at another, even though all the general circumstances should be the same in both cases.—To judge by this rule, the domestic and the gradual revolutions of a state must be a more proper subject of reasoning and observation than the foreign and the violent, which are commonly produced by single persons, and are more influenced by whim, folly, or caprice, than by general passions and interests. The depression of the lords, and rise of the commons in England, after the statutes of alienation and the increase of trade and industry, are more easily accounted for by general principles, than the depression of the Spanish and rise of the French monarchy after the death of Charles V. Had Henry IV. Cardinal Richelieu, and Louis XIV. been Spaniards, and Philip II. III. and IV. and Charles II. been Frenchmen, the history of these two nations had been entirely reversed.

For the same reason, it is more easy to account for the rise and progress of commerce in any kingdom, than for that of learning; and a state which should apply itself to the encouragement of the one, would be more assured of success than one which should cultivate the other. Avarice, or the desire of gain, is an universal passion, which operates at all times, in all places, and upon all persons. But curiosity, or the love of knowledge, has a very limited influence; and requires youth, leisure, education, genius, and example, to make it govern any person. You will never want booksellers while there are buyers of books: But there may frequently be readers where there are no authors. Multitudes of people, necessity, and liberty, have begot commerce in Holland: But study and application have hardly produced any eminent writers.

We may therefore conclude, that there are subjects in which we must proceed with caution in tracing their history, lest we assign causes which never existed, and reduce what is merely contingent to stable and universal principles.

HUME.

CHARACTER.

THIS term comes from a Greek word, signifying impression and graving. It is what nature has engraven in us: Then can we efface it? This is a weighty question. Religion and morality lay a check on the force of a natural temper, but cannot extirpate it. A sot, when in a convent, reduced to half a pint of cyder at each meal, will no longer be seen drunk, but his love of wine will ever be the same.—Age weakens the natural character: it is a tree which only produces some degenerate fruits; still are they of one and the same nature. It grows knotty, and over-run with moss, and worm-eaten; but amidst all this, it continues what it was, whether oak or pear tree. Could a man change his character, he would give himself one; he would be superior to nature. Can we give ourselves any thing? What have we that we have not received? Endeavour to raise the indolent to a constant activity, to freeze the impetuous into an apathy, to give a taste for poetry or music to one who has neither taste nor ears; you may as well go about washing the blackmoor white, or giving sight to one born blind. We only improve, polish, and conceal what nature has put into us; we have nothing of our own putting.—*Naturam expellas furca, tamen usque redibit.*

VOLTAIRE.

National CHARACTERS.

NO species of government, religion, opinion, or moral cause, can make any material alterations in the people of countries situated in the extremes of heat and cold. Heat deprives the body of all vigour and strength, and the imbecillity is communicated to the intellectual faculties; the inclinations

tions are all paffive; indolence conftitutes the utmoft happinefs. In cold countries the inhabitant finds a fufficient tafk in fcreening himfelf from the feverity of the feafon, and in providing a fubfiftence: Not that the nature of man is altered or impaired, either in the quality or number of its faculties; but thefe capabilities are not fuffered to exert themfelves. There can be no vigorous applications, no long watchings, nothing of that progreffive and accumulated improvement of ages and generations linked together, which is indifpenfably neceffary to the perfection of arts and fciences. CHATTELUR.

DIGNITY OF CHARACTER.

THE fublime, fays Longinus, is often nothing but the echo or image of magnanimity; and where this quality appears in any one, even though not a fyllable be uttered, it excites our applaufe and admiration; as may be obferved of the famous filence of Ajax in the Odyffey, which expreffes more noble difdain and refolute indignation than any language can convey.——*Were I Alexander*, faid Parmenio, *I would accept of thefe offers made by Darius. So would I too*, replied Alexander, *were I Parmenio*. This faying is admirable, fays Longinus, from a like principle.

Go! cries the same hero to his soldiers, when they refused to follow him to the Indies; *go tell your countrymen, that you left Alexander completing the conquest of the world.* "Alexander," said the Prince of Condé, who always admired this passage, "abandoned by his soldiers among "barbarians not yet fully subdued, felt in himself "such a dignity and right of empire, that he could "not believe it possible that any one should re- "fuse to obey him. Whether in Europe or in "Asia, among Greeks or Persians, all was indif- "ferent to him; wherever he found men, he fan- "cied he would find subjects."—The confidant of Medea, in the tragedy, recommends caution and submission; and enumerating all the distresses of the unfortunate heroine, asks her what she has to support her against her numerous and implacable enemies. *Myself*, replies she; *myself, I say; and it is enough.* Boileau justly recommends this passage as an instance of true sublime.

When Phocion, the modest, the gentle Phocion, was led to execution, he turned to one of his fellow-sufferers who was lamenting his own hard fate: *Is it not glory enough for you,* says he, *that you die with Phocion.*

Place in opposition the picture which Tacitus draws of Vitellius fallen from empire; prolonging his ignominy from a wretched love of life; delivered over to the merciless rabble; tossed, buffeted,

feted, and kicked about; constrained, by their holding a poinard under his chin, to raise his head and expose himself to every contumely. What abject infamy! What low humiliation! Yet even here, says the historian, he discovered some symptoms of a mind not wholly degenerate. To a tribune who insulted him, he replied, I am still your emperor.

We never excuse the absolute want of spirit and dignity of character, or a proper sense of what is due to one's self in society and the common intercourse of life. This vice constitutes what we properly call meanness; when a man can submit to the basest slavery, in order to gain his ends; fawn upon those who abuse him, and degrade himself by intimacies and familiarities with undeserving inferiors. A certain degree of generous pride or self-value is so requisite, that the absence of it in the mind displeases after the same manner as the want of a nose, eye, or any of the most material features of the face or members of the body. The absence of a virtue may often be a vice, and that of the highest kind; as in the instance of ingratitude as well as meanness. Where we expect a beauty, the disappointment gives an uneasy sensation, and produces a real deformity. An abjectness of character, likewise, is disgustful and contemptible in another view. Where a man has no sense of value in himself, we are

are not likely to have any higher eftimate of him. And if the fame perfon who crouches to his fuperiors, is infolent to his inferiors (as often happens), this contrariety of behaviour, inftead of correcting the former vice, aggravates it extremely, by the addition of a vice ftill more odious.—He muft be a very fuperficial thinker, who imagines that all inftances of mutual deference are to be underftood in earneft, and that a man would be more efteemable for being ignorant of his own merits and accomplifhments. A fmall bias towards modefty, even in the internal fentiments, is favourably regarded, efpecially in young people; and a ftrong bias is required in the outward behaviour. But this excludes not a noble pride and fpirit, which may openly difplay itfelf in its full extent when one lies under calumny or oppreffion of any kind. The generous contumacy of Socrates, as Cicero calls it, has been highly celebrated in all ages; and when joined to the ufual modefty of his behaviour, forms a fhining character. Iphicrates the Athenian, being accufed of betraying the intereft of his country, afked his accufer, *Would you,* fays he, *on a like occafion, have been guilty of that crime? By no means,* replied the other. *And can you then imagine,* cries the hero, *that Iphicrates would be guilty?* In fhort, a generous fpirit and felf-value, well-founded, decently difguifed, and courageoufly ously supported under distress and calumny, is a great excellency, and seems to derive its merit from the noble elevation of its sentiment, or its immediate agreeableness to its possessor. In ordinary characters, we approve of a bias towards modesty, which is a quality immediately agreeable to others. The vicious excess of the former virtue, namely, insolence or haughtiness, is immediately disagreeable to others: the excess of the latter is so to the possessor. Thus are the boundaries of these two duties adjusted.

HUME.

A Defence of the Punishment of CHARLES I.

CHARLES I. whatever he was in his private character, which is out of the question here, was certainly a very bad king of England. During a course of many years, and notwithstanding repeated remonstrances, he governed by maxims utterly subversive of the fundamental and free constitution of this country; and therefore he deserved the severest punishment. If he was misled by his education or his friends, he was like any other criminal in the like circumstances, to be pitied, but by no means to be spared on that account.—From the nature of things, it was necessary that the opposition should begin from a few, who may therefore be styled a Faction: but after the civil war (which necessarily ensued from the King's obstinacy, and in which he had given repeated instances of dissimulation and treachery), there was evidently no safety either for the faction or the nation short of his death. It is to be regretted that the situation of things was such, that the sentence could not be passed by the whole nation, or their representatives, solemnly assembled for that purpose. I am sensible indeed that the generality of the nation at that time would not have voted the death of their Sovereign; but this was not owing to any want of a just sense of the wrongs he had done them, but to an opinion of the sacredness of kingly power, from which very few of the friends of liberty in those times, especially among the Presbyterians who were the majority, could entirely divest themselves. Such a transaction would have been an immortal honour to this country, whenever that superstitious notion shall be obliterated: a notion which has been extremely useful in the infant state of society; but which, like other superstitions, subsists long after it hath ceased to be of use.

PRIESTLEY.

The Merit of CHASTITY derived from its Utility.

The long and helpless infancy of man requires the combination of parents for the subsistence of their young; and that combination requires the virtue of chastity or fidelity to the marriage-bed. Without such an *utility*, it will readily be owned, that such a virtue would never have been thought of. An infidelity of this nature is much more pernicious in women than in men: hence the laws of chastity are much stricter over the one sex than over the other.—These rules have all a reference to generation; and yet women past child-bearing are no more supposed to be exempted from them than those in the flower of their youth and beauty. General rules are often extended beyond the principle whence they first arise; and this in all matters of taste and sentiment. The imagination is influenced by associations of ideas; which, though they arise at first from the judgement, are not easily altered by every particular exception that occurs to us. To which we may add, in the present case of chastity, that the example of the old would be pernicious to the young; and that women, continually foreseeing that a certain time would naturally bring them the liberty of indulgence, would naturally advance that period, and think more lightly of this whole duty so requisite to society.

Those who live in the same family, have such frequent opportunities of licence of this kind, that nothing could preserve purity of manners, were marriage allowed among the nearest relations, or any intercourse of love between them ratified by law and custom. *Incest* therefore being *pernicious* in a superior degree, has also a superior turpitude and moral deformity annexed to it.—What is the reason why, by the Athenian law, one might marry a half-sister by the father but not by the mother? Plainly this: The manners of the Athenians were so reserved, that a man was never permitted to approach the womens apartment, even in the same family, unless where he visited his own mother. His step-mother and her children were as much shut up from him as the women of any other family; and there was as little danger of any criminal correspondence between them. Uncles and nieces for a like reason might marry at Athens; but neither these, nor half brothers and sisters, could contract that alliance at Rome, where the intercourse was more open between the sexes. Public utility is the cause of all these variations.

HUME.

The different Capacities of CHILDREN.

Forward prating children usually make but ordinary men: I know no observation more certain or general than this. There is nothing more difficult, than to distinguish in children between real stupidity and that apparent dulness which is the usual indication of strong intellects. It may appear strange at first sight, that two such different extremes should be indicated by the same signs; and yet it is nevertheless what we ought to expect: For at an age when we have as yet acquired no true ideas, all difference between a child of genius and one that has none, is, that the latter admits only of false ideas of things; while the former, meeting with none but such, refuses to admit any. Both therefore appear to be equally dull; the one, because he has no capacity for the comprehension of things; and the other, because the representations of things are not adapted to his capacity. The only means to distinguish between them depend on accident, which may offer to the latter some idea within his comprehension; whereas the former is always the same in all places and circumstances. Cato himself, during his infancy, was esteemed by his whole family as almost a fool: he was particularly

ticularly reserved and obstinate, which was all they could judge of him. It was in the antichamber of Sylla that his uncle first learnt to know him better. Possibly, had he not been introduced thither, he might have passed for a mere brute till he had arrived at years of discretion. If Cæsar had not also survived, that very Cato might have been treated as a visionary and a madman, who had penetration enough to read his destructive genius, and to foresee, at so great a distance, his fatal projects.——How subject are those who judge precipitately of children to be egregiously deceived! They often betray in this less judgment than the children of whom they judge.

The apparent facility with which children seem to learn, operates greatly to their prejudice; and though we do not observe it, it is a plain proof they learn nothing. The delicate texture of their brain reflects, like a mirror, every object presented to them; but nothing penetrates the substance, or remains behind: a child retains the words, but the ideas accompanying them are reflected back again; those who hear him repeat may understand what he means, but he himself knows nothing of the matter.—Although the memory and judgment are two faculties essentially different; yet the one cannot unfold itself without the other. Before a child arrives at years of understanding, he entertains not the ideas, but simply the images of things; the difference between which confists in this, that such images are only the direct paintings of perceptible objects, and ideas are the notions of such objects determined by their respective relations to each other. A single image may subsist in the mind that is sensible of it; but every idea necessarily supposes the concomitance of others. To simple imagination, or the mere formation of images, nothing more is necessary than to have seen objects; but to conceive any thing about their existence, or to form ideas of them, it is required that we should be able to compare them. Our sensations are merely passive; whereas our perceptions, or the ideas formed in consequence of those sensations, arise from an active principle capable of judging of them.

ROUSSEAU.

THE CHRISTIAN RELIGION,
ITS PROGRESS AND ESTABLISHMENT IN THE ROMAN EMPIRE.

RELIGION in man is the effect of a sense of his misfortunes, and of the fear of invisible powers.

Most legislators have availed themselves of these motives to govern the people, and still more to enflave them. Some of them have afferted, that they held the right of commanding from heaven itfelf; and it is thus that theocracy has been eftablifhed.

If the religion of the Jews has had a more fublime origin, it has not always been exempt from thofe inconveniences which neceffarily arife from the ambition of priefts in a theocratic form of government.

Chriftianity fucceeded the Jewifh inftitution. The fubjection that Rome, miftrefs of the world, was under to the moft favage tyrants; the dreadful miferies which the luxury of a court and the maintenance of armies had occafioned throughout this vaft empire under the reign of the Neros; the fucceffive irruptions of the barbarians, who difmembered this great body; the lofs of provinces either by revolt or invafion; all thefe natural evils had already prepared the minds of men for a new religion; and the changes in politics muft probably have induced an innovation in the form of worfhip. In Paganifm, which had exifted for fo many ages, there remained only the fables to which it owes its origin, the folly or the vices of its gods, the avarice of its priefts, and the infamy and licentious conduct of the kings who fupported them. Then the people, defpairing to obtain relief from their tyrants upon earth, had recourfe to heaven for protection.

Chri-

Chriftianity appeared, and afforded them comfort, at the fame time that it taught them to fuffer with patience. While the tyranny and licentioufnefs of princes tended to the deftruction of Paganifm as well as to that of the empire, the fubjects who had been oppreffed and fpoiled, and who had embraced the new doctrines, were completing its ruin by the examples they gave of thofe virtues which always accompany the zeal of new-made profelytes. But a religion that arofe in the midft of public calamity, muft neceffarily give its preachers a confiderable influence over the unhappy perfons who took refuge in it. Thus the power of the clergy commenced, as it were, with the gofpel.

From the remains of Pagan fuperftitions and philofophic fects a code of rights and tenets was formed, which the fimplicity of the primitive Chriftians fanctified with real and affecting piety; but which at the fame time left the feed of debates and controverfies, from whence arofe a variety of paffions, difguifed and dignified under the name of zeal. Thefe diffentions produced fchools, doctors, a tribunal, and a hierarchy. Chriftianity had begun to be preached by a fet of fifhermen, deftitute of every knowledge but that of the gofpel; it was entirely eftablifhed by bifhops, who formed the church. After this it gained ground by degrees, till at length it attracted

tracted the notice of the emperors. Some of these tolerated Christianity either from motives of contempt, or humanity; others persecuted it. Persecution hastened its progress, for which toleration had paved the way. Connivance and proscription, clemency and rigour, were all equally advantageous to it. The sense of freedom so natural to the human mind, induced many persons to embrace it in its infancy, as it has made others reject it since it has been established. This spirit of independency, rather adapted to truth than to novelty, would necessarily have induced a multitude of persons of all ranks to become converts to Christianity, if even the characters it bore had not been calculated to inspire veneration and respect.

RAYNAL.

CHRISTIANITY,

NOT ADAPTED TO MAKE A CONSTITUTIONAL PART IN ANY SYSTEM OF LEGISLATION.

CHRISTIANITY is in its principles an universal religion; having nothing exclusive, nothing local, nothing peculiar to one country any more than to another. Its Divine Author, embracing all mankind in his boundless charity, came to remove those barriers that separated the nations from each other, and to unite all mankind in a people of brethren: such is the true spirit of the gospel.

Those, therefore, who would make Christianity to be a national religion, and introduce it as a constitutional part in a system of legislation, have been guilty of two faults; the one pernicious to religion, and the other to the state. They have departed from the spirit of Jesus Christ, whose kingdom is not of this world; and, confounding our sublunary interests with those of religion, have sullied its celestial purity; converted it into a scourge in the hands of tyrants, and an instrument of persecution. They have done no less injury to the salutary maxims of policy; as instead of simplifying the machine of government, they have rendered it more complicated; they have added to it foreign and superfluous resources, and by subjecting it to two different and frequently contrary motions, have occasioned those convulsions which are felt in all Christian states, in which religion hath entered into the political system.—Perfect Christianity is an universal social institution; but not a political establishment, nor doth it concur to the support of any good particular institution. All human establishments are founded on human passions, and are supported by them: whatever combats and destroys the passions, therefore, is by no means proper to strengthen those establishments. How can that which

which detaches our hearts from the things of the world, induce us to interest ourselves more strongly in what is doing here? How can that which engages our thoughts only towards another country attach us more powerfully to this? Christianity, by making men just, moderate, and peaceable, is very advantageous to society in general: but it weakens the force of the political spring; it renders the movements of the machine more complex; it breaks the unity of the body moral;.and being insufficiently appropriated to the purposes of government, must either degenerate, or remain a detached and embarrassing subject.—The science of salvation and government are very different. To insist that the former includes all others, is the fanaticism of a narrow mind. Such a way of thinking is like that of the alchemists, who, in the art of making gold, conceive they also see that of the universal medicine; or like that of the Mahometans, who pretend that all arts and sciences are to be found in the Alcoran. The doctrines of the gospel have but one object in view, which is the universal salvation of mankind. Their liberties and properties here below have nothing to do with it. The gospel inspires humanity rather than patriotism, and tends rather to the forming of men than citizens. Patriotism and humanity are two virtues incompatible with each other in

any

any great degree, and particularly in a whole people. The legiflator who would unite them both, will obtain neither one nor the other. Their union never was, nor ever will be, known; becaufe it is contrary to nature, and becaufe it is impoffible to give two objects to one paffion.

ROUSSEAU.

CIVIL COMMOTIONS.

ALWAYS to throw, without diftinction, the blame of all diforders in the ftate upon the prince, would introduce a fatal error in politics, and ferve as a perpetual apology for treafon and rebellion: as if the turbulency of the great, and madnefs of the people, were not, equally with the tyranny of princes, an evil incident to human fociety, and no lefs carefully to be guarded againft in every well-regulated conftitution.—We muft not, therefore, imagine, that all the ancient princes, who were unfortunate in their government, were alfo tyrannical in their conduct, and that the feditions of the people proceeded always from fome invafion of their liberties and privileges by the monarch.—Men, inftead of complaining againft the manners of the age and the form of conftitution, are very apt to impute all errors to the perfon who has the mif-

fortune

fortune to be entrusted with the reins of empire. HUME.

The Difference of Men in different CLIMATES.

A COLD air constringes the extremities of the external fibres of the body, (this appears in the countenance; in cold weather people look thinner): this increases their strength, and favours the return of the blood from the extreme parts to the heart. It contracts those very fibres; of course it increases their force and elasticity.—People are therefore more vigorous in cold climates: here the action of the heart and the reaction of the extremities of the fibres are better performed; the circulation goes on much brisker; the heart has more power. This superiority of strength must produce various effects; for instance, a greater boldness, that is, more courage; a greater sense of superiority, that is, less desire of revenge; a greater opinion of security, that is, more frankness, less suspicion, policy, and cunning. In short, this must be productive of very different tempers. Put a man into a close warm place, and, for the reasons above given, he will feel a great faintness. If under this circumstance you propose a bold enterprise to him, you will find him very little difpofed towards it: his prefent weaknefs will throw him into defpondency; he will be afraid of every thing, being in a ftate of total incapacity. The inhabitants of warm countries are, like old men, timorous; the people in cold countries are, like young men, brave.

The nerves that terminate from all parts in the furface of the body, form each a nervous bundle or papilla. In warm climates, where the fkin is relaxed, the ends of the nerves are expanded, and laid open to the weakeft actions of the fmalleft objects. In cold countries the fkin is conftringed, and the papillæ compreffed; the fenfation does not reach the brain, but when it is very ftrong. Now imagination, tafte, fenfibility, and vivacity, depend on an infinite number of fmall fenfations.

The outermoft part of a fheep's tongue, to the naked eye, feems covered with papillæ. On thefe papillæ are feen through a microfcope fmall filaments like a kind of down; between the papillæ are pyramids, fhaped towards the end like pincers. Very likely, thefe pyramids are the principal organs of tafte.

I caufed the half of a tongue to be frozen, and obferving it with the naked eye, I found the papillæ confiderably diminifhed; even fome rows of them were funk into their fheath. The outermoft part I examined with the microfcope, and
per-

perceived no pyramids. In proportion as the frost went off, the papillæ seemed to the naked eye to rise, and with the microscope the miliary glands began to appear.

This observation confirms what I have been saying, that in cold countries the cutaneous glands and the nervous papillæ are less expanded: they sink deeper into their sheaths, or they are sheltered from the action of external objects; consequently they are less capable of lively sensations.——In cold countries, people have very little sensibility for pleasure; in temperate countries, they have more; in warm countries, their sensibility is exquisite. As climates are distinguished by degrees of latitude, we might distinguish them also in some measure by those of sensibility. I have been at the opera in England and in Italy, where I have seen the same pieces and the same performers: and yet the same music produces such different effects on the two nations; one is so cold and phlegmatic, and the other so lively and enraptured, that it seems almost inconceivable.

It is the same with regard to pain. The fibres of the people of the north are stronger, and less capable of irritation and sensibility, than those of the inhabitants of warm countries; consequently they are less sensible of pain. You must flay a Muscovite alive to make him feel.

From

—From this delicacy of organs peculiar to warm climates, it follows that the mind is moſt ſenſibly moved by whatever relates to the union of the two ſexes: here every thing leads to this object.— In northern climates, ſcarce has the animal part of love a power of making itſelf felt. In temperate climates, love, attended by a thouſand appendages, endeavours to pleaſe by things that have at firſt the appearances, though not the reality, of this paſſion. In warmer climates, it is liked for its own ſake; it is the only cauſe of happineſs; it is life itſelf.—In ſouthern countries, a machine of a delicate frame, but ſtrong ſenſibility, reſigns itſelf either to a love which riſes, and is inceſſantly laid, in a ſeraglio; or to a paſſion which leaves women in greater independence, and is conſequently expoſed to a thouſand inquietudes. In northern regions, a machine robuſt and vigorous finds a pleaſure in whatever is apt to throw the ſpirits into motion; ſuch as hunting, travelling, war, wine. If we travel towards the north, we meet with people who have few vices, many virtues, and a great ſhare of frankneſs and ſincerity. If we draw near the ſouth, we fancy ourſelves entirely removed from the verge of morality: here the ſtrongeſt paſſions are productive of all manner of crimes, each man endeavouring, let the means be what they will, to indulge his inordinate deſires. In temperate climates, we find

find the inhabitants inconstant in their manners, as well as in their vices and virtues: the climate has not a quality determinate enough to fix them.

The heat of the climate may be so excessive as to deprive the body of all vigour and strength. Then the faintness is communicated to the mind; there is no curiosity, no enterprise, no generosity of sentiment; the inclinations are all positive; indolence constitutes the utmost happiness; scarcely any punishment is so severe as mental employment, and slavery is more supportable than force and vigour of mind necessary for human conduct.

MONTESQUIEU.

The Influence of CLIMATE on Mankind.

The soil is not a matter of indifference in the cultivation of mankind: they are not all such as they might have been if born in temperate climates. The disadvantage is visible in either extreme. A man is not planted like a tree in any country to grow there continually, but is frequently changing his place; and he who removes from one extreme to the other, is obliged to go twice as far to arrive at the same point, as he who sets out from a line drawn between both. If the inhabitant of a temperate clime visits successively both extremes, his advantages are further evident

evident: for although he should undergo the same modification as one that should pass from one extreme to the other, yet he would depart each way the less by half from his natural constitution. Thus a Frenchman may live in Guinea or in Lapland; but a negro would not live so well at Torneo, nor a Samoyad at Benin. It appears also that the organization of the brain is less perfect in the two extremes. Neither the Negroes nor the Laplanders have the natural understandings of the nations of milder climates.

ROUSSEAU.

The Influence of CLIMATE.

IF the greater or less strength of mind depended on the different climate of countries, it would be impossible, considering the age of the world, but that what was in this respect most favoured, should by its progress have acquired a great superiority over all others. The esteem which different nations have by turns obtained with respect to science, and the contempt into which they have successively fallen, prove the little influence climates have on the mind. The superiority of certain nations over others in the arts and sciences, can only be attributed to moral causes; there are no people privileged in point of virtue, genius, and courage: Nature, in this respect, has not made a partial distribution of her favours. HELVETIUS.

COMMERCE
FAVOURABLE TO CIVILIZATION AND PEACE.

THERE are many things which in themselves are morally neither good nor bad; but they are productive of consequences which are strongly marked with one or other of these characters. Thus commerce, though in itself a moral nullity, has had a considerable influence in tempering the human mind. It was the want of objects in the ancient world which occasioned such a rude and perpetual turn for war. Their time hung on their hands without the means of employment. The indolence they lived in afforded leisure for mischief; and being all idle at once, and equal in their circumstances, they were easily provoked or induced to action.

But the introduction of commerce furnished the world with objects, which in their extent reach every man, and give him something to think about, and something to do: by these his attention is mechanically drawn from the pursuits which a state of indolence and an unemployed

ployed mind occafioned; and he trades with the fame countries which former ages, tempted by their productions, and too indolent to purchafe them, would have gone to war with.

The condition of the world is materially changed by the influence of fcience and commerce; it is put into a fitnefs not only to admit of, but to defire an extenfion of, civilization. The world has undergone its divifions of empire, the feveral boundaries of which are known and fettled. The idea of conquering countries like the Greeks and Romans, does not now exift; and experience has exploded now the notion of going to war for the fake of profit. In fhort, the objects of war are exceedingly diminifhed, and there is now left fcarcely any thing to quarrel about, but what arifes from the demon of fociety, Prejudice, and the confequent fullennefs and untractablenefs of the temper.

THO^s. PAINE.

CONSCIENCE.

ALL the morality of our actions lies in the judgment we ourfelves form of them. All the rules of morality are written in indelible characters on the heart of man. I have only to confult myfelf to know what I ought to do; all that I feel

feel to be right is right; whatever I feel to be wrong, is wrong: Confcience is the ableft of all cafuifts, and it is only when we are trafficking with her that we have recourfe to the fubtilties of reafon. It is pretended, that every one contributes to the public good for his own intereft; but whence comes it that the virtuous man contributes to it to his prejudice? Can a man lay down his life for his own intereft? The chief of our concerns, indeed, is that of ourfelves; yet how often have we been told by the monitor within, that to purfue our own intereft at the expence of others would be to do wrong! Which is moft agreeable for us to do, and leaves the moft pleafing reflection behind it, an act of benevolence or of mifchief? For whom are we moft interefted at our theatres? Do we take pleafure in acts of villany? or do we fhed tears at feeing the authors of them brought to punifhment? It has been faid, that every thing is indifferent to us in which we are not interefted: the contrary, however, is certain, as the foothing endearments of friendfhip and humanity confole us under afflictions; and even in our pleafures we fhould be too folitary, too miferable, if we had nobody to partake them with us. If there be nothing moral in the heart of man, whence arife thofe tranfports of admiration and efteem we entertain for heroic actions, and great minds?

What

What has this virtuous enthusiasm to do with our private interest? Wherefore do I rather wish to be an expiring Cato, than a triumphant Cæsar? Of what hurt is the wickedness of a Cataline to me? Am I afraid of falling a victim to his villany? Wherefore do I then look upon him with the same horror as if he was my cotemporary? We do not hate the wicked only because their vices are hurtful, but also because they are wicked.

Amidst all the inhuman absurd forms of worship, amidst all the prodigious diversity of manners and characters, you will every where find the same ideas of justice and honesty, the same notions of good and evil. Antient Paganism adopted the most abominable deities, which it would have punished on earth as infamous criminals; deities that presented no other picture of supreme happiness than the commission of crimes, and the gratification of their passions. But vice, armed even with sacred authority, descended in vain on earth; moral instinct influenced the human heart to revolt against it. Even in celebrating the debaucheries of Jupiter, the world admired and respected the continence of Zenocrates; the chaste Lucretia adored the impudent Venus. There exists therefore evidently in the heart of man an innate principle of justice and goodness; by which, in spite of our own

own maxims, we approve or condemn the actions of ourselves and others. To this principle I give the appellation of *conscience*. But we are told by some philosophers, that there is nothing in the human mind but what is instilled by experience; nor can we judge of any thing but from the ideas we have acquired. To confute this opinion, we need only to distinguish between our acquired ideas and our natural sentiments; for we are sensible before we are intelligent; and as we do not learn to desire our own good, and to avoid what is evil, but possess this desire immediately from nature; so the love of virtue and hatred of vice, are as natural as the love of ourselves. The operations of conscience are not intellectual, but sentimental: for though all our ideas are acquired from without, the sentiments which estimate them arise from within; and it is by these alone that we know the agreement or disagreement which exists between us and those things which we ought to seek or shun.

To exist, is, with us, to be sensible; our sensibility is incontestably prior to our intelligence; and we were possessed of sentiment before we formed ideas. Whatever was the cause of our being, it hath provided us with sentiments agreeable to our constitution; nor can it possibly be denied that these at least are innate. These sentiments are, in the individual, the love of himself,
aver-

averſion to pain, dread of death, and the deſire of happineſs. But if, as it cannot be doubted, man is by nature a ſociable being, or at leaſt formed to become ſuch, his ſociability abſolutely requires that he ſhould be furniſhed with other innate ſentiments relative to his ſpecies: For to conſider only the phyſical wants of men, it would certainly be better for them to be diſperſed than aſſembled.

Now it is from this moral ſyſtem, formed by its duplicate relation to himſelf and his fellow-creatures, that the impulſe of conſcience ariſes. To know what is virtuous, is not to love virtue. Man has no innate knowledge of virtue; but no ſooner is it made known to him by reaſon, than conſcience induces him to love and admire it. This is the innate ſentiment I mean.

ROUSSEAU.

ON THE SAME SUBJECT.

THE conſcience is not an original infallible guide appointed by God in our breaſts; it is formed as reaſon, imagination, and the other powers of the mind, by education, habits, examples, principles, and laws; and it differs greatly according as we have been differently affected by thoſe circumſtances. A perſon who has been taught to conſider happineſs as the end of life,

and

and to acquire real knowledge and virtue as the means of that happiness, has a virtuous sensibility formed, which will ever direct him right, and will make him always happy. By a process something similar, an infinite variety of false consciences are formed. A man who has been taught to consider interest as the end of life, and industry, attention, servility, as means, makes his experiments and trials with that object in view; and his understanding and conscience will be totally different from the former. Religion, that first and best of blessings, has been misinterpreted and misunderstood, so as to furnish an infinite variety of false principles of conduct. The intent and purpose of it is to lead men by virtue to happiness. But there is no species of vice which men have not committed on one or more of those false systems, which they have denominated true religion. The reason of this is obvious. A man is brought up to his religion as he is brought up to his trade. He is told of what articles and doctrines it is to consist: and that if he does not induce his mind to believe and practise it, he will lose the good opinion of his friends; he will make them his implacable enemies; his fortune will be injured; his person punished; and after he has been tormented in in this world, he will be consigned to the devil in the next. Thus are most religions taught;

thus

thus are the consciences of men formed to every species of villany and cruelty: for the genuine principle of a bigot is hatred of all his fellow-creatures beyond the inclosures of his own party. And yet he not only imagines he has a good conscience, but triumphs in its execrable testimony.

If we descend into the common walks of life, and consider the difference of mens apprehensions on the subject of right and wrong, we shall see that the satisfaction arising from the testimony of their consciences must be extremely different. A scale might be formed on the customs and principles of trade and commerce, graduated from dishonesty and fraud to the extreme points of honour and justice. Mens consciences, in their various employments, are adjusted on this kind of scale; and we may generally judge of the nature of a man's understanding, the elevation of his mind, and the delicacy and genuineness of his moral sensibility, from the nature of his employment.

False consciences, when they are formed with care on some political, moral, or religious prepossessions, are incurable sources of ill. They are like many disorders in the animal œconomy, where the patient is sensible of his danger; where temporary and fallacious gratifications render him secure and satisfied; and where no
re-

remedies can be applied, because his own concurrence and his own endeavours are requisite, and he cannot see the necessity of them.——It is to be hoped no person will be so puerile as to say, that if men think themselves right, they must be so; and the utmost that can be expected of them, is to act on their opinions. It may be a desirable matter, that men should proceed thus far in the path of morality, and act sincerely and honestly on those principles which they profess, whether good or evil. Hypocrisy, added to ignorance and vicious principles, increases the mischief of them; and yet we find it generally attending them. Men have not only false ideas and false consciences given them; but they are also taught to wear masques, whenever they think proper to act contrary even to their wretched principles. If we remove this hypocrisy, it is true we remove an evil. We should only then have errors to encounter with, which might either be prevented by a rational and just education, or by a diligent and careful attention to the nature and happiness of man. Persons, ill-educated, ill-formed, and with false and delusive consciences, are, however, in a much worse state than common and flagrant sinners, whose actions are in opposition to their minds, and who are often restored to virtue by experiencing the miseries of vice. It is not uncommon to see those who have
been,

been led into excesses by their passions recover themselves, and become regular and happy. It is very uncommon to see a man in any profession acting above the prepossessions of it. It is very uncommon to see a charitable sectary, or a person who has had his mind formed on narrow gloomy cruelty, recover any degree of liberality, good-nature, and humanity. Men in this situation are like lunatics, the main spring of whose minds is a false and insufficient one. And we might as well say lunatics are as they ought to be, because they think so; as that men who act ill on religious or political principles are right, because they are of that opinion. The proper and real happiness of man, as an individual, as a member of society, and a part of the universal empire of God, is to be procured only by real knowledge and virtue. It is therefore as much our duty, in every case, to consider and examine our principles, as it is honestly to act on them when we are satisfied they are right. WILLIAMS.

Liberty of CONSCIENCE.

WE can comprehend things no otherwise than as they present themselves to our perceptions; nor is it possible for any one to restrain his mind from receiving a variety of propositions either as true or as false, when clearly understood.
It

It is not in our power to think or judge according to the opinions of another; nor are we at liberty, in any cafe, to believe or difbelieve, or fufpend our affent, juft as humour or fancy may direct, or others command. In thefe particulars, we muft be guided by that light which arifes from the nature of things, fo far as it is perceived; and by thofe evidences and arguments which may appear to the mind, and convince the judgment. No one can give a rational affent to any thing but in the ufe of his reafon. How then is it poffible he fhould receive as reafonable what appears to him to be unreafonable? or that he fhould receive as a certain truth what does not come to his own mind with clear and convincing evidences? Nor can thofe arguments which may be urged, although valid in themfelves, ever produce an alteration in opinion, if they do not appear to his own judgment obvious in their connexion, and fufficient for that purpofe.

FELL.

CONTEMPT.

IF the contempt of mankind be infupportable, it is becaufe it prefages evil, as it in part deprives us of the advantages that arife from the union of men in fociety: for contempt implies a want of attention in mankind to serve us, and presents the time to come as void of pleasures, and filled with pains. HELVETIUS.

CONTROVERSY.

WHERE is the opinion, so rational, and so plausible, that the spirit of controversy cannot shake it? Can any position be so absurd, as to render specious arguments incapable of supporting it? When a person is once convinced, either of the truth or of the falsity of any thing, he immediately from a passion for disputation, becomes attached to his own idea, and soon seeks solely, to acquire a superiority over his adversary, by dint of the powers of imagination and by subtilty; especially when some obscure question, involved by its nature in darkness, is the point in debate. ARNOBIUS.

RELIGIOUS CONTROVERSIES.

Two men, travelling on the highway, the one east, the other west, can easily pass each other, if the way be broad enough. But two men, reasoning upon opposite principles of religion, cannot so easily pass without shocking; though one should think that the way were also, in that case, sufficiently broad, and that each

VOL. I. N † might

might proceed without interruption in his own courſe. But ſuch is the nature of the human mind, that it always takes hold of every mind that approaches it; and as it is wonderfully fortified and corroborated by an unanimity of ſentiments, ſo it is ſhocked and diſturbed by any contrariety. Hence the eagerneſs which moſt people diſcover in a diſpute; and hence their impatience of oppoſition, even in the moſt ſpeculative and indifferent opinions.

This principle, however frivolous it may appear, ſeems to have been the origin of all religious wars and diviſions. But as this principle is univerſal in human nature, its effects would not have been confined to one age, and to one ſect of religion, did it not there concur with other more accidental cauſes, which raiſe it to ſuch a height as to produce the greateſt miſery and devaſtation. Moſt religions of the ancient world aroſe in the unknown ages of government, when men were as yet barbarous and uninſtructed, and the prince as well as peaſant was diſpoſed to receive with implicit faith, every pious tale or fiction, which was offered him. The magiſtrate embraced the religion of the people, and entering cordially into the care of ſacred matters, naturally acquired an authority in them, and united the eccleſiaſtical with the civil power. But the Chriſtian religion ariſing, while principles directly op-

oppofite to it were firmly eftablifhed in the polite part of the world, who defpifed the nation who broached this novelty; no wonder that, in fuch circumftances, it was but little countenanced by the civil magiftrate, and that the prieflhood were allowed to engrofs all the authority in the new fect. So bad a ufe did they make of this power, even in thofe early times, that the perfecutions of Chriftianity may, perhaps, in *part*, be afcribed to the violence inftilled by them into their followers; though it muft not be diffembled that there were laws againft external fuperftition amongft the Romans as ancient as the time of the twelve tables; and the Jews as well as Chriftians were fometimes punifhed by them; though, in general, thefe laws were not rigoroufly executed. Immediately after the conqueft of Gaul, they forbad all but the natives to be initiated into the religion of the Druids ; and this was a kind of perfecution. In about a century after this conqueft, the Emperor Claudius, quite abolifhed that fuperftition by penal laws ; which would have been a very grievous perfecution, if the imitation of the Roman manners had not, before hand, weaned the Gauls from their ancient prejudices. (*Suetonius in vita Claudii.*) Pliny afcribes the abolition of Druid fuperftitions to Tiberius, probably becaufe that emperor had taken fome fteps towards reftraining them. This is an inftance of the usual caution and moderation of the Romans in such cases; and very different from their violent and sanguinary method of treating the Christians. Hence we may entertain a suspicion, those furious persecutions of Christianity were in some measure owing to the imprudent zeal and bigotry of the first propagators of that sect; and ecclesiastical history affords us many reasons to confirm this suspicion. After Christianity became the established religion, the principles of priestly government continued; and engendered a spirit of persecution, which has ever since been the poison of human society, and the source of the most inveterate factions in every government.—There is another cause (besides the authority of the priests, and the separation of the ecclesiastical and civil powers) which has contributed to render Christendom the scene of religious wars and divisions. Religions, that arise in ages totally ignorant and barbarous, consist mostly of traditional tales and fictions, which may be very different in every sect, without being contrary to each other; and even when they are contrary, every one adheres to the tradition of his own sect, without much reasoning and disputation. But as philosophy was widely spread over the world at the time when Christianity arose, the teachers of the new sect were obliged to form a system of speculative opinions;

to

to divide with some accuracy their articles of faith; and to explain, comment, confute, and defend with all the subtilty of argument and science. Hence naturally arose keenness in dispute, when the Christian religion came to be split into new divisions and heresies. And this keenness assisted the priests in their policy, of begetting a mutual hatred and antipathy among their deluded followers. Sects of philosophy, in the ancient world, were more zealous than parties of religion; but in modern times, parties of religion are more furious and enraged than the most cruel factions that ever arose from interest and ambition.—The civil wars which arose some years ago in Morocco between the blacks and whites, merely on account of their complexion, are founded on a pleasant difference. We laugh at them; but were things rightly examined, we afford much more occasion of ridicule to the moors. For what are all the wars of religion which have prevailed in this polite and knowing part of the world? They are certainly more absurd than the Moorish civil wars. The difference of complexion is a sensible and real difference: But the difference about an article of faith, which is utterly absurd and unintelligible, is not a difference in sentiment, but a difference in a few phrases and expressions, which one party accepts of without underſtanding them, and the other refuſes in the ſame manner.

HUME.

CONVERSATION.

A VERBAL converſation may be miſtaken by a ſlowneſs of underſtanding, or by a haſte of zeal; may be miſtated by a weakneſs of memory, or by arts of deſign. The force and ſpirit of a converſation may depend upon the occaſion which introduced it; upon the obſervations which preceded it; upon the time in which it was pronounced; upon the geſture by which it was accompanied. A converſation related with verbal accuracy may have diminiſhed or increaſed its force, may have acquired a milder or a more malignant ſpirit, in the hands of an artful or an unſkilful reporter. * *

ON THE SAME SUBJECT.

THE laws of converſation are, in general, not to labour over any ſubject, but to paſs over eaſily, without effort or affectation, from one to another; to ſpeak occaſionally on frivolous as well as on ſerious ſubjects; to remember that converſation is a relaxation, and not a fencing-ſchool,

school, nor a game of chess; in a word, to allow the fancy to range at freedom. You are not to engross the discourse to yourself, nor to deliver your opinions in a magisterial tone; as this must be very disgusting to the hearers, and prepossess them against you.—There can be no situation in which we are less able to conceal our self-love than in conversation; and we are always sure to lose by mortifying the pride of others, who will naturally be desirous of revenging themselves; and their ingenuity seldom fails instantly to discover an opportunity. Another defect to be shunned is speaking like one reading, and having what is called a well-written conversation. A conversation ought no more to be like a written discourse, than the latter like a conversation. What is pretty singular is, that those who fall into the former blemish, seldom escape the other: because being in the habit of speaking as they would write, they imagine they ought to write as they speak. It should be a rule, that a man cannot be too much on his guard when he writes to the public, and never too easy towards those with whom he converses.

D'ALEMBERT.

The Exportation of CORN.

IN inland high countries, remote from the sea, and whose rivers are small, running *from* the country, and not *to* it, as is the case of Switzerland, great distress may arise from a course of bad harvests, if public granaries are not provided and kept well stored.—Anciently, too, before navigation was so general, ships so plenty, and commercial connections so well established, even maritime countries might be occasionally distressed by bad crops: But such is now the facility of communication between those countries, that an unrestrained commerce can scarce ever fail of procuring a sufficiency for any of them. If indeed any government is so imprudent as to lay its hands on imported corn, forbid its exportation, or compel its sale at limited prices, there the people may suffer some famine, from merchants avoiding their ports. But wherever commerce is known to be always free, and the merchant absolute master of his commodity, as in Holland, there will always be a reasonable supply.—When an exportation of corn takes place, occasioned by a higher price in some foreign countries, it is common to raise a clamour, on the supposition that we shall thereby produce a domestic famine. Then follows a prohibition, founded on the imaginary

ginary diſtreſs of the poor. The poor to be ſure, if in diſtreſs, ſhould be relieved; but if the farmer could have a high price for his corn from the foreign demand, muſt he by a prohibition of exportation be compelled to take a low price, not of the poor only, but of every one that eats bread, even the richeſt? The duty of relieving the poor is incumbent on the rich; but by this operation the whole burden of it is laid on the farmer, who is to relieve the rich at the ſame time. Of the poor, too, thoſe who are maintained by the pariſhes, have no right to claim this ſacrifice of the farmer; as, while they have their allowance, it makes no difference to them whether bread be cheap or dear. Thoſe working poor, who now mind buſineſs only five or four days in the week, if bread ſhould be ſo dear as to oblige them to work the whole ſix required by the commandment, do not ſeem to be aggrieved, ſo as to have a right to public redreſs. There will then remain, comparatively, only a few families in every diſtrict, who from ſickneſs, or a great number of children, will be ſo diſtreſſed by a high price of corn, as to need relief; and they ſhould be taken care of by particular benefactions, without reſtraining the farmer's profit.—Thoſe who fear that exportation may ſo far drain the country of corn as to ſtarve ourſelves, fear what never did, nor ever can happen. They may as well, when

they

they view the tide ebbing towards the sea, fear that all the water will leave the river. The price of corn, like water, will find its level. The more we export, the dearer it becomes at home; the more is received abroad, the cheaper it becomes there: and as soon as these prices are equal, the exportation stops of course. As the seasons vary in different countries, the calamity of a bad harvest is never universal. If then all ports were always open, and all commerce free, every maritime country would generally eat bread at the medium price or average of all the harvests; which would probably be more equal than we can make it by our artificial regulations, and therefore a more steady encouragement to agriculture. The nation would all have bread at the middle price; and that nation which at any time inhumanly refuses to relieve the distresses of another nation, deserves no compassion when in distress itself. FRANKLIN.

COUNTRY.

A COUNTRY is composed of several families: and as self-love generally leads us to stand up for and support our particular families when a contrary interest does not intervene; so, from the like self-love, a man stands up for his town or village; which he calls his native home.——The

more

more extended this native home is, the lefs we love it; for divifion weakens love: it is impoffible in nature to have a tender love for a family fo numerous as fcarce to be known.—The candidate, amidft his ambitious intrigues to be chofen Ædile, Tribune, Prætor, Conful, Dictator, makes a noife about his love for his country; whereas it is only himfelf that he loves. Every one is for fecuring to himfelf the freedom of laying at his own home, and that it fhall be in no man's power to turn him out; every one is for being fure of his life and fortune. Thus the whole fociety coinciding in the like wifhes, private intereft becomes that of the public; and an individual in praying only for himfelf, prays in effect for the whole community.——Every ftate on the whole earth indifputably has originally been a republic; it is the natural progrefs of human nature: a number of families at firft entered into an alliance to fecure one another againft bears and wolves; and that which had plenty of grain, bartered with another which had nothing but wood.

On our difcovery of America, all the feveral tribes throughout that vaft part of the world were found divided into republics; but there were only two kingdoms. Of a thoufand nations, only two were fubdued.

VOLTAIRE.

Religious and Political Corruption.

The name of religious corruption is given to all kinds of libertinism, and principally to that of men with women. This species of corruption is not incompatible with the happiness of a nation. The people of different countries have believed, and believe still, that this corruption is not criminal. It could not be criminal in any state, if women were in common, and their offspring declared the children of the state: this crime would then, in a political view, be attended with no danger. In fact, if we take a survey of the earth, we shall see different nations of people, among whom what we call *libertinism* is not only considered as no corruption of manners, but is found authorised by the laws, and even confecrated by religion. What innumerable evils, will it be said, are annexed to this kind of corruption? May it not be answered: That diffoluteness is then only politically dangerous in a state, when it contravenes the law of the country, or is blended with some other defect of government. It is in vain to add, that the nations where such diffoluteness prevails, are the contempt of the world. What nation ever excelled the Greeks? a people which to this day is the admiration and honour of human

man nature. Before the Peleponefian war, an æra fatal to their virtue, what nation, what country, produced so many virtuous and great men? Yet the taste of the Greeks for the most indecent and unnatural lust is well known; and the most virtuous of the Greeks, according to our ideas of morality, would have been looked upon in Europe as most wicked and contemptible debauchees. This kind of corruption of manners was in Greece carried to the utmost excess, at the very time that country produced such great men of every kind as made Persia to tremble. We may therefore observe, that religious corruption does not seem incompatible with the greatness and felicity of a state; but political corruption is preparative to the fall of an empire, and presages its ruin. With this a people is infected when the bulk of the individuals separate their interest from that of the public. This kind of corruption, which sometimes is blended with the preceding, has led many moralists to confound them: if the question be only of the political interest of a state, the latter would perhaps be the most dangerous. A people, however pure its manners might have been at first, when this corruption becomes common, must necessarily be unhappy at home, and little feared abroad: the duration of such an empire is precarious; it is chance which either delays or hastens the fall of it.

it. The public happinefs or mifery depends folely on the agreement or oppofition of the intereft of individuals with the general intereft; and the religious corruption of manners may, as hiftory abundantly proves, be often joined with magnanimity, elevation of foul, wifdom, abilities; in fine, with all the qualities which form great men. There are two different fpecies of bad actions; fome vicious in every form of government; others, which in a ftate are pernicious, and confequently criminal only, as thofe actions are contradictory to the laws of thofe countries.

HELVETIUS.

COURTESANS.

COUTESANS were more honoured by the Romans than by us; and more than either by the Greeks. All the world have heard of the two Afpafias, one of whom inftructed even Socrates in politics and eloquence; of Phryne, who at her own expence built the walls of Thebes deftroyed by Alexander, and whofe lewdnefs repaired in fome meafure the evil done by that conqueror; of Lais, who captivated fo many philofophers, even Diogenes, whom fhe made happy, and of whom Ariftippus faid, " I poflefs Lais, " but Lais does not poflefs me:" A good maxim for every man of fenfe. But the moft celebrated
of

of all was Leontium, who wrote books of philofophy, and was beloved by Epicurus and his difciples. The famous Ninon l'Enclos may be looked upon as the modern Leontium: but how few others have refembled her! Nothing is more uncommon than philofophical ladies of pleafure: perhaps it is a profanation to join the former to the latter term. We will not enlarge on this article; but it may be proper to obferve, that, independent of our religion, viewing it only in a moral light, a paffion for *common women* equally enervates the foul and the body, and is attended with the worft of confequences, with regard to fortune, health, repofe, and happinefs. On this occafion we may recal the faying of Demofthenes, " I will not buy repentance at fo " dear a price;" and alfo that of the Emperor Adrian, who on being afked why Venus was painted naked, replied, *Quia nullos dimittit.*

But are not falfe and coquetifh women more contemptible in one fenfe, and more dangerous to the heart and underftanding, than courtefans? This queftion we fhall leave others to determine.

A celebrated philofopher (Buffon) now living, examines in his natural hiftory, Why love makes the happinefs of all other beings and the mifery of man? He anfwers " That the only thing " valuable in that paffion is the inftinctive attrac- " tion (le phyfique), and that the moral fentiment
" (le

"(le moral) which accompanies it is good for no-thing." This philosopher does not maintain that the moral adds nothing to the physical pleasure; for here experience would be against him: nor that the moral is only an illusion (which is the case), but destroys not the vivacity of the pleasure. His meaning is, undoubtedly, that from the moral sentiment proceed all the evils of love: and here one cannot be of his opinion.

From this, let us only infer, that if a light superior to our reason did not promise us a happier state, we might well complain of Nature, who with one hand presenting us the most alluring of pleasures, would seem with the other to push us from it, in surrounding it with so many rocks and shelves, and placing it in a manner on the brink of a precipice between grief and privation.

Qualibus in tenebris, vitæ quantique periclis. Degitur hoc ævi quodcunque est!

D'ALEMBERT.

CREATION.

WE have no ideas of matter being created and endued with the qualities which it possesses. Things having certainly very much the appearance which they might have had, if we could suppose a certain portion of space occupied by a confused mass

mass of such materials as form this world; and if we could suppose Almighty God immediately employed in keeping this mass from universal dissipation till the laws of motion, attraction, and gravitation took place: then, from the motion of this substance, we can account for the present form of the earth; the constituent parts of it; the beds or strata and laminæ of which it is composed; the subsiding of those heavier matters; the raising water to the surface;. of the air above it; and of that ether,. that pure electric fire, which seems to be the last and simplest of our elements. In the disposition of these things, we find most eminently those qualities which we admire; Wisdom, Power, Goodness. These qualities uniformly co-operate with each other; we therefore refer them to one great principle, which we call God. Whether this great Almighty Being produced matter, and gave it principles and laws, it would be impious assurance in us either to assert or deny; because it is a subject on which we can have no conceptions, no ideas: But that the materials of this world have been brought into such order, and have such effects either with or without the industry of man, as to show wisdom, power, and goodness in the great principle which uniformly and constantly actuates it;—this we understand. WILLIAMS..

CREDULITY and AUTHORITY.

Nations in general are made more for feeling than thinking. The greatest part of them never had an idea of analysing the nature of the power by which they are governed. They obey without reflection, because they have the habit of obeying. The lover of power has no other fulcrum than opinion. The origin and the object of the first national associations being unknown to them, all resistance to government appears to them a crime. It is chiefly in those states where the principles of legislation are confounded with those of religion that this blindness is to be met with. The habit of believing favours the habit of suffering. Man renounces not any object with impunity. It seems as if nature would revenge herself upon him who dares thus to degrade her. The servile disposition which she stamps upon his soul in consequence, extends itself throughout. It makes a duty of resignation as of meanness; and, kissing chains of all kinds with respect, trembles to examine either its doctrines or its laws. In the same manner that a single extravagance in religious opinions is sufficient to make many more to be adopted by minds once deceived, a first usurpation of government opens the door to all the rest. He, who believes the greater, believes the less;

he who can do the greater, can do the lefs. It is by this double abufe of credulity and authority that all the abfurdities in matters of religion and policy have been introduced into the world, for the harraffing and the crufhing of the human race.　　　　　　　　　　　RAYNAL.

THE DEGREE OF CRIMES.

CRIMES are only to be meafured by the injury done to fociety.—They err, therefore, who imagine that a crime is greater or lefs according to the intention of the perfon by whom it is committed: for this will depend on the actual impreffion of objects on the fenfes, and on the previous difpofition of the mind; both which will vary in different perfons, and even in the fame perfon at different times, according to the fucceffion of ideas, paffions, and circumftances. Upon that fyftem it would be neceffary to form, not only a particular code for every individual, but a new penal law for every crime. Men, often with the beft intention, do the greateft injury to fociety; and with the worft, do it the moft effential fervices.—Others have eftimated crimes rather by the dignity of the perfon offended, than by their confequences to fociety. If this were the true ftandard, the fmalleft irreverence to the Divine Being ought to be punifhed with infinitely more feverity severity than the assassination of a monarch.—Others have imagined, that the greatness of the sin should aggravate the crime. But the fallacy of this opinion will appear on the slightest consideration of the relations between man and man, and between God and man. The relations between man and man are relations of equality. Necessity alone hath produced, from the opposition of private passions and interests, the idea of public utility; which is the foundation of human justice. The degree of sin depends on the malignity of the heart, which is impenetrable to finite beings. How then can the degree of sin serve as a standard to determine the degree of crimes? If that were admitted, men may punish when God pardons, and pardon when God condemns; and thus act in opposition to the Supreme Being. BECCARIA.

Evidence of CRIMES.

When the proofs of a crime are dependent on each other; that is, when the evidence of each witness, taken separately, proves nothing, or when all proofs are dependent upon one, the number of proofs neither increase nor diminish the probability of the fact: for the force of the whole is no greater than the force of that on which they depend; and if this fails, they all fall to the ground.

ground. When the proofs are independent on each other, the probability of the fact increases in proportion to the number of proofs; for the falsehood of one does not diminish the veracity of another.—Moral certainty, with respect to crimes, is here called probability; though it is a certainty which every man in his senses assents to from an habit produced by the necessity of acting, and which is anterior to all speculation. That certainty, which is necessary to decide that the accused is guilty, is the very same which determines every man in the most important transactions of his life.—The proofs of a crime may be divided into two classes, perfect and imperfect. I call those perfect which exclude the possibility of innocence; imperfect, those which do not exclude this possibility. Of the first, one only is sufficient for condemnation; of the second, as many are required as form a perfect proof; that is to say, that though each of these, separately taken, does not exclude the possibility of innocence, it is nevertheless excluded by their union. It should be also observed, that the imperfect proofs of which the accused, if innocent, might clear himself, and does not, become perfect.

BECCARIA.

The proportion between CRIMES and Punishments.

IT is not only the common interest of mankind that crimes should not be committed, but that crimes of every kind should be less frequent in proportion to the evil they produce to society. Therefore the means made use of by the legislature to prevent crimes, should be more powerful in proportion as they are destructive of the public safety and happiness; and as the inducements to commit them are stronger, therefore there ought to be a fixed proportion between crimes and punishments.—The disorders in society increase in proportion to the number of people, and the opposition of private interests. If we consult history, we shall find them increasing in every state with the extent of dominion. In political arithmetic, it is necessary to substitute a calculation of probabilities to mathematical exactness. That force which continually impels us to our own private interest like gravity, acts incessantly, unless it meets with an obstacle to oppose it. The effects of this force are the confused series of human actions. Punishments, which I would call political obstacles, prevent the fatal effects of private interest, without destroying the impelling cause, which is that sensibility inseparable from man.

man. The legiflator acts in this cafe like a fkilful architect, who endeavours to counteract the force of gravity by combining the circumftances which may contribute to the ftrength of his edifice.—The neceffity of uniting in fociety being granted, together with the conventions which the oppofite interefts of individuals muft neceffarily require, a fcale of crimes may be formed; of which the firft degree fhould confift of thofe which immediately tend to the diffolution of fociety; and the laft, of the fmalleft poffible injuftice done to a private member of that fociety. If an equal punifhment be ordained for two crimes that injure fociety in different degrees, there is nothing to deter men from committing the greater as often as it is attended with greater advantages.

BECCARIA.

The Influence of the CROWN in the British Parliament.

THE influence of the crown has perhaps not been induftrioufly augmented in a view to undermine the fabric of civil liberty: it appears rather to have infenfibly arifen to its prefent pitch, from the increafe of empire and commerce, from the augmentation of our armies, navies, debts, and revenues. But refer its origin to what caufe you pleafe, its exiftence is certain, and its tendency

dency obvious. In the hands of a wife and good prince, this influence may not be prejudicial; but the freedom of a people should not depend on the accidental good disposition of the prince. It is our duty by social compact to be loyal; it is our right by nature to be free. When the servility of the Roman Senate had given up to Augustus the liberties of the state, the people enjoyed under him a mild and moderate government; but did they do the same under Tiberius, Caligula, Nero, Domitian, and many other weak and wicked princes who succeeded him? Rome was once free. France heretofore had the three estates which were the guardians of its liberty. Spain had many rights and privileges, of which nothing now but the shadow remains. Denmark and Sweden had once constitutions something like that of England; but all these countries have been enslaved by their own corruption.

* *

The Origin of barbarous and ridiculous Customs in various Ages and Nations.

Some maintain, that we have an idea of virtue absolutely independent of different ages and government; and that virtue is always one and the same. Others maintain, on the contrary, that every nation forms a different idea of virtue, and consequently that the idea of virtue is merely arbitrary. These two philosophical sects are deceived; but they would both have escaped error, had they with an attentive eye considered the history of the world. They would then have perceived, that time must necessarily produce in the physical and moral world revolutions that change the face of empires; that in the great catastrophes of kingdoms the people always experience great changes; that the same actions may successively become useful and prejudicial, and consequently by turns assume the name of virtuous and vicious: for by the word *virtue* can only be understood a desire of the general happiness, and the object of virtue is the public welfare, and the actions it enjoins are the means it makes use of to accomplish that end: and therefore the idea of virtue is not arbitrary; but in different ages and countries all men, at least those who live in society, ought to form the same idea of it: and, in short, if the people represent it under different forms, it is because they take for virtue the various means they employ to accomplish the end.——However stupid we suppose mankind, it is certain, that, enlightened by their own interest, they have not without motives adopted the ridiculous customs we find among some of them: the fantasticalness of these customs proceeds then from the diversity of the interests of different nations; and in fact, if they have always, though confusedly, understood by the word *virtue* the desire of the public happiness; if they have consequently given the name of *virtuous* only to actions of public utility; and if the idea of utility has always been secretly connected with the idea of virtue; we may assert, that the most ridiculous, and even the most barbarous customs, have always had for their foundation either a real or apparent utility.—Theft was permitted at Sparta: they only punished the awkwardness of the thief. By the laws of Lycurgus, and the contempt for gold and silver in that country, few things could be stolen; and these thefts inured the Lacedemonians to a habit of courage and vigilance, who could only oppose these virtues to the ambition of the Persians and the treachery of the Ilotes. It is therefore certain, that theft, which is always prejudicial to a rich people, was of use to Sparta.

At the end of winter, when hunger calls the savage to the chase, there are some savage nations who massacre all the old and infirm men which are unable to sustain the fatigues of hunting: were they left in their cabins or in the forests, they would fall a prey to hunger or the wild beasts; they, therefore, choose rather to preserve them from those dreadful misfortunes by a speedy and a necessary parricide. And this execrable custom originates

nates from the same principle of humanity that makes us look upon it with horror.———But without having recourse to savage nations, let us direct our views to China: If it be asked why an absolute authority is there given to fathers over the lives of their children? we find that the lands of that empire, how extensive soever they are, cannot sometimes furnish subsistence for the numerous inhabitants. Now, as the too great disproportion between the multiplicity of men and the fertility of the lands would necessarily occasion wars fatal to that empire, we see that in time of famine, and to prevent an infinite number of murders and unnecessary misfortunes, the Chinese nation, humane in its intentions, but barbarous in the choice of the means, has through a sentiment of humanity, though a mistaken one, considered the permission to murder their infants as necessary to the repose of the empire. We sacrifice, say they, for this purpose some unfortunate victims, from whom infancy and ignorance conceal the horrors of death, in which perhaps consist its most formidable terrors.———It was equally a motive of public utility, and the desire of protecting modest beauty, that formerly engaged the Swiss to publish an edict, by which it was not only permitted, but even ordained, that each priest should provide himself a concubine.

These examples might be multiplied without end; and all would concur to prove, that customs, even the most foolish and barbarous, have always their source in the real or apparent utility of the public. But it is said, that these customs are not on this account the less odious or ridiculous. It is true, but it is only, because we are ignorant of the motives of their establishment; and because these customs, consecrated by antiquity and superstition, subsist, by the negligence or weakness of governments, long after the causes of their establishment are removed. All the customs that procure only transient advantages, are like scaffolds that should be pulled down when the palaces are raised. The interest of states, like all human things, is subject to a thousand revolutions. The same laws and the same customs become successively useful and prejudicial to the same people; from whence we may conclude, that those laws ought by turns to be adopted and rejected, and that the same actions ought successively to be named virtuous and vicious: a proposition that cannot be denied, without confessing that there are actions which at one and the same time are virtuous and prejudicial to the state, and consequently without sapping the foundations of all government and all society. HELVETIUS.

D.

D.

LOCKE'S OPINION CONCERNING DARKNESS CONSIDERED.

IT is Mr Locke's opinion, that darkness is not naturally an idea of terror; and that though an exceſſive light is painful to the ſenſe, that the greateſt exceſs of darkneſs is noways troubleſome. He obſerves, indeed, in another place, that a nurſe or an old woman, having once aſſociated the idea of ghoſts and goblins with that of darkneſs, night ever after becomes painful and horrible to the imagination. The authority of this great man is doubtleſs as great as that of any man can be. But it ſeems that an aſſociation of a more general nature, an aſſociation which takes in all mankind, may make darkneſs terrible: for in utter darkneſs it is impoſſible to know in what degree of ſafety we ſtand; we are ignorant of the objects which ſurround us; we may every moment ſtrike againſt ſome dangerous obstruction; we may fall down a precipice the first step we take; and if an enemy approach, we know not in what quarter to defend ourselves. In such a case strength is no sure protection; wisdom can only act by guess; the boldest are staggered; and he who would pray for nothing else towards his defence, is forced to pray for light.

Ζευ πατερ, αλλα συ ρυσαι απ ηερος υιας Αχαιων
Ποισον δ' αιθρην, δος δ' οφθαλμοισιν ιδισθαι
Εν δε φαει και ολεσσον.

As to the association of ghosts and goblins, surely it is more natural to think that darkness being originally an idea of terror, was chosen as a fit scene for such terrible rerpesentations, than that such representations have made darkness terrible. The mind of man very easily slides into an error of the former sort; but it is very hard to imagine that the effect of an idea, so universally terrible in all times and in all countries, as darkness, could possibly have been owing to a set of idle stories, or to any cause of a nature so trivial and of an operation so precarious.

Perhaps it may appear on inquiry, that blackness and darkness are in some degree painful by their natural operation, independent of any associations whatsoever. It must be observed, that the ideas of darkness and blackness are much the same; and they differ only in this, that blackness is a more confined idea. Dr Chefelden has

DARKNESS.

has given us a very curious story of a boy who had been born blind, and continued so until he was thirteen or fourteen years old. He was then couched for a cataract; by which operation he received his sight. Among many remarkable particulars that attended his first perceptions and judgments on visual objects, Cheselden tells us, that the first time the boy saw a black object it gave him great uneasiness; and that some time after, upon accidentally seeing a negro woman, he was struck with great horror at the sight. The horror, in this case, can scarcely be supposed to arise from any association. The boy appears by the account to have been particularly observing and sensible for one of his age; and therefore it is probable, if the great uneasiness he felt at the first sight of black had arisen from its connection with any other disagreeable ideas, he would have observed and mentioned it: For an idea, disagreeable only by association, has the cause of its ill effect on the passions, evident enough at the first impression. In ordinary cases it is indeed frequently lost; but this is because the original association was made very early, and the consequent impression repeated often. In this instance there was no time for such an habit; and there is no reason to think that the ill effects of black on his imagination were more owing to its connection with any disagreeable ideas, than that the
good

good effects of more cheerful colours were derived from their connection with pleasing ones. They had both probably their effects from their natural operation.

It may be worth while to examine how darkness can operate in such a manner as to cause pain. It is observable, that still as we recede from the light, nature has so contrived it, that the pupil is enlarged by the retiring of the iris in proportion to our recess. Now, instead of declining from it but a little, suppose that we withdraw entirely from the light: it is reasonable to think that the contraction of the radial fibres of the iris is proportionably greater; and that this part by great darkness may come to be so contracted, as to strain the nerves that compose it beyond their natural tone, and by this means to produce a painful sensation. Such a tension, it seems, there certainly is whilst we are involved in darkness; for in such a state, while the eye remains open, there is a continual nisus to receive light: This is manifest from the flashes and luminous appearances which often seem in these circumstances to play before it, and which can be nothing but the effect of spasms produced by its own efforts in pursuit of its object. Several other strong impulses will produce the idea of light in the eye besides the substance of light itself, as we experience on many occasions. Though the circular ring of the

iris

iris be in some sense a sphincter, which may possibly be dilated by a simple relaxation; yet in one respect it differs from most of the sphincters of the body, that it is furnished with antagonist muscles, which are the radial fibres of the iris. No sooner does the circular muscle begin to relax, than these fibres, wanting their counterpoise, are forcibly drawn back, and open the pupil to a considerable wideness. But though we were not apprised of this, every one, it is to be presumed, will find, if he opens his eyes and makes an effort to see in a dark place, that a very perceivable pain ensues. It hath also been a complaint of some ladies, that after having worked a long time upon a ground of black, their eyes were so pained and weakened they could hardly see. It may perhaps be objected to this theory of the mechanical effect of darkness, that the ill effects of darkness or blackness seem rather mental than corporeal: and it is true that they do so; and so do all those that depend on the affections of the finer parts of our system.

The ill effects of bad weather appear no otherwise than in a melancholy and dejection of of spirits; though without doubt, in this case, the bodily organs suffer first, and the mind through these organs.

BURKE.

DEITY

DEITY.

A PURPOSE, an intention, a design, strikes every where the most careless thinker; and no man can be so hardened in absurd systems as at all times to reject it.——*That nature does nothing in vain*, is a maxim established in all the schools, merely from the contemplation of the books of nature, without any religious purpose: and from a firm conviction of its truth, an anatomist, who had observed a new organ or canal, would never be satisfied till he had discovered its use and intention.—One great foundation of the Copernican system is the maxim, *that nature acts by the simplest methods, and chooses the most proper means to any end*: and astronomers, without thinking of it, often lay this strong foundation of piety and religion.—The same thing is observable in other parts of philosophy: And thus all the sciences almost lead us insensibly to acknowledge a first intelligent Author; and their authority is often so much the greater, as they do not directly professs that intention.—It is with pleasure I hear Galen reason concerning the structure of the human body.--The anatomy of a man, says he, discovers above 600 different muscles; and whoever duly considers these will find, that in each of them nature must have adjusted at least ten different

cir-

circumstances in order to attain the end which she proposed; proper figure, just magnitude, right disposition of the several ends, upper and lower position of the whole, the due insertion of the several nerves, veins, and arteries; so that in the muscles alone, above 6000 several views and intentions must have been formed and executed. —The bones he calculates to be 284.—The distinct purposes aimed at in the structure of each above forty.—What a prodigious display of artifice even in these simple and homogeneous parts! But if we consider the skin, ligaments, vessels, glandules, humours, the several limbs and members of the body, how must our astonishment rise upon us, in proportion to the number and intricacy of the parts so artificially adjusted? The further we advance in these researches, we discover new scenes of art and wisdom; but descry at a distance further scenes beyond our reach, in the fine internal structure of the parts, in the œconomy of the brain, in the fabric of the seminal vessels.— All these artifices are repeated in every different species of animal with wonderful variety and with exact propriety, suited to the different intentions of nature in framing each species.— And if the infidelity of Galen, even when these natural sciences were still imperfect, could not withstand such striking appearances; to what pitch of pertinacious obstinacy must a philosopher in this age have attained, who can now doubt of a Supreme Intelligence?——Could I meet with a man of this kind, I would afk him, Suppofing there were a God who did not difcover himfelf immediately to the fenfes; were it poffible for him to give ftronger proofs of his exiftence, than what appear on the whole face of nature? What indeed could fuch a divine being do, except copy the prefent œconomy of things; render many of his artifices fo plain, that no ftupidity could miftake them; afford glimpfes of ftill greater artifices, which demonftrate this prodigious fuperiority above our narrow apprehenfions; and conceal altogether a great many from fuch imperfect creatures? Now, according to all rules of juft reafoning, every fact muft pafs for undifputed, when it is fupported by all the arguments which its nature admits of; even though thefe arguments be not very forcible or numerous: how much more in the prefent cafe, where no human imagination can compute their number, and no underftanding eftimate their cogency?—The comparifon of the univerfe to a machine is fo obvious and natural, and is juftified by fo many inftances of order and defign in nature, that it muft immediately ftrike all unprejudiced apprehenfions, and procure univerfal approbation.—That the works of nature bear a great analogy to the productions of art, is evident; and according to all the rules of good reasoning we ought to infer, if we argue at all concerning them, that their causes have a proportional analogy.—But as there are also considerable differences, we have reason to suppose a proportional difference in the causes; and in particular ought to attribute a much higher degree of power and energy to the Supreme Cause than any we have ever observed in mankind.—Here then the existence of a Deity is plainly ascertained by reason: and if we make it a question, Whether on account of these analogies we can properly call him a Mind or Intelligence, notwithstanding the vast difference which may reasonably be supposed between him and human minds; what is this but a mere verbal controversy? No man can deny the analogies between the effects: to restrain ourselves from inquiring concerning the causes is scarcely possible. From this inquiry the legitimate conclusion is, that the causes have also an analogy: and if we are not contented with calling the first and supreme cause a God or Deity, but desire to vary the expression, what can we call him but Mind or Thought, to which he is justly supposed to bear a considerable resemblance? So that this controversy is a dispute of words. HUME.

On the same Subject.

TO difcover a Deity, mankind muft open the facred volume of God's works; confider the obvious fitnefs of every caufe to produce its effect; the proof which this affords of intention and defign; the harmony and order which prevails wherever we have clear and perfect views; and the invariable certainty with which virtue and happinefs arife to individuals and nations from the laws of this order. Let them go one ftep, and one ftep only, into the region of analogy and imagination; let them fuppofe thefe great qualities—thefe intentions, this defign, this goodnefs, not to be fcattered through the univerfe, but to belong to one being who actuates it; and they will know all that can poffibly be known of God. Beware of trufting your imagination one moment longer. She has foared her utmoft height; and every effort fhe makes will be towards the earth, and will generate error and abfurdity. You are to glance only by the utmoft exertion of your abilities at that Being who is incomprehenfible; and you are to be fatisfied with few and general ideas on fo great a fubject.—When a man has obtained general proofs, that the univerfe is replete with the effects of wifdom, directed to the happinefs of its inhabitants,

tants, he has all the knowledge he can ever have of God. All his further inquiries, when judiciously made, will only furnish additional evidence to the same general truth. But whether he be Nature itself, or a principle distinct from and animating it; whether he consist of matter or spirit, whether he be infinite space or a mathematical point; whether he be undefinable and have no form, or have any determinate figure, and reside in a particular place? these are ridiculous and mischievous questions; because we have no possibility of being informed on the subjects of them; because they mislead us from truth, the principle of virtue, to visions and errors, the principles of vice; they create differences, generate divisions, and destroy the general harmony and benevolence which were designed to reign through the whole universe.—All nature is an altar to the unknown God.

WILLIAMS.

The Idea and Belief of a GOD, not innate.

The belief of an invisible, intelligent Power has been very generally diffused over the human race in all places and in all ages; but it has neither, perhaps, been so universal as to admit of no exceptions, nor has it been in any degree uniform in the ideas which it has suggested. Some nations have been discovered, who entertain no sentiments of religion, if travellers and historians may be credited; and no two nations, and scarce any two men, have ever agreed precisely in the same sentiments. It would appear, then, that this preconception springs not from an original instinct or primary impression of Nature; since every instinct of that kind must be absolutely universal in all nations and ages, and must have always a precise determinate object which it inflexibly pursues. The first religious principles, therefore, are secondary; such as may easily be perverted by various accidents and causes, and whose operation, too, in some cases, may by an extraordinary concurrence of circumstances, be altogether prevented. HUME.

The Worship of the DEITY.

TO know God, says Seneca, is to worship him. All other worship is indeed absurd, superstitious, and even impious.—It degrades him to the low condition of mankind, who are delighted with intreaty, solicitation, presents, and flattery.—Yet is this impiety the smallest of which superstition is guilty.—Commonly it depresses the Deity far below the condition of mankind; and represents him as a capricious dæmon, who exercises

cises his power without reason and without humanity!—And were the Divine Being disposed to be offended at the vices and follies of silly mortals, who are his own workmanship, ill would it surely fare with the votaries of most popular superstitions.—Nor would any of the human race merit his favour, but a very few, the philosophical Theists, who entertain suitable notions of his divine perfections: as the only persons intitled to his compassion and indulgence would be the philosophical Sceptics, a sect almost equally rare; who from a natural diffidence of their own capacity, suspend, or endeavour to suspend, all judgment with regard to such sublime and such extraordinary subjects. HUME.

DELICACY OF TASTE AND OF PASSION.

SOME people are subject to a certain delicacy of passion, and others enjoy a delicacy of taste. The first quality makes them extremely sensible to all the accidents of life, and gives them a lively joy upon every prosperous event, as well as a piercing grief when they meet with misfortunes and adversity. Favours and good offices easily engage their friendship; while the smallest injury provokes their resentment. Any honour, or mark of distinction elevates them above measure;

sure; but they are sensibly touched with contempt.

Delicacy of taste much resembles this delicacy of passion, and produces the same sensibility to beauty and deformity of every kind as that does to prosperity and adversity, obligations and injuries. When you present a poem or a picture to a man possessed of this talent, the delicacy of his feeling makes him be touched very sensibly with every part of it; nor are the masterly strokes perceived with more exquisite relish and satisfaction, than the negligences or absurdities with disgust and uneasiness. A polite and judicious conversation affords him the highest entertainment; rudeness or impertinence is a great punishment to him.—Delicacy of passion gives us more lively enjoyments as well as more pungent sorrows than are felt by men of cool and sedate tempers: but when every thing is balanced, there is no one who would not, perhaps, rather be of the latter character, were he entirely master of his own disposition. Good or ill fortune is very little at our disposal: and when a person, that has this sensibility of temper, meets with any misfortune, his sorrow or resentment takes entire possession of him, and deprives him of all relish in the common occurrences of life; the right enjoyment of which forms the chief part of our happiness. Not to mention that men of such lively passions are

are apt to be tranfported beyond all bounds of prudence and difcretion, and to take falfe fteps in the conduct of life, which are often irretrievable.—Delicacy of tafte has alfo the fame effect as delicacy of paffion: it enlarges the fphere both of our happinefs and mifery, and makes us fenfible to pains as well as pleafures which efcape the reft of mankind.—A delicacy of tafte is favourable to love and friendfhip, by confining our choice to few people, and making us indifferent to the company and converfation of the greateft part of mankind. Mere men of the world, whatever ftrong fenfe they may be endowed with, are feldom very nice in diftinguifhing characters, or marking thofe infenfible differences and gradations which make one man preferable to another. Any one that has competent fenfe is fufficient for their entertainment. But one that has well digefted his knowledge both of books and men, has little enjoyment but in the company of a few felect companions. He feels too fenfibly, how much all the reft of mankind fall fhort of the notions which he has entertained.

How far delicacy of tafte and that of paffion are connected together in the original frame of the mind, it is hard to determine. However, there appears a very confiderable connection between them; but notwithftanding this connection, delicacy of tafte is as much to be defired and cultivated,

vated, as delicacy of paſſion is to be lamented, and to be remedied if poſſible. The good or ill accidents of life are very little at our diſpoſal; but we are pretty much maſters what books we ſhall read, what diverſions we ſhall partake of, and what company we ſhall keep.   HUME.

DELIRIUMS.

DELIRIUMS ſometimes attend diſeaſes, eſpecially acute ones. In theſe a diſagreeable ſtate is introduced into the nervous ſyſtem by the bodily diſorder, which checks the riſe of pleaſant aſſociations, and gives force and quickneſs to diſguſtful ones; and which conſequently would of itſelf alone, if ſufficient in degree, vitiate and diſtort all the reaſonings of the ſick perſon. But beſides this, it ſeems that in deliriums attending diſtempers, a vivid train of viſible images forces itſelf upon the patient's eye; and that either from a diſorder of the nerves and blood-veſſels of the eye itſelf, or from one in the brain or one in the alimentary duct; or, which is moſt probable, from a concurrence of all theſe. It ſeems alſo, that the wild diſcourſe of delirious perſons is accommodated to this train in ſome imperfect manner; and that it becomes ſo wild, partly from the incoherence of the parts of this train, partly from its not expreſſing even this incoherent train adequately,

quately, but deviating into such phrases as the vibrations excited by the distemper in parts of the brain corresponding to the auditory nerves, or in parts still more internal, and consequently the seats of ideas purely intellectual, produce by their associated influence over the organs of speech.

That delirious persons have such trains forced upon the eye from internal causes, appears probable from hence; that when they first begin to be delirious and talk wildly, it is generally at those times only when they are in the dark, so as to have all visible objects excluded: for upon bringing a candle to them, and presenting common objects, they recover themselves, and talk rationally till the candle be removed again. From hence we may conclude, that the real objects overpower the visible train from internal causes, while the delirium is in its infancy; and that the patient relapses as soon as he is shut up in the dark, because the visible train from internal causes overpowers that which would rise up, was the person's nervous system in a natural state, according to the usual course of association and the recurrent recollection of the place and circumstances in which he is situated. By degrees the visible train from internal causes, grows so vivid by the increase of the distemper, as even to overpower the impressions from real objects, at least frequently and in a great degree, and so as to intermix

termix itself with them, and to make an inconsistency in the words and actions: and thus the patient becomes quite delirious.

Persons inclining to be delirious in distempers, are most apt to be so going to sleep, and in waking from sleep; in which circumstances the visible trains are more vivid than when we are quite awake.

It casts also some light on this subject, that tea and coffee will sometimes occasion such trains; and that they arise in our first attempts to sleep after those liquors.

As death approaches, the deliriums attending diseases abound with far more incoherencies and inconsistencies than any other species of alienations of the mind, the natural result of the entire disorder of the nervous system. However, there are some cases of death where the nervous system continues free from disorder to the last, as far as the by-standers can judge.

HARTLEY.

DELUGE.

THAT ever the whole globe was at one time totally overflowed with water, is physically impossible. The sea may have covered all parts successively one after the other; and this could be only in a gradation so very slow, as to take up a
pro-

prodigious number of ages. The sea, in the space of five hundred years, has withdrawn from Aigues-mortes, from Frejus, and from Ravenna, once large ports, leaving about two leagues of land quite dry. This progreſſion ſhows, that to make the circuit of the globe, it would require two millions two hundred thouſands years. A very remarkable circumſtance is, that this period comes very near to that which the earth's axis would take up in raiſing itſelf again and coinciding with the equator. A motion ſo far from improbable, that for theſe fifty years paſt ſome apprehenſion has been entertained of it; but it cannot be accompliſhed under two millions three hundred thouſand years.——The ſtrata or beds of ſhells every where found, ſixty, eighty, and even a hundred leagues from the ſea, prove beyond all diſpute, that it has inſenſibly depoſited thoſe maritime products on ground which was once its ſhores: but that the water at one and the ſame time covered the whole earth, is a phyſical abſurdity, which the laws of gravitation, as well as thoſe of fluids, and the deficiency of the quantity of water, demonſtrates to be impoſſible. The univerſal deluge was a miracle.

VOLTAIRE.

DESTINY.

THE world subsists either by its own nature, by its physical laws, or a Supreme Being has formed it by his primitive laws. In either case these laws are immutable; in either case every thing is necessary. Heavy bodies gravitate towards the centre of the earth, and cannot tend to remain in the air; pear-trees can never bear pine-apples; the instinct of a spaniel can never be the instinct of an ostrich; every thing is arranged, set in motion, and limited.—Man can have but a certain number of teeth, hair, and ideas; and a time comes when he necessarily loses them. It is a contradiction that what was yesterday has not been, and what is to-day should not be: No less a contradiction is it that a thing which is to be should not come to pass.—If thou could give a turn to the destiny of a fly, I see no reason why thou mightest not as well determine the destiny of all other flies, of all other animals, of all men, and of all nature; so that at last thou wouldst be more powerful than God himself.—It is common for weak people to say, Such a physician has cured a person of a dangerous illness; he has added to his life ten years. Others as weak, but in their own opinion very wise, say, The prudent man owes his fortune to himself.

self. But the prudent man oftentimes is crushed by his destiny, instead of making it: it is their destiny that renders men prudent.—The physician has saved a person; allowed: But herein he certainly did not reverse the order of nature; he conformed to it. It is evident that the person could not hinder his being born in such a town, and having a certain illness at such a time; that the physician could be no where but in the town where he was; that the person was to send for him; and that he was to prescribe those medicines which effected the cure.—A peasant imagines that the hail which is fallen in his ground is purely matter of chance: but the philosopher knows that there is no such thing as chance; and that by the constitution of the world, it must necessarily have hailed that day in that very place.

Some, alarmed at this truth, say there are necessary events, and others which are not so: but it would be odd indeed that one part of this world were fixed and not the other; that some things which happen were to happen, and that others which happen were not necessarily to happen. On a close examination, the doctrine which opposes that of destiny must appear loaded with absurdities, and contrary to the idea of an eternal Providence. But many are destined to reason wrongly; others not to reason at all; and others to persecute those who do reason. VOLTAIRE.

DISCRETION.

The quality the most necessary for the execution of any useful enterprize is *discretion;* by which we carry on a safe intercourse with others; give due attention to our own and to their character; weigh each circumstance of the business which we undertake; and employ the surest and safest means for the attainment of any end or purpose. To a *Cromwell*, perhaps, or a *De Retz*, discretion may appear an alderman-like virtue as Dr Swift calls it; and being incompatible with those vast designs to which their courage and ambition prompted them, it might really in them be a fault or imperfection. But in the conduct of ordinary life, no virtue is more requisite, not only to obtain success, but to avoid the most fatal miscarriages and disappointments. The greatest parts without it, as observed by an elegant writer, may be fatal to their owner: as Polyphemus, deprived of his eye, was only the more exposed on account of his enormous strength and stature.

The best character, indeed, were it not rather too perfect for human nature, is that which is not swayed by temper of any kind; but alternately employs enterprise and caution, as each is useful to the particular purpose intended. Such is the excellence which St Evremond ascribes to Mareschal

Marefchal Turenne, who difplayed, every campaign as he grew older, more temerity in his military enterprifes; and being now, from long experience, perfectly acquainted with every incident in war, he advanced with greater firmnefs and fecurity in a road fo well known to him. Fabius, fays Machiavel, was cautious; Scipio enterprifing: and both fucceeded; becaufe the fituation of Roman affairs, during the command of each, was peculiarly adapted to his genius; but both would have failed had thefe fituations been reverfed. He is happy whofe circumftances fuit his temper; but he is more excellent who can fuit his temper to any circumftances.

HUME.

DIVISIBILITY of MATTER.

In matter we have no clear ideas of the fmallnefs of parts much beyond the fmalleft that occurs to any of our fenfes: and therefore when we talk of the divifibility of matter *in infinitum*, though we have clear ideas of divifion and divifibility, and have alfo clear ideas of parts made out of a whole by divifion; yet we have but very obfcure and confufed ideas of corpufcles or minute bodies fo to be divided, when by former divifions they are reduced to a fmallnefs much exceeding the perception of any of our fenfes: and fo all that we we have clear and diſtinct ideas of, is of what diviſion in general or abſtractedly is, and the relation of *totum* and *pars* : But of the bulk of the body, to be thus infinitely divided after certain progreſſions, I think we have no clear nor diſtinct idea at all. For I aſk any one, Whether taking the ſmalleſt atom of duſt he ever ſaw, he has any diſtinct idea (bating ſtill the number which concerns extenſion) betwixt the 100,000th, and the 1,000,000th part of it? Or if he thinks he can refine his ideas to that degree without loſing ſight of them, let him add ten cyphers to each of theſe numbers. Such a degree of ſmalneſs is not unreaſonable to be ſuppoſed ; ſince a diviſion carried on ſo far brings it no nearer the end of infinite diviſion than the firſt diviſion in two halves does. I muſt confeſs, that I have no clear diſtinct ideas of the different bulk or extenſion of thoſe bodies; having but a very obſcure one of either of them. So that I think, when we talk of diviſion of bodies *in infinitum*, our ideas of their diſtinct bulks, which is the ſubject and foundation of diviſion, comes after a little progreſſion to be confounded and almoſt loſt in obſcurity. For that idea which is to repreſent only bigneſs, muſt be very obſcure and confuſed which we cannot diſtinguiſh from one ten times as big but only by number: So that we have clear diſtinct ideas, we may ſay, of ten and one, but no

dif-

distinct ideas of two such extensions. It is plain from hence, that when we talk of infinite divisibility of body or extension, our distinct and clear *ideas* are only of numbers.

- LOCKE.

DIVORCE AND REPUDIATION.

THERE is this difference between a divorce and a repudiation, that the former is made by mutual consent arising from a mutual antipathy; while the latter is formed by the will and for the advantage of one of the two parties, independently of the will and advantage of the other.

The necessity there is sometimes for women to repudiate, and the difficulty there always is in doing it, render that law very tyrannical which gives this right to men, without granting it to women. A husband is the master of the house; he has a thousand ways of confining his wife to her duty, or of bringing her back to it: So that, in his hands, it seems as if repudiation could be only a fresh abuse of power. But a wife who repudiates, only makes use of a dreadful kind of remedy. It is always a great misfortune for her to go in search of a second husband, when she has lost the most part of her attractions with another. One of the advantages attending the charms of youth in the female sex is, that in an advanced age the hufband is led to complacency and love by the remembrance of paft pleafures.

It is, then, a *general rule,* that in all countries where the laws have given to men the power of repudiating, they ought alfo to grant it to women. Nay, in climates where women live in domeftic flavery, one would think that the law ought to favour women with the right of repudiation, and hufbands only with that of divorce.

When wives are confined in a feraglio, the hufband ought not to repudiate on account of an oppofition of manners; it is the hufband's fault if their manners are incompatible.

Repudiation on account of the barrennefs of the woman ought never to take place but where there are many: this is of no importance to the hufband.

The law of the Maldivians permitted them to take a wife whom they had repudiated. A law of Mexico forbad their being reunited under pain of death. The law of Mexico was more rational than that of the Maldivians: at the time even of the diffolution, it tended to the perpetuity of marriage. Inftead of this, the law of the Maldivians feemed equally to fport with marriage and repudiation.

The law of Mexico admitted only of divorce. This was a particular reafon for their not permitting thofe who were voluntarily feparated to be be ever reunited. Repudiation seems chiefly to proceed from a hastiness of temper, and from the dictates of passion; while divorce appears to be an affair of deliberation.

Divorces are frequently of great political use: but as to the civil utility, they are established only for the advantage of the husband and wife; and are not always favourable to their children.

MONTESQUIEU.

DOTAGE.

THE dotage of old persons is oftentimes something more than a mere decay of memory: For they mistake things present for others; and their discourse is often foreign to the objects that are presented to them. However, the imperfection of their memories, in respect of impressions just made, or at short intervals of past time, is one principal source of their mistakes. One may suppose here, that the part of the brain which receives ideas is decayed in a peculiar manner, perhaps from too great use; while the parts appropriated to the natural, vital, and animal motions, remained tolerably perfect. The sinuses of the brain are probably considerably distended in these cases, and the brain itself in a languishing state; for there seems to be a considerable resemblance between the inconsistencies of some kinds of
do-

dotage and thofe of dreams. Befides which, it may be obferved, that in dotage the perfon is often fluggifh and lethargic; and that as a defect of the nutritive faculty in the brain will permit the finufes to be more eafily diftended, fo a diftenfion of the finufes from this or any other caufe may impede the due nutrition of the brain. We fee that in old perfons all the parts, even the bones themfelves, wafte and grow lefs. Why may not this happen to the brain, the origin of all, and arife from an obftruction of the infinitely fmall veffels of the nervous fyftem; this obftruction caufing fuch a degree of opacity, as greatly to abate, or even deftroy, the powers of affociation and memory? When old perfons relate the incidents of their youth with great precifion, it is rather owing to the memory of many preceding memories, recollections, and relations, than to the memory of the thing itfelf.

HARTLEY.

DREAMS.

WE have many ftriking inftances of dreaming in men and animals. The poet verfifies, the mathematician views figures, the metaphyfician reafons, and the dog hunts in his dreams. Is this the action of the body's organs, or is it merely the foul, which, now freed from the power of the fenfes, senses, acts in the full enjoyment of its properties? If the organs alone produce our dreams by night, why not our ideas by day? If it be merely the soul acting of itself, and quiet by the suspension of the senses, which is the only cause and subject of all our sleeping ideas; whence is it that they are almost ever irrational, irregular, and incoherent? Can it be that, in the time of the soul's most abstract quietude, its imagination would be the most confused? Is it fantastical when free? Were it born with metaphysical ideas, as some writers, who were troubled with waking dreams, have affirmed, its pure and luminous ideas of being, of infinitude, and of all primary principles, naturally should awake in her with the greatest energy when the body is sleeping, and men should philosophise best in their dreams.— Whatever system you espouse, however you may labour to prove that memory stirs the brain, and your brain your soul; you must allow that, in all your ideas in sleep, you are entirely passive; your will has no share in those images. Thus it is clear, that you can think seven or eight hours on a stretch, without having the least inclination to think, and even without being certain that you do think. Consider this, and tell me what is man's compound? Superstition has always dealt much in dreams; nothing, indeed, was more natural. A man deeply concerned about

about his mistress who lies ill, dreams that he sees her dying; and the next day she actually dies: then, to be sure, God had given him previous knowledge of his beloved's death.—A commander of an army dreams much of gaining a battle; gains it: then the gods had intimated to him that he should be conqueror.—It is only such dreams as meet with some accomplishment that are taken notice of; the others we think not worth remembrance. Dreams make full as great a part of ancient history as oracles.

Somnia quæ ludunt animos volitantibus umbris,
Non delubra deûm, nec ab æthere numina mittunt,
Sed sua quisque facit.

VOLTAIRE.

Female DRESS.

IT is well known that a loose and easy dress contributes much to give both sexes those fine proportions of body that are observable in the Grecian statues, and which serve as models to our present artists; nature being too much disfigured among us to afford them any such. The Greeks knew nothing of those Gothic shackles, that multiplicity of ligatures and bandages, with which our bodies are compressed. Their women were ignorant of the use of whalebone stays, by which ours distort their shape instead of displaying it.

This

This practice, carried to so great an excess as it is in England, must in time degenerate the species, and is an instance of bad taste. Can it be a pleasing sight to behold a woman cut in two in the middle, as it were, like a wasp? on the contrary, it is as shocking to the eye as it is painful to the imagination. A fine shape, like the limbs, hath its due size and proportion; a diminution of which is certainly a defect. Such a deformity also would be shocking in a naked figure; wherefore then should it be esteemed a beauty in one that is dressed?—Every thing that confines and lays nature under a restraint, is an instance of bad taste: This is as true in regard to the ornaments of the body as to the embellishments of the mind. Life, health, reason, and convenience, ought to be taken first into consideration. Gracefulness cannot subsist without ease; delicacy is not debility; nor must a woman be sick in order to please. Infirmity and sickness may excite our pity; but desire and pleasure require the bloom and vigour of health. ROUSSEAU.

DURATION.

IT is evident to any one who will but observe what passes in his own mind, that there is a train of ideas which constantly succeed one another in his understanding as long as he is awake.
Re-

Reflection on these appearances of several ideas, one after another in our minds, is that which furnishes us with the idea of *succession:* and the distance between any parts of that succession, or between the appearance of any two ideas in our minds, is that we call *duration.* For whilst we are thinking, or whilst we receive successively several ideas in our mind, we know that we do exist, and so we call the existence, or the continuation of the existence of ourselves, or any thing else, commensurate to the succession of any ideas in our minds, the *duration* of ourselves, or any other thing coexisting with our thinking.

That we have our notion of *succession* and *duration* from this original, viz. from reflection on the train of ideas, which we find to appear one after another in our own minds, seems plain to me, in that we have no perception of *duration*, but by considering the train of ideas that take their turns in our understanding. When that succession of ideas ceases, our perception of duration ceases with it; which every one clearly experiences in himself whilst he sleeps soundly, whether an hour, or a day, or a month, or a year; of which duration of things, whilst he sleeps, or thinks not, he has no perception at all, but it is quite lost to him; and the moment wherein he leaves off to think, until the moment he begins to think again, seems to him to have no distance.

distance. And so I doubt not but it will be to a waking man, if it were possible for him to keep only one *idea* in his mind, without variation, and the succession of others. And we see, that one who fixes his thoughts very intently on one thing, so as to take but little notice of the succession of ideas that pass in his mind whilst he is taken up with that earnest contemplation, lets slip out of his account a good part of that duration, and thinks that time shorter than it is. But if sleep commonly unites the distant parts of duration, it is because during that time we have no succession of ideas in our minds. For if a man during his sleep dreams, and variety of ideas make themselves perceptible in his mind one after another, he hath then, during such a dreaming, a sense of *duration*, and of the length of it. By which it is to me very clear, that men derive their ideas of duration from their *reflection on the train of the ideas* they observe to succeed one another in their own understandings; without which observation they can have no notion of *duration*, whatever may happen in the world.

LOCKE.

E.

ECCLESIASTICAL Power and its Influence.

IN all Christian churches the benefices of the clergy are a sort of freeholds, which they enjoy, not during pleasure, but during life or good behaviour. If they held them by a more precarious tenure, and were liable to be turned out upon every slight disobligation either of the Sovereign or of his ministers, it would perhaps be impossible for them to maintain their authority with the people; who would then consider them as mercenary dependents upon the court, in the sincerity of whose instructions they could no longer have any confidence. But should the Sovereign attempt irregularly, and by violence, to deprive any number of clergymen of their freeholds

holds on account perhaps of their having propagated, with more than ordinary zeal, some factious or seditious doctrine; he would only render by such persecution both them and their doctrine ten times more popular, and therefore ten times more troublesome and dangerous than they had been before. Fear is in almost all cases a wretched instrument of government, and ought in particular never to be employed against any order of men who have the smallest pretensions to independency. To attempt to terrify them, serves only to irritate their bad humour, and to confirm them in an opposition, which more gentle usage perhaps might easily induce them either to soften or to lay aside altogether. The violence which the French government usually employed in order to oblige all their parliaments, or sovereign courts of justice, to enregister any unpopular edict, very seldom succeeded. The means commonly employed, however, the imprisonment of all the refractory members, one would think were forcible enough. The princes of the house of Stuart sometimes employed the like means in order to influence some of the members of the Parliament of England; and they generally found them equally intractable. The Parliament of England is now managed in another manner; and a very small experiment which the Duke of Choiseul made about twelve years ago upon the

Parliament of Paris, demonstrated sufficiently that all the Parliaments of France might have been managed still more easily in the same manner. That experiment was not pursued. For though management and persuasion are always the easiest and the safest instruments of government, as force and violence are the worst and the most dangerous; yet such, it seems, is the natural insolence of man, that he almost always disdains to use the good instrument, except when he cannot or dare not use the bad one. The French government could and durst use force, and therefore disdained to use management and persuasion. But there is no order of men, it appears, I believe, from the experience of all ages, upon whom it is so dangerous, or rather so pefectly ruinous, to employ force and violence, as upon the respected clergy of any established church. The rights, the privileges, the personal liberty of every individual ecclesiastic who is upon good terms with his own order, are even in the most despotic governments more respected than those of any other person of nearly equal rank and fortune. It is so in every gradation of despotism, from that of the gentle and mild government of Paris, to that of the violent and furious government of Constantinople. But though this order of men can scarce be ever forced, they may be managed as easily as any other; and the security of the Sovereign, as well as the

public

public tranquillity, seems to depend very much upon the means which he has of managing them; and those means seem to consist altogether in the preferment which he has to bestow upon them.

In the ancient constitution of the Christian church, the bishop of each diocese was elected by the joint votes of the clergy and of the people of the Episcopal city. The people did not long retain their right of election; and while they did retain it, they almost always acted under the influence of the clergy, who in such spiritual matters appeared to be their natural guides. The clergy, however, soon grew weary of the trouble of managing them, and found it easier to elect their own bishops themselves. The abbot in the same manner was elected by the monks of the monastery, at least in the greater part of abbacies. All the inferior ecclesiastical benefices comprehended within the diocese were collated by the bishop, who bestowed them upon such ecclesiastics as he thought proper. All church preferments were in this manner in the disposal of the church. The Sovereign, though he might have some indirect influence in those elections, and though it was sometimes usual to ask both his consent to elect, and his approbation of the election, yet had no direct or sufficient means of managing the clergy. The ambition of every clergyman naturally led him to pay court, not so much to his Sovereign, as to his own order, from which only he could expect preferment.

Through the greater part of Europe the Pope gradually drew to himself, first the collation of almost all bishoprics and abbacies, or of what were called Consistorial benefices; and afterwards, by various machinations and pretences, of the greater part of inferior benefices comprehended within each diocese; little more being left to the bishop than what was barely necessary to give him a decent authority with his own clergy. By this arrangement the condition of the Sovereign was still worse than it had been before. The clergy of all the different countries of Europe were thus formed into a sort of spiritual army; dispersed in different quarters indeed, but of which all the movements and operations could now be directed by one head, and conducted upon one uniform plan. The clergy of each particular country might be considered as a particular detachment of that army, of which the operations could easily be supported and seconded by all the other detachments quartered in the different countries round about. Each detatchment was not only independent of the Sovereign of the country in which it was quartered, and by which it was maintained, but dependent upon a foreign sovereign, who could at any time turn its arms

arms againſt the Sovereign of that particular country, and ſupport them by the arms of all the other detachments.

Thoſe arms were the moſt formidable that can well be imagined. In the ancient ſtate of Europe, before the eſtabliſhment of arts and manufactures, the wealth of the clergy gave them the ſame ſort of influence over the common people, which that of the great barons gave them over their reſpective vaſſals, tenants, and retainers. In the great landed eſtates, which the miſtaken piety both of princes and private perſons had beſtowed upon the church, juriſdictions were eſtabliſhed of the ſame kind with thoſe of the great barons; and for the ſame reaſon. In thoſe great landed eſtates, the clergy, or their bailiffs, could eaſily keep the peace without the ſupport or aſſiſtance either of the King or of any other perſon; and neither the King nor any other perſon could keep the peace there without the ſupport and aſſiſtance of the clergy. The juriſdictions of the clergy, therefore, in their particular baronies or manors, were equally independent, and equally excluſive of the authority of the King's courts, as thoſe of the great temporal lords. The tenants of the clergy were, like thoſe of the great barons, almoſt all tenants at will, entirely dependent upon their immediate lords; and therefore liable to be called out at pleaſure, in order to fight in any quarrel

in

in which the clergy might think proper to engage them. Over and above the rents of thofe eftates, the clergy poffeffed, in the tythes, a very large portion of the rents of all the other eftates in every kingdom of Europe. The revenues arifing from both thofe fpecies of rents were, the greater part of them, paid in kind, in corn, wine, cattle, poultry, &c. The quantity exceeded greatly what the clergy could themfelves confume; and there were neither arts nor manufactures for the produce of which they could exchange the furplus. The clergy could derive advantage from this immenfe furplus in no other way than by employing it, as the great barons employed the like furplus of their revenues, in the moft profufe hofpitality and in the moft extenfive charity. Both the hofpitality and the charity of the ancient clergy, accordingly, are faid to have been very great. They not only maintained almoft the whole poor of every kingdom, but many knights and gentlemen had frequently no other means of fubfiftence than by travelling about from monaftery to monaftery, under pretence of devotion, but in reality to enjoy the hofpitality of the clergy. The retainers of fome particular prelates were often as numerous as thofe of the greateft lay lords; and the retainers of all the clergy taken together were, perhaps, more numerous than thofe of all the lay lords. There was always

much

much more union among the clergy than among the lay-lords. The former were under a regular difcipline and fubordination to the papal authority: The latter were under no regular difcipline or fubordination, but almoft always equally jealous of one another, and of the King. Though the tenants and retainers of the clergy, therefore, had both together been lefs numerous than thofe of the great lay lords, and their tenants were probably much lefs numerous; yet their union would have rendered them more formidable. The hofpitality and charity of the clergy, too, not only gave them the command of a great temporal force, but increafed very much the weight of their fpiritual weapons. Thofe virtues procured them the higheft refpect and veneration among all the inferior ranks of people; of whom many were conftantly, and almoft all occafionally, fed by them. Every thing belonging or relating to fo popular an order, its poffeffions, its privileges, its doctrines, neceffarily appeared facred in the eyes of the common people; and every violation of them, whether real or pretended, the higheft act of facrilegious wickednefs and profanenefs. In this ftate of things, if the Sovereign frequently found it difficult to refift the confederacy of a few of the great nobility, we cannot wonder that he fhould find it ftill more fo to refift the united force of the clergy of his own

own dominions, fupported by that of the clergy of all the neighbouring dominions. In fuch circumftances, the wonder is, not that he was fometimes obliged to yield, but that he ever was able to refift.

The privileges of the clergy in thofe ancient times (which to us who live in the prefent times appear the moft abfurd), their total exemption from the fecular jurifdiction, for example, or what in England was called the benefit of clergy, were the natural or rather the neceffary confequences of this ftate of things. How dangerous muft it have been for the Sovereign to attempt to punifh a clergyman for any crime whatever, if his own order were difpofed to protect him, and to reprefent either the proof as infufficent for convicting fo holy a man, or the punifhment as too fevere to be inflicted upon one whofe perfon had been rendered facred by religion? The Sovereign could, in fuch circumftances, do no better than leave him to be tried by the ecclefiaftical courts; who, for the honour of their own order, were interefted to reftrain, as much as poffible, every member of it from committing enormous crimes, or even from giving occafion to fuch grofs fcandal as might difguft the minds of the people.

In the ftate in which things were through the greater part of Europe during the tenth, eleventh, twelfth,

twelfth, and thirteenth centuries, and for some time both before and after that period, the conſtitution of the church of Rome may be conſidered as the moſt formidable combination that ever was formed againſt the authority and ſecurity of civil government, as well as againſt the liberty, reaſon, and happineſs of mankind, which can flouriſh only where civil government is able to protect them. In that conſtitution, the groſſeſt deluſions of ſuperſtition were ſupported in ſuch a manner by the private intereſts of ſo great a number of people, as put them out of all danger from any aſſault of human reaſon : becauſe though human reaſon might perhaps have been able to unveil, even to the eyes of the common people, ſome of the deluſions of ſuperſtition; it could never have diſſolved the ties of private intereſt. Had this conſtitution been attacked by no other enemies but the feeble efforts of human reaſon, it muſt have endured for ever. But that immenſe and well-built fabric, which all the wiſdom and virtue of man could never have ſhaken, much leſs have overturned, was, by the natural courſe of things, firſt weakened, and afterwards in part deſtroyed; and is now likely, in the courſe of a few centuries more, perhaps, to crumble into ruins altogether.

The gradual improvements of arts, manufactures, and commerce, the ſame cauſes which
de-

destroyed the power of the great barons, destroyed in the same manner, through the greater part of Europe, the whole temporal power of the clergy. In the produce of arts, manufactures, and commerce, the clergy, like the great barons, found something for which they could exchange their rude produce; and thereby discovered the means of spending their whole revenues upon their own persons, without giving any considerable share of them to other people. Their charity became gradually less extensive, their hospitality less liberal or less profuse. Their retainers became consequently less numerous, and by degrees dwindled away altogether. The clergy, too, like the great barons, wished to get a better rent from their landed estates, in order to spend it, in the same manner, upon the gratification of their own private vanity and folly. But this increase of rent could be got only by granting leases to their tenants; who thereby became in a great measure independent of them. The ties of interest, which bound the inferior ranks of people to the clergy, were in this manner gradually broken and dissolved. They were even broken and dissolved sooner than those which bound the same ranks of people to the great barons: because the benefices of the church being, the greater part of them, much smaller than the estates of the great barons, the possessor of each benefice was much

soon-

sooner able to spend the whole of its revenue upon his own person. During the greater part of the fourteenth and fifteenth centuries, the power of the great barons was, through the greater part of Europe, in full vigour. But the temporal power of the clergy, the absolute command which they had once had over the great body of the people, was very much decayed. The power of the church was by that time very nearly reduced through the greater part of Europe to what arose from her spiritual authority; and even that spiritual authority was much weakened when it ceased to be supported by the charity and hospitality of the clergy. The inferior ranks of people no longer looked upon that order, as they had done before, as the comforters of their distress, and the relievers of their indigence. On the contrary, they were provoked and disgusted by the vanity, luxury, and expence of the richer clergy, who appeared to spend upon their own pleasures what had always before been regarded as the patrimony of the poor.

In this situation of things, the sovereigns in the different states of Europe endeavoured to recover the influence which they had once had in the disposal of the great benefices of the church, by procuring to the deans and chapters of each diocese the restoration of their ancient right of electing the bishop, and to the monks of each abbacy that of electing the abbot. The re-establishing of this ancient order was the object of several statutes enacted in England during the course of the fourteenth century, particularly of what is called the Statute of Provisors; and of the Pragmatic Sanction established in France in the fifteenth century. In order to render the election valid, it was necessary that the Sovereign should both consent to it before-hand, and afterwards approve of the person elected; and though the election was still supposed to be free, he had, however, all the indirect means which his situation necessarily afforded him, of influencing the clergy in his own dominions. Other regulations of a similar tendency were established in other parts of Europe. But the power of the Pope in the collation of the great benefices of the church seems, before the Reformation, to have been no where so effectually and so universally restrained as in France and England. The Concordat afterwards, in the sixteenth century, gave to the kings of France the absolute right of presenting to all the great, or what are called the Consistorial, benefices of the Gallican church.

Since the establishment of the Pragmatic sanction and of the Concordat, the clergy of France have in general shown less respect to the decrees of the Papal court than the clergy of any other Catholic country. In all the disputes which their

Sovereign has had with the Pope, they have almoſt conſtantly taken party with the former. This independency of the clergy of France upon the court of Rome, ſeems to be principally founded upon the Pragmatic ſanction and the Concordat. In the earlier periods of the monarchy, the clergy of France appear to have been as much devoted to the Pope as thoſe of any other country. When Robert, the ſecond Prince of the Capetian race, was moſt unjuſtly excommunicated by the court of Rome, his own ſervants, it is ſaid, threw the victuals which came from his table to the dogs, and refuſed to taſte any thing themſelves which had been polluted by the contact of a perſon in his ſituation. They were taught to do ſo, it may very ſafely be preſumed, by the clergy of his own dominions.

The claim of collating to the great benefices of the church, a claim in defence of which the court of Rome had frequently ſhaken, and ſometimes overturned, the thrones of ſome of the greateſt ſovereigns in Chriſtendom, was in this manner either reſtrained or modified, or given up altogether, in many different parts of Europe, even before the time of the Reformation. As the clergy had now leſs influence over the people, ſo the ſtate had more influence over the clergy. The clergy therefore had both leſs power and leſs inclination to diſturb the ſtate.——The authority

thority of the church of Rome was in this state of declenfion at the time of the Reformation.

A. SMITH.

THE ADVANTAGE OF UNITING THE CIVIL AND ECCLESIASTICAL POWERS IN EVERY GOVERNMENT.

THE union of the civil and ecclefiaftical powers ferves extremely in every civilized government to the maintenance of peace and order, and prevents thofe mutual encroachments which, as there can be no ultimate judge between them, are often attended with the moft dangerous confequences. Whether the fupreme magiftrate who unites thefe powers, receives the appellation of Prince or Prelate, it is not material. The fuperior weight which temporal interefts commonly bear in the apprehenfions of men above fpiritual, renders the civil part of his character moft prevalent; and in time prevents thofe grofs impoftures and bigotted perfecutions which in all falfe religions are the chief foundation of clerical authority.

HUME.

ECONOMY.

THE purfuit of the objects of private intereft in all common, little, and ordinary cafes, ought to flow rather from a regard to the general rules which prefcribe fuch conduct, than from any paf-paſſion for the objects themſelves. To be anxious, or to be laying a plot either to gain or ſave a ſingle ſhilling, would degrade the moſt vulgar tradeſman in the opinion of all his neighbours. Let his circumſtances be ever ſo mean, no attention to any ſuch ſmall matters, for the ſake of the things themſelves, muſt appear in his conduct. His ſituation may require the moſt ſevere economy, and the moſt exact aſſiduity; but each particular exertion of that economy and aſſiduity muſt proceed, not ſo much from a regard to that particular ſaving or gain, as from the general rule which to him preſcribes, with the utmoſt rigour, ſuch a tenor of conduct. His parſimony to-day muſt not ariſe from a deſire of the particular three-pence which he will ſave by it; nor his attendance in his ſhop from a paſſion for the particular ten-pence which he will acquire by it: both the one and the other ought to proceed ſolely from a regard to the general rule, which preſcribes with the moſt unrelenting ſeverity this plan of conduct to all perſons in his way of life. In this conſiſts the difference between the character of a miſer and that of a perſon of exact economy and aſſiduity. The one is anxious about ſmall matters for their own ſake; the other attends to them only in conſequence of the ſcheme of life which he has laid down to himſelf.

A. SMITH.

EDUCATION.

The time which we usually bestow on the instruction of our children in principles, the reasons of which they do not understand, is worse than lost: it is teaching them to resign their faculties to authority; it is improving their memories instead of their understandings; it is giving them credulity instead of knowledge; and it is preparing them for any kind of slavery which can be imposed on them. Whereas, if we assisted them in making experiments on themselves; induced them to attend to the consequence of every action, to adjust their little deviations, and fairly and freely to exercise their powers; they would collect facts which nothing could controvert. These facts they would deposite in their memories as in secure and eternal treasures; they would be materials for reflection, and in time be formed into principles of conduct, which no circumstances or temptations could remove. This would be a method of forming a man who would answer the end of his being, and make himself and others happy.

WILLIAMS.

On the same Subject.

IF men were educated to use the powers of their minds freely; to investigate by their own industry all the principles they want; to consider nothing as an intellectual acquisition but in consequence of such investigation: this knowledge would be a sure foundation of virtue, and human life would have few crimes or miseries to infest it. Instead of this, they are educated to take almost every thing from others, and to suffer their own powers to lie inactive. Most of the vices of the world have arisen from the habit men have so long been in of believing instead of inquiring. A mind that is trained to inquiry, is trained in a kind of activity which will lead to virtue. A mind in which this activity is suppressed, has a greater difficulty in becoming virtuous, and is a much easier prey to vice. It seems to acquire knowledge, and has none; and false knowledge is worse than none. All the wisdom we obtain, by believing as we are commanded, and committing to memory principles, doctrines, and opinions, which we have never considered or do not understand, is so much poison in the mind, which acts the more surely and fatally as we have no apprehension of danger from it. We see men overwhelmed with what they call doctrines and prin-

principles both of religion and morality, without being of any use to the world, and without ever performing a religious or moral action. It was not so when men were educated to inquire, to think, to form to themselves a few principles which they comprehended and felt, and to act on them. This was the case in the best ages of Greece. Education had a few simple and important objects; and they always related to private and public virtue. It underwent some modifications, according to the circumstances of the different pupils. It would astonish a modern tutor to know the time and pains which were taken on these few things; and to see what wonderful men were formed in this manner. Education was then the art of developing the mind to principles and employments which were suited to it, and giving it habits which would lead to any degree of real knowledge. Education at present is a different thing: it is the art of loading the memory with the imperfect and useless knowledge of all languages and all sciences; and our youth are often sent into the world without one principle of real wisdom, and almost incapable of any act of public or private virtue.

WILLIAMS.

On the same Subject.

The most important and most useful rule of education is, not to gain time, but to lose it. If children took a leap from their mother's breast, and at once arrived at the age of reason, the methods of education now usually taken with them would be very proper: but according to the progress of nature, they require those which are very different. We should not tamper with the mind till it has acquired all its faculties: for it is impossible it should perceive the light we hold out to it while it is blind; or that it should pursue, over an immense plain of ideas, that route which reason hath so slightly traced, as to be perceptible only to the sharpest sight.

The first part of education therefore ought to be purely negative: It consists neither in teaching virtue nor truth; but in guarding the heart from vice, and the mind from error. Take the road directly opposite to that which is in use, and you will almost always do right. Never argue with a child, particularly in striving to reconcile him to what he dislikes: for to use him to reason only upon disagreeable subjects, is the way to disgust him, and bring argument early into discredit with a mind incapable of understanding it. Exercise his corporeal organs, senses, and faculties

ties as much as you pleafe; but keep his intellectual ones inactive as long as poffible. Be cautious of all the fentiments he acquires previous to the judgment which fhould enable him to fcrutinize them: Prevent or reftrain all foreign impreffions; and in order to hinder the rife of evil, be not in too great hurry to inftil good; for it is only fuch when the mind is enlightened by reafon. Look upon every delay as an advantage; it is gaining a great deal, to advance without lofing any thing: let the infancy of children therefore have time to ripen. In fhort, whatever inftruction is neceffary for them, take care not to give it them to-day, if it may be deferred without danger till to-morrow. Another confideration which confirms the utility of this method, is the particular genius of the child; which ought to be known before it can be judged what moral regimen is adapted to it. Every mind has its peculiar turn, according to which it ought to be educated; and it is of very material confequence to our endeavours that it be educated according to that turn, and not to any other. The prudent governor will watch a long time the workings of nature, and will lay the natural character under no unneceffary reftraints. If we fet about any thing before we know in what manner to act, we proceed at random; liable to miftake, we are frequently obliged to undo what is done, and find ourfelves further

from

from the end designed than if we had been less precipitate to begin the work.

ROUSSEAU.

On the same Subject.

IN the education of children, excessive severity, as well as excessive indulgence, should be equally avoided. If you leave children to suffer, you expose their health, endanger their lives, and make them actually miserable. On the other hand, if you are too anxious to prevent their being sensible of any kind of pain and inconvenience, you only pave their way to feel much greater: you enervate their constitutions, make them tender and effeminate: in a word, you remove them out of their situation as men, into which they must hereafter return in spite of all your solicitude. In order not to expose them to the few evils nature would inflict on them, you provide for them many which they would otherwise never have suffered.

Can you conceive any being can be truly happy in circumstances inconsistent with its constitution? And is it not inconsistent with the constitution of man to endeavour to exempt him from all the evils incident to his species? Man is capacitated to experience great pleasure only by being inured to slight pain: Such is the nature of man

man. If his physical constitution be too vigorous, his moral constitution tends to depravity. The man who should be ignorant of pain, would be a stranger also to the sensations of humanity, and the tender feelings of compassion for his species: his heart would be unsusceptible of sympathy; he would be unsocial; he would be a monster among his fellow-creatures.

Would you know the most infallible way to make your child miserable? It is to accustom him to obtain every thing he desires: For those desires still increasing from the facility of gratification, your incapacity to satisfy them must sooner or later reduce you to the necessity of a refusal; and that refusal, so new and uncommon, will give him more trouble than even the want of that which he desires. From wanting your cane he will proceed to your watch; he will next want the bird that flies in the air, the star that glitters in the firmament; in short, every thing he sees: nothing less than omnipotence would enable you to satisfy it.

Nature has constituted children to claim our love and assistance; but has she made them to be obeyed and feared? A child should obtain nothing merely because he asks for it, but because he stands in need of it: A child should be made to do nothing out of obedience, but only out of necessity. Thus the words *command* and *obey* should have no place in his dictionary, much lefs thofe of *duty* and *obligation:* but thofe of power, neceffity, impotence, and reftraint, ought to ftand forth in capitals. It ought to be obferved, that as pain is often a neceffity, fo pleafure is fometimes a natural want. Children have therefore but one defire only which fhould not be gratified; and this is the defire of exacting obedience. Hence it follows, that in every thing they demand, it is the motive which excites them to make fuch demand which ought to engage our attention. Indulge them as much as poffible in every thing which may give them real pleafure; but conftanly refufe them what they require from motives of caprice, or merely to exercife their authority.

ROUSSEAU.

A COMPARATIVE VIEW OF ANCIENT AND MODERN EDUCATION.

DIFFERENT plans and different inftitutions for education feem to have taken place in different ages and nations.—In the republics of ancient Greece, every free citizen was inftructed, under the direction of the public magiftrate, in gymnaftic exercifes and in mufic. By gymnaftic exercifes it was intended to harden his body, to fharpen his courage, and to prepare him for the fatigues and dangers of war; and as the Greek militia was, by all accounts, one of the beft that ever

ever was in the world, this part of their public education must have answered completely the purpose for which it was intended. By the other part, music, it was proposed, at least by the philosophers and historians who have given us an account of those institutions, to humanize the mind, to soften the temper, and to dispose it for performing all the social and moral duties both of public and private life.

In ancient Rome, the exercises of the Campus Martius answered the same purpose as those of the Gymnasium in ancient Greece, and they seem to have answered it equally well. But among the Romans there was nothing which corresponded to the musical education of the Greeks. The morals of the Romans, however, both in private and public life, seem to have been not only equal, but upon the whole a good deal superior, to those of the Greeks. That they were superior in private life, we have the express testimony of Polybius and of Dionysius of Halicarnassus, two authors well acquainted with both nations; and the whole tenor of the Greek and Roman history bears witness to the superiority of the public morals of the Romans. The good temper and moderation of contending factions seems to be the most essential circumstance in the public morals of a free people. But the factions of the Greeks were almost always violent and sanguinary;

nary: whereas, till the time of the Gracchi, no blood had ever been shed in any Roman faction; and from the time of the Gracchi the Roman republic may be considered as in reality dissolved. Notwithstanding, therefore, the very respectable authority of Plato, Aristotle, and Polybius, and notwithstanding the very ingenious reasons by which Mr Montesquieu endeavours to support that authority, it seems probable that the musical education of the Greeks had no great effect in mending their morals; since, without any such education, those of the Romans were upon the whole superior. The respect of those ancient sages for the institutions of their ancestors, had probably disposed them to find much political wisdom in what was, perhaps, merely an ancient custom, continued without interruption from the earliest period of those societies to the times in which they had arrived at a considerable degree of refinement. Music and dancing are the great amusements of almost all barbarous nations, and the great accomplishments which are supposed to fit any man for entertaining his society. It is so at this day among the negroes on the coast of Africa. It was so among the ancient Celtes, among the ancient Scandinavians, and, as we may learn from Homer, among the ancient Greeks in the times preceding the Trojan war. When the Greek tribes had formed themselves into little republics, it was natural that the study of those accomplishments should for a long time make a part of the public and common education of the people.

The masters, who instructed the young people either in music or in military exercises, do not seem to have been paid, or even appointed by the state, either in Rome, or even in Athens; the Greek republic of whose laws and customs we are the best informed. The state required that every free citizen should fit himself for defending it in war, and should, upon that account, learn his military exercises. But it left him to learn them of such masters as he could find; and it seems to have advanced nothing for this purpose, but a public field or place of exercise, in which he should practise and perform them.

In the early ages both of the Greek and Roman republics, the other parts of education seem to have consisted in learning to read, write, and account according to the arithmetic of the times. Those accomplishments the richer citizens seem frequently to have acquired at home by the assistance of some domestic pedagogue, who was generally either a slave or a freed-man; and the poorer citizens, in the schools of such masters as made a trade of teaching for hire. Such parts of education, however, were abandoned altogether to the care of the parents or guardians of each individual. It does not appear that the state ever assumed any inspection or direction of them. By a law of Solon, indeed, the children were acquitted from maintaining those parents in their old age who had neglected to instruct them in some profitable trade or business.

In the progress of refinement, when philosophy and rhetoric came into fashion, the better sort of people used to send their children to the schools of philosophers and rhetoricians, in order to be instructed in these fashionable sciences: But those schools were not supported by the public; they were for a long time barely tolerated by it. The demand for philosophy and rhetoric was for a long time so small, that the first professed teachers of either could not find constant employment in any one city, but were obliged to travel about from place to place. In this manner lived Zeno of Elea, Protagoras, Gorgias, Hippias, and many others. As the demand increased, the schools both of philosophy and rhetoric became stationary; first in Athens, and afterwards in several other cities. The state, however, seems never to have encouraged them further than by assigning to some of them a particular place to teach in, which was sometimes done too by private donors. The state seems to have assigned the Academy to Plato, the Lyceum to Aristotle, and the Portico to Zeno of Citta the founder of the Stoics.

Stoics. But Epicurus bequeathed his gardens to his own school. Till about the time of Marcus Antoninus, however, no teacher appears to have had any salary from the public, or to have had any other emoluments but what arose from the honoraries or fees of his scholars. The bounty which that philosophical emperor, as we learn from Lucian, bestowed upon one of the teachers of philosophy, probably lasted no longer than his own life. There was nothing equivalent to the privileges of graduation; and to have attended any of those schools was not necessary, in order to be permitted to practise any particular trade or profession. If the opinion of their own utility could not draw scholars to them, the law neither forced any body to go to them, nor rewarded any body for having gone to them. The teachers had no jurisdiction over their pupils, nor any other authority besides that natural authority, which superior virtue and abilities never fail to procure from young people, towards those who are entrusted with any part of their education.

At Rome, the study of the civil law made a part of the education, not of the greater part of the citizens, but of some particular families. The young people, however, who wished to acquire knowledge in the law, had no public school to go to, and had no other method of studying it, than by frequenting the company of such of their
rela-

relations and friends as were fuppofed to underſtand it. It is perhaps worth while to remark, that though the laws of the twelve tables were, many of them, copied from thoſe of ſome ancient Greek republics, yet law never ſeems to have grown up to be a ſcience in any republic of ancient Greece. In Rome it became a ſcience very early, and gave a confiderable degree of illuſtration to thoſe citizens who had the reputation of underſtanding it. In the republics of ancient Greece, particularly in Athens, the ordinary courts of juſtice confiſted of numerous, and therefore diforderly, bodies of people, who frequently decided almoſt at random, or as clamour, faction, and party-ſpirit happened to determine. The ignominy of an unjuſt deciſion, when it was to be divided among five hundred, a thouſand, or fifteen hundred people (for ſome of their courts were ſo very numerous), could not fall very heavy upon any individual. At Rome, on the contrary, the principal courts of juſtice confiſted either of a ſingle judge, or of a ſmall number of judges, whoſe characters, eſpecially as they deliberated always in public, could not fail to be very much affected by any raſh or unjuſt deciſion. In doubtful cafes, ſuch courts, from their anxiety to avoid blame, would naturally endeavour to ſhelter themſelves under the example, or precedent, of the judges who had

ſat

fat before them, either in the fame or in fome other court. This attention to practice and precedent, neceffarily formed the Roman law into that regular and orderly fyftem in which it has been delivered down to us; and the like attention has had the like effects upon the laws of every other country where fuch attention has taken place. The fuperiority of character in the Romans over that of the Greeks, fo much remarked by Polybius and Dionyfius of Halicarnaffus, was probably more owing to the better conftitution of their courts of juftice, than to any of the circumftances to which thofe authors afcribe it. The Romans are faid to have been particularly diftinguifhed for their fuperior refpect to an oath. But the people who were accuftomed to make oath only before fome diligent and well-informed court of juftice, would naturally be much more attentive to what they fwore, than they who were accuftomed to do the fame thing before mobbifh and diforderly affemblies.

The abilities, both civil and military, of the Greeks and Romans, will readily be allowed to have been at leaft equal to thofe of any modern nation. Our prejudice is perhaps rather to overrate them. But except in what related to military exercifes, the ftate feems to have been at no pains to form thofe great abilities: for I cannot be induced to believe that the mufical education

tion of the Greeks could be of much confequence in forming them. Mafters, however, had been found, it feems, for inftructing the better fort of people among thofe nations in every art and fcience in which the circumftances of their fociety rendered it neceffary or convenient for them to be inftructed. The demand for fuch inftruction produced, what it always produces, the talent for giving it; and the emulation which an unreftrained competition never fails to excite, appears to have brought that talent to a very high degree of perfection. In the attention which the ancient philofophers excited in the empire, which they acquired over the opinions and principles of their auditors, in the faculty which they poffeffed of giving a certain tone and character to the conduct and converfat.on of thofe auditors; they appear to have been much fuperior to any modern teachers. In modern times, the diligence of public teachers is more or lefs corrupted by the circumftances, which render them more or lefs independent of their fuccefs and reputation in their particular profeffions. Their falaries too put the private teacher, who would pretend to come into competition with them, in the fame ftate with a merchant who attempts to trade without a bounty, in competition with thofe who trade with a confiderable one. If he fells his goods at nearly the fame price, he cannot have

the

the same profit; and poverty and beggary at least, if not bankruptcy and ruin, will infallibly be his lot. If he attempts to sell them much dearer, he is likely to have so few customers that his circumstances will not be much mended. The privileges of graduation, besides, are in many countries necessary, or at least extremely convenient, to most men of learned professions, that is, to the far greater part of those who have occasion for a learned education. But those privileges can be obtained only by attending the lectures of the public teachers. The most careful attendance upon the ablest instructions of any private teacher cannot always give any title to demand them. It is from these different causes that the private teacher of any of the sciences which are commonly taught in universities, is in modern times generally considered as in the very lowest order of men of letters. A man of real abilities can scarce find out a more humiliating or a more unprofitable employment to turn them to. The endowments of schools and colleges have, in this manner, not only corrupted the diligence of public teachers, but have rendered it almost impossible to have any good private ones.

Were there no public institutions for education, no system, no science would be taught for which there was not some demand; or which the circumstances of the times did not render it, either

ther neceffary, or convenient, or at leaft fashionable to learn. A private teacher could never find his account in teaching, either an exploded and antiquated fyftem of a fcience acknowledged to be ufeful, or a fcience univerfally believed to be a mere ufelefs and pedantic heap of fophiftry and nonfenfe. Such fyftems, fuch fciences, can fubfift no where, but in thofe incorporated focieties for education whofe profperity and revenue are in a great meafure independent of their reputation, and altogether independent of their induftry. Were there no public inftitutions for education, a gentleman, after going through, with application and abilities, the moft complete courfe of education which the circumftances of the times were fuppofed to afford, could not come into the world completely ignorant of every thing which is the common fubject of converfation among gentlemen and men of the world.

There are no public inftitutions for the education of women; and there is accordingly nothing ufelefs, abfurd, or fantaftical in the common courfe of their education. They are taught what their parents or guardians judge it neceffary or ufeful for them to learn; and they are taught nothing elfe. Every part of their education tends evidently to fome ufeful purpofe; either to improve the natural attractions of their perfon, or to form their mind to referve, to modefty, to chaftity, chaſtity, and to œconomy: to render them both likely to become the miſtreſſes of a family, and to behave properly when they have become ſuch. In every part of her life, a woman feels ſome conveniency or advantage from every part of her education. It ſeldom happens that a man, in any part of his life, derives any conveniency or advantage from ſome of the moſt laborious and troubleſome parts of his education.

A. SMITH.

ATTENTION TO THE EDUCATION OF THE COMMON PEOPLE, INCUMBENT UPON THE PUBLIC.

OUGHT the public to give no attention, it may be aſked, to the education of the people? Or if it ought to give any, what are the different parts of education which it ought to attend to in the different orders of the people? and in what manner ought it to attend to them?

In ſome caſes, the ſtate of the ſociety neceſſarily places the greater part of individuals in ſuch ſituations as naturally form in them, without any attention of government, almoſt all the abilities and virtues which that ſtate requires, or perhaps can admit of. In other caſes, the ſtate of the ſociety does not place the greater part of individuals in ſuch ſituations; and ſome attention of government

ment is necessary, in order to prevent the almost entire corruption and degeneracy of the great body of the people.

In the progress of the division of labour, the employment of the far greater part of those who live by labour, that is, of the great body of the people, comes to be confined to a few very simple operations; frequently to one or two. But the understandings of the greater part of men are necessarily formed by their ordinary employments. The man whose whole life is spent in performing a few simple operations, of which the effects too are, perhaps, always the same, or very nearly the same, has no occasion to exert his understanding, or to exercise his invention in finding out expedients for removing difficulties which never occur. He naturally loses, therefore, the habit of such exertion, and generally becomes as stupid and ignorant as it is possible for a human creature to become. The torpor of his mind renders him, not only incapable of relishing or bearing a part in any rational conversation, but of conceiving any generous, noble, or tender sentiment; and consequently of forming any just judgment concerning many even of the ordinary duties of private life. Of the great and extensive interests of his country, he is altogether incapable of judging; and unless very particular pains have been taken to render him otherwise, he is equally incapable of defending his country in war. The uniformity of his stationary life naturally corrupts the courage of his mind, and makes him regard with abhorrence the irregular, uncertain, and adventurous life of a soldier. It corrupts even the activity of his body, and renders him incapable of exerting his strength with vigour and perseverance in any other employment than that to which he has been bred. His dexterity at his own particular trade seems, in this manner, to be acquired at the expence of his intellectual, social, and martial virtues. But in every improved and civilized society this is the state in which the labouring poor, that is, the great body of the people, must necessarily fall, unless government takes some pains to prevent it.

It is otherwise in the barbarous societies, as they are commonly called, of hunters, of shepherds, and even of husbandmen in that rude state of husbandry which precedes the improvement of manufactures, and the extension of foreign commerce. In such societies, the varied occupations of every man oblige every man to exert his capacity, and to invent expedients for removing difficulties which are continually occurring. Invention is kept alive, and the mind is not suffered to fall into that drowsy stupidity, which, in a civilized society, seems to benumb the understanding of almost all the inferior ranks of people. In those
bar-

barbarous focieties, as they are called, every man, it has already been obferved, is a warrior. Every man too is in fome meafure a ftatefman, and can form a tolerable judgment concerning the intereft of the fociety, and the conduct of thofe who govern it. How far their chiefs are good judges in peace, or good leaders in war, is obvious to the obfervation of almoft every fingle man among them. In fuch a fociety, indeed, no man can well acquire that improved and refined underftanding, which a few men fometimes poffefs in a more civilized ftate. Though in a rude fociety there is a good deal of variety in the occupations of every individual, there is not a great deal in thofe of the whole fociety. Every man does, or is capable of doing, almoft every thing which any other man does, or is capable of doing. Every man has a confiderable degree of knowledge, ingenuity, and invention; but fcarce any man has a great degree. The degree, however, which is commonly poffeffed, is generally fufficient for conducting the whole fimple bufinefs of the fociety. In a civilized ftate, on the contrary, though there is little variety in the occupations of the greater part of individuals, there is an almoft infinite variety in thofe of the whole fociety. Thefe varied occupations prefent an almoft infinite variety of objects to the contemplation of thofe few, who, being attached to no particular occupation themselves, have leisure and inclination to examine the occupations of other people. The contemplation of so great a variety of objects necessarily exercises their minds in endless comparisons and combinations, and renders their understandings, in an extraordinary degree, both acute and comprehensive. Unless those few, however, happen to be placed in some very particular situations, their great abilities, though honourable to themselves, may contribute very little to the good government or happiness of their society. Nothwithstanding the great abilities of those few, all the nobler parts of the human character may be, in a great measure, obliterated and extinguished in the great body of the people.

The education of the common people requires, perhaps, in a civilized and commercial society, the attention of the public more than that of people of some rank and fortune. People of some rank and fortune are generally eighteen or nineteen years of age before they enter upon that particular business, profession, or trade, by which they propose to distinguish themselves in the world. They have before that full time to acquire, or at least to fit themselves for afterwards acquiring, every accomplishment which can recommend them to the public esteem, or render them worthy of it. Their parents or guardians are generally sufficiently anxious that they should be so accomplished;

plifhed; and are, in moft cafes, willing enough to lay out the expence which is neceffary for that purpofe. If they are not always properly educated, it is feldom from the want of expence laid out upon their education ; but from the improper application of that expence. It is feldom from the want of mafters; but from the negligence and incapacity of the mafters who are to be had, and from the difficulty, or rather from the impoffibility which there is, in the prefent ftate of things, of finding any better. The employments, too, in which people of fome rank or fortune fpend the greater part of their lives, are not, like thofe of the common people, fimple and uniform. They are almoft all of them extremely complicated; and fuch as exercife the head more than the hands. The underftandings of thofe who are engaged in fuch employments can feldom grow torpid for want of exercife. The employments of people of fome rank and fortune, befides, are feldom fuch as harrafs them from morning to night. They generally have a good deal of leifure; during which they may perfect themfelves in every branch either of ufeful or ornamental knowledge of which they may have laid the foundation, or for which they may have acquired fome tafte in the earlier part of life.

It is otherwife with the common people. They have little time to fpare for education. Their parents

rents can scarce afford to maintain them even in infancy. As soon as they are able to work, they must apply to some trade by which they can earn their subsistence. That trade too is generally so simple and uniform as to give little exercise to the understanding; while, at the same time, their labour is both so constant and so severe, that it leaves them little leisure and less inclination to apply to, or even to think of any thing else.

But though the common people cannot, in any civilized society, be so well instructed as people of some rank and fortune, the most essential parts of education, however, to read, write, and account, can be acquired at so early a period of life, that the greater part even of those who are to be bred to the lowest occupations, have time to acquire them before they can be employed in those occupations. For a very small expence, the public can facilitate, can encourage, and can even impose upon almost the whole body of the people, the necessity of acquiring those most essential parts of education.

The public can facilitate this acquisition by establishing in every parish or district a little school, where children may be taught for a reward so moderate, that even a common labourer may afford it; the master being partly, but not wholly, paid by the public; because if he was wholly, or even principally paid by it, he would soon learn to neglect

glect his bufinefs. In Scotland, the eſtabliſhment of ſuch pariſh-ſchools has taught almoſt the whole common people to read, and a very great proportion of them to write and account. In England, the eſtabliſhment of charity ſchools has had an effect of the ſame kind; though not ſo univerſally, becauſe the eſtabliſhment is not ſo univerſal. If in thoſe little ſchools the books, by which the children are taught to read, were a little more inſtructive than they commonly are; and if, inſtead of a little ſmattering of Latin, which the children of the common people are ſometimes taught there, and which can ſcarce ever be of any uſe to them, they were inſtructed in the elementary parts of geometry and mechanics, the literary education of this rank of people would perhaps be as complete as it can be. There is ſcarce a common trade which does not afford ſome opportunities of applying to it the principles of geometry and mechanics, and which would not therefore gradually exerciſe and improve the common people in thoſe principles; the neceſſary introduction to the moſt ſublime as well as to the moſt uſeful ſciences.

The public can encourage the acquiſition of thoſe moſt eſſential parts of education, by giving ſmall premiums and little badges of diſtinction to the children of the common people who excel in them.

The

The public can impose upon almost the whole body of the people the necessity of acquiring those most essential parts of education, by obliging every man to undergo an examination or probation in them before he can obtain the freedom in any corporation, or be allowed to set up any trade either in a village or town corporate.

It was in this manner, by facilitating the acquisition of their military and gymnastic exercises, by encouraging it, and even by imposing upon the whole body of the people the necessity of learning those exercises, that the Greek and Roman republics maintained the martial spirit of their respective citizens. They facilitated the acquisition of those exercises, by appointing a certain place for learning and practising them, and by granting to certain masters the privilege of teaching in that place. Those masters do not appear to have had either salaries or exclusive privileges of any kind. Their reward consisted altogether in what they got from their scholars; and a citizen who had learnt his exercises in the public Gymnasia, had no sort of legal advantage over one who had learnt them privately, provided the latter had learnt them equally well. Those republics encouraged the acquisition of those exercises, by bestowing little premiums and badges of distinction upon those who excelled in them. To have gained a prize in the Olympic, Isthmian, or Nemæan games,

games, gave illuftration, not only to the perfon who gained it, but to his whole family and kindred. The obligation which every citizen was under to ferve a certain number of years, if called upon, in the armies of the republic, fufficiently impofed the neceffity of learning thofe exercifes, without which he could not be fit for that fervice.

That in the progrefs of improvement, the practice of military exercifes, unlefs government takes proper pains to fupport it, goes gradually to decay, and, together with it, the martial fpirit of the great body of the people, the example of modern Europe fufficiently demonftrates. But the fecurity of every fociety muft always depend, more or lefs, upon the martial fpirit of the great body of the people. In the prefent times, indeed, that martial fpirit alone, and unfupported by a well-difciplined ftanding army, would not, perhaps, be fufficient for the defence and fecurity of any fociety. But where every citizen had the fpirit of a foldier, a fmaller ftanding army would furely be requifite. That fpirit, befides, would neceffarily diminifh very much the dangers to liberty, whether real or imaginary, which are commonly apprehended from a ftanding army. As it would very much facilitate the operations of that army againft a foreign invader, fo it would obftruct them as much if unfortunately they fhould ever be directed againft the conftitution of the ftate.

The

The ancient inftitutions of Greece and Rome feem to have been much more effectual for maintaining the martial fpirit of the great body of the people than the eftablifhment of what are called the militias of modern times. They were much more fimple. When they were once eftablifhed, they executed themfelves, and it required little or no attention from government to maintain them in the moft perfect vigour. Whereas to maintain even in tolerable execution the complex regulations of any modern militia, requires the continual and painful attention of government; without which they are conftantly falling into total neglect and difufe. The influence, befides, of the ancient inftitutions was much more univerfal. By means of them the whole body of the people was completely inftructed in the ufe of arms: whereas it is but a very fmall part of them who can ever be fo inftructed by the regulations of any modern militia; except, perhaps, that of Switzerland. But a coward, a man incapable either of defending or of revenging himfelf, evidently wants one of the moft effential parts of the character of a man. He is as much mutilated and deformed in his mind as another is in his body, who is either deprived of fome of its moft effential members, or has loft the ufe of them. He is evidently the more wretched and miferable of the two; becaufe happinefs and mifery, which refide

alto-

altogether in the mind, muſt neceſſarily depend more upon the healthful or unhealthful, the mutilated or entire ſtate of the mind, than upon that of the body. Even though the martial ſpirit of the people were of no uſe towards the defence of the ſociety, yet to prevent that ſort of mental mutilation, deformity, and wretchedneſs, which cowardice neceſſarily involves in it, from ſpreading themſelves through the great body of the people, would ſtill deſerve the moſt ſerious attention of government; in the ſame manner as it would deſerve its moſt ſerious attention to prevent a leproſy or any other loathſome and offenſive diſeaſe, though neither mortal nor dangerous, from ſpreading itſelf among them; though, perhaps, no other public good might reſult from ſuch attention beſides the prevention of ſo great a public evil.

The ſame thing may be ſaid of the groſs ignorance and ſtupidity which, in a civilized ſociety, ſeem ſo frequently to benumb the underſtandings of all the inferior ranks of people. A man, without the proper uſe of the intellectual faculties of a man, is, if poſſible, more contemptible than even a coward; and ſeems to be mutilated and deformed in a ſtill more eſſential part of the character of human nature. Though the ſtate was to derive no advantage from the inſtruction of the inferior ranks of people, it would ſtill deſerve its
at-

attention that they should not be altogether uninstructed. The state, however, derives no inconsiderable advantage from their instruction. The more they are instructed, the less liable they are to the delusions of enthusiasm and superstition; which, among ignorant nations, frequently occasion the most dreadful disorders. An instructed and intelligent people, besides, are always more decent and orderly than an ignorant and stupid one. They feel themselves, each individually, more respectable, and more likely to obtain the respect of their lawful superiors; and they are therefore more disposed to respect those superiors. They are more disposed to examine, and more capable of seeing, through the interested complaints of faction and sedition; and they are, upon that account, less apt to be misled into any wanton or unnecessary opposition to the measures of government. In free countries, where the safety of government depends very much upon the favourable judgment which the people may form of its conduct, it must surely be of the highest importance that they should not be disposed to judge rashly or capriciously concerning it.

A. SMITH.

The Causes of the Decadency of an Empire.

The introduction and improvement of the arts and sciences in an empire do not occasion its decadency; but the same causes that accelerate the progress of the sciences, sometimes produce the most fatal effects.—There are nations where, by a peculiar series of circumstances, the seeds of the arts and sciences do not spring up till the moment the manners begin to corrupt.——A certain number of men assemble to form a society. These men found a city: Their neighbours see it rise up with a jealous eye. The inhabitants of that city, forced to be at once labourers and soldiers, make use by turns of the spade and the sword. What in such a country is the necessary science and virtue? The military arts and valour, they alone are there respected. Every other science and virtue are there unknown. Such was the state of rising Rome, when, weak and surrounded by warlike nations, it with difficulty sustained their attacks: Its glory and power extended over the whole earth: it acquired, however, the one and the other very slowly; ages of triumphs were necessary to subject their neighbours. Now when the surrounding nations were subdued, there arose from the form

of their government civil wars, which were succeeded by those with foreigners; so that it cannot be imagined, while the citizens were engaged in the different employments of magistrates and soldiers, and incessantly agitated with strong hopes and fears, they could enjoy the leisure and tranquillity necessary to the study of the sciences.
——In every country where these events succeed each other in a regular series, the only period favourable to letters is unfortunately that when the civil wars, the troubles and factions being extinguished, liberty is expiring, as in the time of Augustus, under the strokes of despotism. Now this period precedes but a short time the decadency of an empire. The arts and sciences, however, then flourish; and that for two reasons.

The first is the force of mens passions. In the first moments of slavery, their minds, still agitated by the remembrance of their lost liberty, are like the sea after a tempest. The citizen still burns with a desire to render himself illustrious, but his situation is altered. He cannot have his bust placed by that of Timoleon, Pelopidas, or Brutus: He cannot deliver his name down to posterity as the destroyer of tyrants, and the avenger of liberty. His statue may however be placed by those of Homer, Epicurus, or Archimedes. This he knows; and therefore if there be but one sort of glory to which he can aspire,

if

if it be with the laurels of the muses alone that he can be crowned, it is in the career of the arts and sciences he prepares to seek them; and it is then that illustrious men of every literary profession arise.——The second of these causes is the interest sovereigns then have to encourage the progress of the sciences. At the moment that despotism is established, what does the monarch desire? To inspire his subjects with the love of the the arts and sciences. What does he fear? That they should reflect on their fetters, blush on their servitude, and again turn their looks towards liberty. He would therefore, by employing their minds, make them forget their base condition. He consequently presents them with new objects of glory. As an hypocritical fautor of the arts and sciences, he shows the more regard to the man of genius, the more he feels the want of his eulogies.—The manners of a nation do not change the moment despotism is established. The spirit of a people is free some time after their hands are tied. During these first moments illustrious men still preserve some consideration. The tyrant therefore loads them with favours, that they may load him with praises; and men of great talents are too often seduced to become the panegyrists of usurpation and tyranny. What motives can induce them to it? Sometimes meanness, and frequently gratitude. It must be con-

fessed,

fessed, that every great revolution in an empire supposes great talents in him by whom it is produced, or at least some brilliant vice that astonishment and gratitude metamorphose into virtue.—Such is, at the time of the establishment of despotism, the productive cause of great accomplishments in the arts and sciences. The first moments past, if the same country become barren in men of talent, it is because the tyrant, being then well established on his throne, is no longer in want of their assistance. So that the reign of the arts and sciences in a state seldom extends above a century or two.——If in each empire the sciences just shoot up and then wither, it is because the motives proper to produce men of genius do not commonly exert themselves there more than once. It is at the highest period of grandeur that a nation commonly produces the fruits of the arts and sciences. While three or four generations of illustrious men pass away, the people change their manners, and sink into servitude; their minds have lost their energy; there is no strong passion remaining to put them in action; the tyrant no longer excites the people to the pursuit of any kind of glory; it is not talents but baseness he now honours; and genius, if it still remain, lives and dies unknown to its own country: It is like the orange tree, that
flourishes,

flourishes, perfumes the air, and dies in a desert.

Despotism, while it is gaining ground, suffers men to say what they will, while they suffer it to do what it will: but once established, it forbids all talking, writing, and thinking. The minds of men then sink into an apathy: all the inhabitants become slaves, curse the breasts that gave them milk, and under such a government every new birth is an increase of misery.———The pomp of an eastern empire can without doubt impose on the vulgar, who may estimate the force of a nation by the magnificence of its palaces. The wise man judges differently; it is by that very magnificence he estimates its weakness. He sees nothing more in that imposing pomp, in the midst of which the tyrant sits enthroned, than a sumptuous and mournful decoration of the dead; than the apparatus of a sumptuous funeral, in the centre of which is a cold and lifeless body, a lump of unanimated earth: in short, a phantom of power ready to disappear before the enemy by whom it is despised. A great nation where despotic power is at last established, resembles an oak that has been crowned by ages; its majestic trunk and the largeness of its branches still declare its pristine force and grandeur; it seems still to be the monarch of the woods: but its true state is that of decadency; its branches despoiled of their leaves, and destitute of the spirit of life, are half withered, and some of them continually broken off by the wind. Such is the state of a nation subdued by arbitrary power.

HELVETIUS.

The ENGLISH constitution.

The constitution of the English government, ever since the invasion of this island by the Saxons, may boast of this pre-eminence, that in no age the will of the monarch was ever entirely absolute and uncontrouled: but in other respects, the balance of power has extremely shifted among the several orders of the state; and this fabric has experienced the same mutability which has attended all human institutions.——The ancient Saxons, like the other German nations, where each individual was enured to arms, and where the independence of men was secured by a great equality of possessions, seem to have admitted a considerable mixture of democracy into their form of government, and to have been one of the freest nations of which there remains any account in the records of history.—After this tribe was settled in England, especially after the dissolution of the Heptarchy, the great extent of the kingdom produced a great inequality of property; and the balance seems to have inclined to the side of the aristocracy.—The Norman conquest threw more authority into the hands of the sovereign, which, however, admitted of great controul; though derived less from the general forms of the constitution, which were inaccurate and irregular, than from the independent power enjoyed by each baron in his particular district or province.— The establishment of the great charter exalted still higher the aristocracy, imposed regular limits on royal power, and gradually introduced some mixture of democracy into the constitution. —But even during this period, from the accession of Edward I. to the death of Richard III. the condition of the Commons was nowise desirable; a kind of Polish aristocracy prevailed; and though the kings were limited, the people were as yet far from being free.—It required the authority almost absolute of the sovereigns, which took place in the subsequent period, to pull down these disorderly and licentious tyrants, who were equally enemies to peace and to freedom, and to establish that regular execution of the laws, which, in a following age, enabled the people to erect a regular and equitable plan of liberty. In each of these successive alterations, the only rule of government, which is intelligible, or carries any authority with it, is the established practice of the age, and the maxims of administration, which are at that time prevalent and universally assented to.

to.—Those who, from a pretended respect to antiquity, appeal at every turn to an original plan of the constitution, only cover their turbulent spirit and their private ambition under the appearance of venerable forms; and whatever period they pitch on for their model, they may still be carried back to a more ancient period, where they will find the measures of power entirely different, and where every circumstance, by reason of the greater barbarity of the times, will appear less worthy of imitation.—Above all, a civilized nation, like the English, who have happily established the most perfect and most accurate system of liberty that ever was found compatible with government, ought to be cautious of appealing to the practice of their ancestors, or regarding the maxims of uncultivated ages as certain rules for their present conduct.—An acquaintance with the history of the ancient periods of their government is chiefly useful, by instructing them to cherish their present constitution from a comparison or contrast with the condition of those distant times.—And it is also curious, by showing them the remote, and commonly faint and disfigured, originals of the most finished and most noble institutions, and by instructing them in the great mixture of accident, which commonly concurs with a small ingredient of wisdom and fore-
fight,

fight, in erecting the complicated fabric of the moſt perfect government. HUME.

ABUSES IN THE ENGLISH CONSTITUTION.

THE Engliſh hiſtory will inform us, that the people of England have always borne extreme oppreſſion for a long time before there has appeared any danger of a general inſurrection againſt the government. What a ſeries of encroachments upon their rights did even the feudal barons, whoſe number was not very conſiderable, and whoſe power was great, bear from William the Conqueror, and his ſucceſſors, before they broke out into actual rebellion on that account, as in the reigns of King John and Henry III. ! And how much were the loweſt orders of the poor Commons trampled upon with impunity by both till a much later period; when, all the while, they were ſo far from attempting any reſiſtance, or even complaining of the groſs infringement of their rights, that they had not ſo much as an idea of their having any right to be trampled upon! After the people had begun to acquire property, independence, and an idea of their natural rights, how long did they bear a load of old and new oppreſſions under the Tudors, but more eſpecially under the Stuarts, before they broke out into what the friends of arbitrary power

power affect to call the grand rebellion! And how great did that obstinate civil war show the power of the King to be, notwithstanding the most intolerable abuse of it! At the close of the year 1642, it was more probable that the King would have prevailed than the Parliament; and his success would have been certain, if his conduct had not been as weak as it was wicked.—So great was the power of the crown, that after the Restoration, Charles II. was tempted to act the same part as his father, and actually did it in a great measure with impunity; till at last he was even able to reign without parliaments; and if he had lived much longer, he would, in all probability, have been as arbitrary as the King of France. His brother James II. had almost subverted both the civil and religious liberties of his country in the short space of four years; and might have done it completely, if he could have been content to have proceeded with more caution: nay, he might have succeeded notwithstanding his precipitancy, if the Divine Being had not, at that critical time, raised William III. of glorious memory, for our deliverence.

* *

ENNUI or THE WEARISOMENESS OF INACTION.

THE ennui, or the wearisomeness of inaction, is a more general and powerful spring of action than is imagined. Of all pains this is the least; but neverthelefs it is one. The desire of happiness makes us always consider the absence of pleasure as an evil. We would have the necessary intervals that separate the lively pleasures always connected with the gratification of our natural wants, filled up with some of those sensations that are always agreeable when they are not painful: we therefore constantly desire new impressions, in order to put us in mind every instant of our existence; because every one of these informations affords us pleasure. Thus the Savage, as soon as he has satisfied his wants, runs to the banks of a river, where the rapid succession of the waves that drive each other forward make every moment new impressions upon him: for this reason, we prefer objects in motion to those at rest: and we proverbially say, that fire makes company; that is, it helps to deliver us from the wearisomeness of inaction. Men search with the greatest eagerness for every thing capable of putting them in motion; it is this desire that makes the common people run to an execution, and the people of fashion to a play; and it is the same motive in a gloomy devotion, and even in the austere exercises of penance, that frequently affords old women a remedy against the tiresomeness of inaction: for God, who by all possible means endeavours to bring sinners to himself, commonly uses with respect to them that of the wearisomeness of inaction.

A man of literature had for his neighbour one of those indolent people who are the pest of society; who being tired of himself, went one day to pay a visit to the man of letters; who received him in a very agreeable manner, and with great politeness continued tired of him, till being weary of staying any longer in the same place, the idler took his leave, in order to plague somebody else. He was no sooner gone, than the man of learning returned to his studies and forgot his vexation. Some days after he was accused of not having returned the visit he had received, and taxed with want of politeness; upon which he, in his turn, went to see the idler: " Sir, (said he),
" I am informed that you complain of me: how-
" ever, you know that it was being weary of
" yourself that brought you to me. I, who tired
" nobody, received you as well as I could; it is
" then you who are obliged, and I who am taxed
" with unpoliteness. Be yourself the judge of
" my proceedings, and see whether you ought

" not to put an end to complaints that prove no-
" thing, but that I have not, like you, occasion
" for visits; and have neither the inhumanity to
" plague my neighbour, nor the injustice to de-
" fame him after I have tired out his patience."

HELVETIUS.

ENTHUSIASM.

IMMEDIATE revelation being a much easier way for men to establish their opinions and regulate their conduct than the tedious and not always successful labour of strict reasoning; it is no wonder that some have been very apt to pretend to revelation, and to persuade themselves, that they are under the peculiar guidance of heaven in their actions and opinions, especially in those of them which they cannot account for by the ordinary methods of knowledge and principles of reason. Hence we see, that in all ages, men in whom melancholy has mixed with devotion, or whose conceit of themselves has raised them into an opinion of a greater familiarity with God, and a nearer admittance to his favour, than is afforded to others, have often flattered themselves with a persuasion of an immediate intercourse with the Deity, and frequent communications from the Divine Spirit. God, I own, cannot be denied to be able to enlighten the understanding by a ray darted into the mind immediately from the fountain of light. This they underſtand he has promiſed to do; and who then has ſo good a title to expect it as thoſe who are his peculiar people, choſen by him, and depending on him?

Their minds being thus prepared, whatever groundleſs opinion comes to ſettle itſelf ſtrongly upon their fancies, is an illumination from the Spirit of God, and preſently of Divine authority; and whatſoever odd action they find in themſelves a ſtrong inclination to do, that impulſe is concluded to be a call or direction from heaven, and muſt be obeyed; it is a commiſſion from above, and they cannot err in executing it.

This I take to be properly enthuſiaſm; which, though founded neither on reaſon nor divine revelation, but riſing from the conceits of a warmed or overweening brain, works yet, where it once gets footing, more powerfully on the perſuaſions and actions of men, than either of thoſe two or both together: men being moſt forwardly obedient to the impulſes they receive from themſelves; and the whole man is ſure to act more vigorouſly, where the whole man is carried by a natural motion. For ſtrong conceit, like a new principle, carries all eaſily with it when got above common ſenſe; and freed from all reſtraint of reaſon and check of reflection, it is heightened into a divine au-

authority in concurrence with our own temper and inclination.
LOCKE.

EQUALITY.

IT is one of the moſt important objects of government, to prevent an extreme inequality of fortunes; not by taking away the wealth of the poſſeſſors, but in depriving them of means to accumulate them; not by building hoſpitals for the poor, but by preventing the citizens from becoming poor. The unequal diſtribution of the inhabitants of a country; ſome being thinly ſcattered over a large tract of land, while others are aſſembled together in crowds in cities; the encouragement of the agreeable inſtead of the uſeful arts; the ſacrifice of agriculture to commerce; the mal-adminiſtration of the finances; and in ſhort, that exceſs of venality which ſets public eſteem at a pecuniary value, and rates even virtue at a market-price: Theſe are all the moſt obvious cauſes of opulence and of poverty; of the public intereſt; the mutual hatred of the citizens; their indifference for the common cauſe; the corruption of the people; and the weakening of all the ſprings of government.
ROUSSEAU.

On the same Subject.

The term Equality does not mean, that individuals should all absolutely possess the same degree of wealth and power; but only, that with respect to the latter, it should never be exercised contrary to good order and the laws; and with respect to the former, that no one citizen should be rich enough to buy another, and that none should be so poor as to be obliged to sell himself.—This supposes a moderation of possessions and credit on the side of the great, and a moderation of desires and covetousness on the part of the little.—Would you give a state consistency and strength, prevent the two extremes as much as possible; let there be no rich persons, nor beggars. These two conditions, naturally inseparable, are equally destructive to the commonwealth: the one furnishes tyrants, and the other the supporters of tyranny. It is by these the traffic of public liberty is carried on; the one buying, the other selling it.—This equality, they tell us, is a mere speculative chimera, which cannot exist in practice. But though abuses are inevitable, does it thence follow they are not to be corrected? It is for the very reason that things always tend to destroy this equality, that the laws should be calculated to preserve it. ROUSSEAU.

On the same Subject.

A TOO great disproportion of wealth among citizens weakens any state. Every person, if possible, ought to enjoy the fruits of his labour, in a full possession of all the necessaries, and many of the conveniences of life. No one can doubt but such an equality is most suitable to human nature, and diminishes much less from the happiness of the rich than it adds to that of the poor. It also augments the power of the state, and makes any extraordinary taxes or impositions be paid with more cheerfulness. Where the riches are engrossed by a few, these must contribute very largely to supplying the public necessities: But when the riches are dispersed among multitudes, the burden feels light on every shoulder; and the taxes make not a sensible difference on any one's way of living.—Add to this, that where the riches are in few hands, these must enjoy all the power; and will readily conspire to lay all the burthen on the poor, and oppress them still farther, to the discouragement of all industry.

HUME.

On the same Subject.

ALL animals are equal; but man is a slave to man almost every where throughout the earth. If man had met every where with an easy, certain, and safe subsistence, and a climate suitable to his nature, it is manifestly impossible that one man could have enslaved another. When this earth shall every where produce salubrious fruits; when the air, which should contribute to our life, shall not bring us sicknesses and death; when man shall stand in need of no other lodging and bed than that of the deer and roe-buck; then the Tamerlanes of the earth will have no other domestics than their children, in this so natural state, which all quadrupeds, birds, and reptiles enjoy. Man would be as happy as they: Dominion would then be a chimera, an absurdity which no one could think of; for who would make a bustle to get servants without any want of their service? Should any individual, of a tyrannical disposition and extraordinary strength, take it into his head to make a slave of his weaker neighbour, the thing would be impracticable; the party oppressed would be an hundred leagues out of the oppressor's reach before he had taken his measures.—Thus a freedom from wants would necessarily make all men equal. It is the distress annexed to our species which subjects one man to another. Not that inequality is a real misfortune; the grievance lies in dependence.—A numerous family has successfully cultivated a good soil, whilst two small neighbouring families cannot

bring

bring the stubborn grounds to produce any thing: the two poor families must either become servants to the opulent family, or extirpate it. This is self-evident: one of the two indigent families, for a subsistence, goes and offers its labour to the rich; the other goes to dispossess it by force of arms, and is beaten. The former is the origin of domestics and labourers; and from the latter slavery is derived.—In our calamitous globe, it is impossible that men, living together in society, should not be divided into two classes; one the rich, who command; the other the poor, who serve or obey. This division originates from nature. The unequal abilities, industry, ambition, and avarice, which are every where found in mankind, produce it.—All the oppressed are not absolutely unhappy. Most of them being born in a servile state, continual labour and a habit of dependence preserve them from too sensible feeling of their situation: but whenever they feel it, wars are the consequence; as at Rome between the Plebeian and Patrician parties; and those of the peasants in Germany. All these wars terminate, soon or late, in the subjection of the people; because the great have riches, and riches do every thing within a state: I say, within a state; for between nation and nation it is otherwise. A nation which handles iron best, will ever be too strong for that which, with its abundance

dance of gold, is deficient in skill and courage: the Mexicans and Peruvians are striking instances of this truth.—Every man is born with no small propensity to power, riches, and pleasure, and has naturally a delight in indolence; consequently every man is for having the riches, wives, or daughters of others; would subject all to his humours, and do no work, or at least what only pleased himself.

Mankind, in the present state, cannot subsist, unless an infinity of useful men have the misfortune of being without any possession whatever; for no man in easy circumstances will plough the ground. Thus equality is, at the same time, both the most natural and the most chimerical thing in the world.

Every man has a right to believe himself naturally equal to other men; the animal functions are alike in both. But it does not from hence follow, that a man is excused in neglecting the duty of his station: were it so, there would be an end of human society.

VOLTAIRE.

ESTABLISHMENTS FOR THE RELIGIOUS INSTRUCTION OF THE PEOPLE.

The institutions for the instruction of the people of all ages are chiefly those for religious instruction.

tion. This is a species of instruction of which the object is not so much to render the people good citizens in this world, as to prepare them for another and a better world in a life to come. The teachers of the doctrine which contains this instruction, in the same manner as other teachers, may either depend altogether for their subsistence upon the voluntary contributions of their hearers; or they may derive it from some other fund to which the law of their country may intitle them; such as a landed estate, a tythe or land-tax, an established salary or stipend. Their exertion, their zeal and industry, are likely to be much greater in the former situation than in the latter. In this respect the teachers of new religions have always had a considerable advantage in attacking those ancient and established systems of which the clergy, reposing themselves upon their benefices, had neglected to keep up the fervour of faith and devotion in the great body of the people; and having given themselves up to indolence, were become altogether incapable of making any vigorous exertion in defence even of their own establishment. The clergy of an established and well-endowed religion frequently become men of learning and elegance, who possess all the virtues of gentlemen, or which can recommend them to the esteem of gentlemen; but they are apt gradually to lose the qualities, both good and bad,

bad, which gave them authority and influence with the inferior ranks of people, and which had perhaps been the original causes of the success and establishment of their religion. Such a clergy, when attacked by a set of popular and bold, though perhaps stupid and ignorant enthusiasts, feel themselves as perfectly defenceless as the indolent, effeminate, and full-fed nations of the southern parts of Asia, when they were invaded by the active, hardy, and hungry Tartars of the north. Such a clergy, upon such an emergency, have commonly no other resource than to call upon the civil magistrate to persecute, destroy, or drive out their adversaries, as disturbers of the public peace. It was thus that the Roman Catholic clergy called upon the civil magistrate to persecute the Protestants; and the church of England, to persecute the Dissenters; and that, in general, every religious sect, when it has once enjoyed for a century or two the security of a legal establishment, has found itself incapable of making any vigorous defence against any new sect which chose to attack its doctrine or discipline. Upon such occasions, the advantage in point of learning and good writing may sometimes be on the side of the established church: But the arts of popularity, all the arts of gaining proselytes, are constantly on the side of its adversaries. In England, those arts have been long

long neglected by the well-endowed clergy of the established church, and are at present chiefly cultivated by the Diffenters and by the Methodists. The independent provisions, however, which in many places have been made for diffenting teachers, by means of voluntary subscriptions, of trust-rights, and other evasions of the law, seem very much to have abated the zeal and activity of those teachers. They have many of them become very learned, ingenious, and respectable men; but they have in general ceased to be very popular preachers. The Methodists, without half the learning of the Diffenters, are much more in vogue.

In the church of Rome, the industry and zeal of the inferior clergy is kept more alive by the powerful motive of self-interest, than perhaps in any established Protestant church. The parochial clergy derive, many of them, a very considerable part of their subsistence from the voluntary oblations of the people; a source of revenue which confession gives them many opportunities of improving. The mendicant orders derive their whole subsistence from such oblations. It is with them, as with the huffars and light infantry of some armies; no plunder, no pay. The parochial clergy are like those teachers whose reward depends partly upon their salary, and partly upon the fees or honoraries which they get from their pupils;

pupils; and these must always depend more or less upon their industry and reputation. The mendicant orders are like those teachers whose subsistence depends altogether upon their industry. They are obliged, therefore, to use every art which can animate the devotion of the common people. The establishment of the two great mendicant orders of St. Dominick and St. Francis, it is observed by Machiavel, revived, in the thirteenth and fourteenth conturies, the languishing faith and devotion of the Catholic church. In Roman Catholic countries, the spirit of devotion is supported altogether by the monks and by the poorer parochial clergy. The great dignitaries of the church, with all the accomplishments of gentlemen and men of the world, and sometimes with those of men of learning, are careful enough to maintain the necessary discipline over their inferiors, but seldom give themselves any trouble about the instruction of the people.

"Most of the arts and professions in a state," says by far the most illustrious philosopher and historian of the present age (David Hume), "are of such a nature, that while they promote the interest of the society, they are also useful or agreeable to some individuals; and in that case the constant rule of the magistrate, except perhaps on the first introduction of any art, is to leave the profession to itself, and trust its encouragement to the individuals who reap the benefit of it.

—The

—The artifans, finding their profits to rife by the favour of their cuftomers, increafe as much as poffible their fkill and induftry; and as matters are not difturbed by any injudicious tampering, the commodity is always fure at all times to be exactly proportioned to the demand.—But there are alfo fome callings which, though ufeful and even neceffary in a ftate, bring no advantage or pleafure to any individual; and the fupreme power is obliged to alter its conduct with regard to the retainers of thofe profeffions.—It muft give them public encouragement in order to their fubfiftence; and it muft provide againft that negligence to which they will naturally be fubject, either by annexing particular honours to the profeffion, by eftablifhing a long fubordination of ranks and a ftrict dependence, or by fome other expedient.—The perfons employed in the finances, armies, fleets, and magiftracy, are inftances of this order of men.—It may naturally be thought at firft view, that the ecclefiaftics belong to the firft clafs; and that their encouragement, as well as that of lawyers and phyficians, may fafely be trufted to the liberality of individuals who are attached to their doctrines, and who find benefit or confolation from their fpiritual miniftry and affiftance.—Their induftry and vigilance will no doubt be whetted by fuch an additional motive; and their fkill in the profeffion, as well as their addrefs

addrefs in governing the minds of the people, muſt receive daily increaſe from their increaſing practice, ſtudy, and attention.—But if we conſider the matter more cloſely, we ſhall find that this intereſted diligence of the clergy is what every wiſe legiſlature will ſtudy to prevent; becauſe in every religion except the true, it is highly pernicious, and has even a natural tendency to pervert the true, by infuſing into it a ſtrong mixture of ſuperſtition, folly, and deluſion.—Each ghoſtly practitioner, in order to render himſelf more precious and ſacred in the eyes of his retainers, muſt inſpire them with the moſt violent abhorrence againſt all other ſects, and continually endeavour by ſome novelty to excite the languid devotion of his audience.—No regard will be paid to truth, morals, or decency, in the doctrines inculcated.—Every tenet will be adopted that beſt ſuits the diſorderly affections of the human frame. —Cuſtomers will be drawn to each conventicle by new induſtry and addreſs in practiſing on the paſſions and credulity of the populace.—And in the end, the civil magiſtrate will find that he has paid dearly for his pretended frugality in ſaving a ſettled foundation for the prieſts; and that in reality the moſt decent and advantageous compoſition which he can make with the ſpiritual guides, is to bribe their indolence, by affixing ſtated ſalaries to their profeſſion, and rendering

it

it superfluous for them to be further active than merely to preserve their flock from straying in quest of new pastures.—And in this manner ecclesiastical establishments, though commonly they arose at first from religious views, prove in the end advantageous to the political interests of society."

But whatever may have been the good or bad effects of the independent provision of the clergy, it has, perhaps, been very seldom bestowed upon them from any view to those effects. Times of violent religious controversy have generally been times of equally violent political faction. Upon such occasions, each political party has either found it, or imagined it, for its interest, to league itself with some one or other of the contending religious sects. But this could be done only by adopting, or at least by favouring, the tenets of that particular sect. The sect which had the good fortune to be leagued with the conquering party, necessarily shared in the victory of its ally, by whose favour and protection it was soon enabled in some degree to silence and subdue all its adversaries. Those adversaries had generally leagued themselves with the enemies of the conquering party, and were therefore the enemies of that party. The clergy of this particular sect having thus become complete masters of the field, and their influence and authority with the great body of the people being in its higheſt vigour, they were powerful enough to over-awe the chiefs and leaders of their own party, and to oblige the civil magiſtrate to reſpect their opinions and inclinations. Their firſt demand was generally, that he ſhould ſilence and ſubdue all their adverſaries; and their ſecond, that he ſhould beſtow an independent proviſion on themſelves. As they had generally contributed a good deal to the victory, it ſeemed not unreaſonable that they ſhould have ſome ſhare in the ſpoil. They were weary, beſides, of humouring the people, and of depending upon their caprice for a ſubſiſtence. In making this demand therefore they conſulted their own eaſe and comfort, without troubling themſelves about the effect which it might have in future times upon the influence and authority of their order. The civil magiſtrate, who could comply with this demand only by giving them ſomething which he would have choſen much rather to take, or to keep to himſelf, was ſeldom very forward to grant it. Neceſſity, however, always forced him to ſubmit at laſt, though frequently not till after many delays, evaſions, and affected excuſes.

But if politics had never called in the aid of religion, had the conquering party never adopted the tenets of one ſect more than thoſe of another, when it had gained the victory, it would probably

bly have dealt equally and impartially with all the different sects, and have allowed every man to choose his own priest and his own religion as he thought proper. There would in this case, no doubt, have been a great multitude of religious sects. Almost every different congregation might probably have made a little sect by itself, or have entertained some peculiar tenets of its own. Each teacher would no doubt have felt himself under the necessity of making the utmost exertion, and of using every art both to preserve and to increase the number of his disciples. But as every other teacher would have felt himself under the same necessity, the success of no one teacher, or sect of teachers, could have been very great. The interested and active zeal of religious teachers can be dangerous and troublesome only where there is either but one sect tolerated in the society, or where the whole of a large society is divided into two or three great sects; the teachers of each acting by concert, and under a regular discipline and subordination. But that zeal must be altogether innocent where the society is divided into two or three hundred, or perhaps into as many thousand, small sects, of which no one could be considerable enough to disturb the public tranquillity. The teachers of each sect, seeing themselves surrounded on all sides with more adversaries than friends, would be obliged to learn that candour

candour and moderation which is so seldom to be found among the teachers of those great sects, whose tenets being supported by the civil magistrate, are held in veneration by almost all the inhabitants of extensive kingdoms and empires, and who therefore see nothing round them but followers, disciples, and humble admirers. The teachers of each little sect, finding themselves almost alone, would be obliged to respect those of almost every other sect; and the concessions which they would mutually find it both convenient and agreeable to make to one another, might in time probably reduce the doctrine of the greater part of them to that pure and rational religion, free from every mixture of absurdity, imposture, or fanaticism, such as wise men have in all ages of the world wished to see established; but such as positive law has perhaps never yet established, and probably never will establish, in any country: because, with regard to religion, positive law always has been, and probably always will be, more or less influenced by popular superstition and enthusiasm. This plan of ecclesiastical government, or more properly of no ecclesiastical government, was what the sect called Independents, a sect no doubt of very wild enthusiasts, proposed to establish in England towards the end of the civil war. If it had been established, though of a very unphilosophical origin, it would probably by this time

time have been productive of the most philosophical good temper and moderation with regard to every sort of religious principle. It has been established in Pensylvania, where, though the Quakers happen to be the most numerous, the law in reality favours no one sect more than another; and it is there said to have been productive of this philosophical good temper and moderation.

But though this equality of treatment should not be productive of this good temper and moderation in all, or even in the greater part of the religious sects of a particular country; yet provided those sects were sufficiently numerous, and each of them consequently too small to disturb the public tranquillity, the excessive zeal of each for its particular tenets could not well be productive of any very hurtful effects, but, on the contrary, of several good ones: and if the government was perfectly decided both to let them all alone, and to oblige them all to let alone one another, there is little danger that they would not of their own accord subdivide themselves fast enough, so as soon to become sufficiently numerous.

A. SMITH.

E V I.

EVIDENCE.

Every one asks, what is truth or evidence? The root of the word indicates the idea we ought to annex to it. Evidence is derived from *videre*.—What is an evident proposition? It is a fact of which all may convince themselves by the testimony of their senses, and whose existence they may moreover verify every instant. Such are these two facts, *two and two make four; the whole is greater than a part*.—If I pretend, for example, that there is in the north sea a polypus named Kraken, and that this polypus is as large as a small island; this fact, though evident to me, if I have seen and examined it with all the attention necessary to convince me of its reality, is not even probable to him who has not seen it; it is more rational in him to doubt my veracity, than to believe the existence of so extraordinary an animal.—But if, after travellers, I describe the true form of the buildings at Pekin, this description, evident to those who inhabit them, is only more or less probable to others; so that the true is not always evident, and the probable is often true. But in what does evidence differ from probability? Evidence is a fact that is subject to our senses, and whose existence all men may verify every instant. As to probability, it is founded on conjectures, on the testimony of men, and on a hundred proofs of the same kind. Evidence is a single point; there are no degrees of evidence. On the contrary, there are various degrees of probability, according to the difference, first, of the people who assert; secondly, of the fact asserted. Five men tell me they have seen a bear in the forests of Poland: this fact not being contradicted by any thing, is to me very probable. But if not five only, but five hundred men, should assure me they met in the same forests ghosts, fairies, demons, their united evidence would not be to me at all probable; for in cases of this nature, it is more common to meet with five hundred romancers, than to see such prodigies.

HELVETIUS.

Historical EVIDENCE.

WERE most historical events traced up to their causes, we should find historical evidence very deficient. Mankind is made up of inconsistencies; and no man acts invariably up to his predominant character. Our best conjectures, as to the true spring of actions, are very uncertain; the actions themselves is all we must pretend to know from history. That Cæsar was murdered by 24 conspirators, I doubt not; but I very much doubt, whether their love of liberty was the sole cause.

CHESTERFIELD.
THE

The Origin of Evil.

Man is an active and free being; he acts of himself: none of his spontaneous actions, therefore, enter into the general system of Providence, nor can be imputed to it. Providence doth not contrive the evil, which is the consequence of man's abusing the liberty his Creator gave him: it only doth not prevent it; either because the evil, which so impotent a being is capable of doing, is beneath its notice; or because it cannot prevent it without laying a restraint upon his liberty, and causing a great evil by debasing his nature. Providence hath left man at liberty, not that he should do evil, but good by choice, in making a proper use of the faculties bestowed on him: his powers, however, are at the same time so limited and confined, that the abuse he makes of his liberty, is not of importance enough to disturb the general order of the universe. The evil done by man falls on his own head, without making any change in the system of the world, without hindering the human species from being preserved in spite of themselves. To complain, therefore, that God doth not prevent man from doing evil, is, in fact, to complain that he hath given a superior excellence to human nature; that he hath ennobled our actions, by annexing

to

to them the merit of virtue. What could Omnipotence itself do more in our favour? Could it have established a contradiction in our nature, or have allotted rewards for well-doing to a being incapable of doing ill? It is the abuse of our faculties which makes us wicked and miserable. Our cares, our anxieties, our griefs, are all owing to ourselves. Moral evil is incontestably our own work; and physical evil would in fact be nothing, did not our vices render us sensible of it. Is it not for our preservation that nature makes us sensible of our wants? Is not pain of body an indication that the machine is out of order, and a caution for us to provide a remedy? And as to death—do not the wicked render both our lives and their own miserable? Who is there desirous of living here for ever? Death is a remedy for all the evils we inflict on ourselves. Nature will not let us suffer perpetually. To how few evils are men subject who live in primeval simplicity! They hardly know any disease, and are irritated by scarcely any passions: they neither foresee death, nor suffer by the apprehensions of it: when it approaches, their miseries render it desirable; and it is to them no evil.

Inquire no longer, man! who is the author of evil: behold him in yourself. There exists no other evil in nature but what you do or suffer; and you are equally the author of both. A general

neral evil could exist only in disorder; but in the system of nature, there is an established order which is never disturbed. Particular evil exists only in the sentiment of the suffering being: and this sentiment is not given to man by nature, but is of his own acquisition. Pain and sorrow have but little hold of those who, unaccustomed to reflections, have neither foresight nor memory. Take away our fatal improvements, take away our errors and vices; take away, in short, every thing that is the work of man; and all the rest is good. Let us be first virtuous, and rest assured we shall be happy sooner or later. Let us not require the prize before we have got the victory, nor demand the price of our labour before the work is finished. It is not in the lists, says Plutrach, that the victors at our games are crowned, but after the conquest is over. The soul is immaterial, and will survive the body; and in that view Providence is justified. When delivered from the delusions of sense, we shall enjoy the contemplation of the Supreme Being, and those eternal truths of which he is the source; when the beauty of the natural order of things shall strike all the faculties of the soul, and when we shall be employed solely in comparing what we have really done with what we ought to have done.

ROUSSEAU.

Observations on Natural and Moral EVIL.

IT muſt be allowed, that if a very limited intelligence, whom we ſhall ſuppoſe utterly unacquainted with the univerſe, were aſſured that it were the production of a very good, wiſe, and powerful being, however finite, he would from his conjectures form *beforehand* a different notion of it from what we find it to be by experience; nor would he ever imagine, merely from theſe attributes of the cauſe, of which he is informed, that the effect could be ſo full of vice and miſery and diſorder as it appears in this life. Suppoſe now that this perſon were brought into the world, ſtill aſſured that it was the workmanſhip of ſuch a ſublime and benevolent Being, he might perhaps be ſurpriſed at the diſappointment; but would never retract his former belief, if founded on a very ſolid argument; ſince ſuch a limited intelligence muſt be ſenſible of his own blindneſs and ignorance, and muſt allow that there may be many ſolutions of thoſe phenomena which will for ever eſcape his comprehenſion. But ſuppoſing, which is the real caſe with regard to man, that this creature is not antecedently convinced of a ſupreme Intelligence, benevolent and powerful, but is left to gather ſuch a belief from the appearances

ances of things; this entirely alters the cafe, nor will he ever find any reafon for fuch a conclufion. He may be fully convinced of the narrow limits of his underftanding; but this will not help him in forming an inference concerning the goodnefs of fuperior powers, fince he muft form that inference from what he knows, and not from what he is ignorant of. The more you exaggerate his weaknefs and ignorance, the more diffident you render him, and give him the greater fufpicion that fuch fubjects are beyond the reach of his faculties. You are therefore obliged to reafon with him merely from the known phenomena, and to drop every arbitrary fuppofition or conjecture.

Did I fhew you a houfe or palace, where there is not one apartment convenient or agreeable; where the windows, doors, fires, paffages, ftairs, and the whole œconomy of the building, were the fource of noife, confufion, fatigue, darknefs, and the extremes of heat and cold; you would certainly blame the contrivance, without any further examination. The architect would in vain difplay his fubtilty, and prove to you, that if this door or that window were altered, greater ills would enfue. What he fays may be ftrictly true: the alteration of one particular, while the other parts of the building remain, may only augment the inconveniences. But ftill you would affert in general, that if the architect had fkill and good inten-

intentions, he might have formed such a plan of the whole, and might have adjusted the parts in such a manner, as would have remedied all or most of these inconveniences. His ignorance, or even your own ignorance, of such a plan, will never convince you of the impossibility of it. If you find many inconveniences and deformities in the building, you will always, without entering into any detail, condemn the architect.

Is the world considered in general, and as it appears to us in this life, different from what a man, or such a limited being, would *beforehand* expect from a very powerful, wise, and benevolent Deity? It must be strange prejudice to assert the contrary. And from thence I conclude, that however consistent the world may be, allowing certain suppositions and conjectures, with the idea of such a Deity, it can never afford us an inference concerning his existence. The consistence is not absolutely denied, but only the inference. Conjectures, especially where infinity is excluded from the divine attributes, may perhaps be sufficient to prove a consistence; but can never be foundations for any inference.

There seem to be *four* circumstances on which depend all the greatest part of the ills that molest sensible creatures; and it is not impossible but all these circumstances may be necessary and unavoidable. We know so little beyond common life,

life, or even of common life, that, with regard to the œconomy of an univerſe, there is no conjecture, however wild, which may not be juſt; nor any one, however plauſible, which may not be erroneous. All that belongs to human underſtanding in this deep ignorance and obſcurity, is to be ſceptical, or at leaſt cautious; and not to admit of any hypotheſis whatever, much leſs of any which is ſupported by no appearance of probability. Now this I aſſert to be the caſe with regard to all the circumſtances on which it depends. None of them appear to human reaſon in the leaſt degree neceſſary or unavoidable; nor can we ſuppoſe them ſuch without the utmoſt licence of imagination.

The *firſt* circumſtance which introduces evil is that contrivance or œconomy of the animal creation, by which pains as well as pleaſures are employed to excite all creatures to action, and make them vigilant in the great work of ſelf-preſervation. Now pleaſure alone, in its various degrees, ſeems to human underſtanding ſufficient for this purpoſe. All animals might be conſtantly in a ſtate of enjoyment: but when urged by any of the neceſſities of nature, ſuch as thirſt, hunger, wearineſs; inſtead of pain, they might feel a diminution of pleaſure, by which they might be prompted to ſeek that object which is neceſſary to their ſubſiſtence. Men purſue pleaſure as eagerly

gerly as they avoid pain, at least might have been so constituted. It seems therefore plainly possible to carry on the business of life without any pain. Why then is any animal ever rendered susceptible of such a sensation? If any animals can be free from it an hour, they might enjoy a perpetual exemption from it; and it required as particular a contrivance of their organs to produce that feeling, as to endow them with sight, hearing, or any of the senses. Shall we conjecture that such a contrivance was necessary, without any appearance of reason? and shall we build on that conjecture as on the most certain truth?

But a capacity of pain would not alone produce pain, were it not for the *second* circumstance, viz. the conducting the world by general laws; and this seems no way necessary to a very perfect being. It is true, if every thing were conducted by particular volitions, the course of nature would be perpetually broken, and no man would employ his reason in the conduct of life. But might not other particular volitions remedy this inconvenience? In short, might not the Deity exterminate all ill, wherever it were to be found; and produce all good, without any preparation or long progress of causes and effects?

Besides, we must consider, that, according to the present œconomy of the world, the course of nature, though supposed exactly regular, yet to us appears not so; and many events are uncertain, and many disappoint our expectations. Health and sickness, calm and tempest, with an infinite number of other accidents, whose causes are unknown and variable, have a great influence both on the fortunes of particular persons, and on the prosperity of public societies; and indeed all human life in a manner depends on such accidents. A being, therefore, who knows the secret springs of the universe, might easily, by particular volitions, turn all these accidents to the good of mankind, and render the whole world happy, without discovering himself in any operation. Some small touches given to Caligula's brain in his infancy might have converted him into a Trajan; one wave a little higher than the rest, by burying Cæsar and his fortune in the ocean, might have restored liberty to a considerable part of mankind. A few such events as these, regularly and wisely conducted, would change the face of the world; and yet would no more seem to disturb the course of nature, or confound human conduct, than the present œconomy of things, where the causes are secret, and variable, and compounded.

If every thing in the universe be conducted by general laws, and if animals be susceptible of pain; yet ill would be very rare, were it not for the *third* circumstance which I proposed to mention,

tion, viz. the great frugality with which all powers and faculties are diftributed to every particular being. So well adjufted are the organs and capacities of all animals, and fo well fitted to their prefervation, that, as far as hiftory or tradition reaches, there appears not to be any fingle fpecies which has yet been extinguifhed in the universe. Every animal has the requifite endowments; but the endowments are beftowed with fo fcrupulous an œconomy, that any confiderable diminution muft entirely deftroy the creature. Whereever one power is increafed, there is a proportional abatement in the others. Nature feems to have formed an exact calculation of the neceffities of her creatures, and, like a *rigid mafter*, has afforded them little more powers or endowments than what are ftrictly fufficient to fupply thofe neceffities. An *indulgent parent* would have beftowed a large ftock, in order to guard againft accidents, and to fecure the happinefs and welfare of the creature in the moft unfortunate concurrence of circumftances. The Author of nature is inconceivably powerful: his force is fuppofed great, if not altogether inexhauftible; nor is there any reafon, as far as we can judge, to make Him obferve this ftrict frugality in His dealings with His creatures.

In order to cure moft of the ills of life, I require not that man fhould have the wings of the eagle,

eagle, the swiftness of the stag, &c. I am contented to take an increase in one single power or faculty of the soul. Let him be endowed with greater propensity to industry and labour; a more vigorous spring and activity of mind; a more constant bent to business and application. Let the whole species possess naturally an equal diligence with that which many individuals are able to attain by habit and reflection; and the most beneficial consequences, without any allay of ill, is the immediate and necessary result of this endowment. Almost all the moral as well as natural evils of human life arise from idleness; and were our species, by the original constitution of their frame, exempt from this vice or infirmity, the perfect cultivation of land, the improvement of arts and manufactures, the exact execution of every office and duty, immediately follow; and men at once may fully reach that state of society, which is so imperfectly attained in the best government. But as industry is a power, and the most valuable of any, nature seems determined, suitably to her usual maxims, to bestow it on men with a sparing hand; and rather to punish him severely for his deficiency in it, than to reward him for his attainments. She has so contrived his frame, that nothing but the most violent necessity can oblige him to labour; and she employs all his other wants to overcome, at least in part, the want

of

of diligence, and to endow him with some share of a faculty, of which she has thought fit naturally to bereave him.

The *fourth* circumstance, whence arises the misery and ill of the universe, is the inaccurate workmanship of all the springs and principles of the great machine of nature. It must be acknowledged, that there are few parts of the universe which seem not to serve some purpose; and whose removal would not produce a visible defect and disorder in the whole. The parts hang all together; nor can one be touched without affecting the rest, in a greater or less degree. But at the same time it must be observed, that none of these parts or principles, however useful, are so accurately adjusted, as to keep precisely within those bounds in which their utility consists; but they are all of them apt, on every occasion, to run into the one extreme or the other. There is nothing so advantageous in the universe but what frequently becomes pernicious by its excess or defect; nor has nature guarded, with the requisite accuracy, against all disorder and confusion. The irregularity is never, perhaps, so great as to destroy any species; but is often sufficient to involve the individuals in ruin and misery.

On the concurrence then of these four circumstances, does all, or the greatest part of natural evil depend. Were all living creatures incapable of pain, or were the world administered by particular volitions, evil could never have found access into the universe: and were animals endowed with a large stock of powers and faculties beyond what strict necessity requires; or were the several springs and principles of the universe so accurately framed as to preserve always the just temperament and medium; there must have been very little ill in comparison of what we feel at present.

Here the Manichean system occurs as a proper hypothesis to solve the difficulty: and, no doubt, in some respects it is very specious, and has more probability than the common hypothesis, by giving a plausible account of the strange mixture of good and ill which appears in life. But if we consider, on the other hand, the perfect uniformity and agreement of the parts of the universe, we shall not discover in it any marks of the combat of a malevolent with a benevolent being. There is, indeed, an opposition of pains and pleasures in the feelings of sensible creatures: but are not all the operations of nature carried on by an opposition of principles; of hot and cold, moist and dry, light and heavy? The true conclusion is, that the original source of all things is entirely indifferent to all these principles; and has no more regard to good above ill, than to heat above cold, or to drought above moisture, or to light above heavy.

There may *four* hypotheses be framed concerning

ing the first causes of the universe: *That* they are endowed with perfect goodness; *that* they have perfect malice; *that* they are opposite, and have both goodness and malice; *that* they have neither goodness nor malice. Mixt phenomena can never prove the two former unmixt principles. And the uniformity and steadiness of general laws seem to oppose the third. The fourth, therefore, seems by far the most probable.

Allowing, what never will be believed, at least what never possibly can be proved, that animal, or at least human happiness, in this life exceeds its misery, is to do nothing: for this is not by any means what we expect from Infinite Power, Infinite Wisdom, and Infinite Goodness. Why is there any misery at all in the world? Not by chance surely. From some cause then. Is it from the intention of the Deity? But he is perfectly benevolent. Is it contrary to his intention? But he is Almighty. Nothing can shake this reasoning; so short, so clear, so decisive: except we assert, that these subjects exceed all human capacity, and that our common measures of truth and falsehood are not applicable to them.

What is here said of natural evil will apply to moral with little or no variation; and we have no more reason to infer, that the rectitude of the Supreme Being resembles human rectitude, than that his benevolence resembles the human. Nay,

it

it will be thought, that we have still greater cause to exclude from him moral sentiments, such as we feel them; since moral evil, in the opinion of many, is much more predominant above moral good, than natural evil above natural good. But even though this should not be allowed; and though the virtue, which is in mankind, should be acknowledged much superior to the vice; yet so long as there is any vice at all in the universe, it will be very difficult to account for it. We must assign a cause for it, without having recourse to the first cause. But every effect must have a cause, and that cause another: you must either carry on the progression *in infinitum*, or rest on that original principle who is the ultimate cause of all things. HUME.

CAUSES AND EFFECTS DISCOVERABLE, NOT BY REASON, BUT BY EXPERIENCE.

THE knowledge of causes and effects is not in any instance attained by reasonings *à priori;* but arises entirely from experience, when we find that any particular objects are constantly conjoined with each other. Adam, though his rational faculties be supposed, at the very first, entirely perfect, could not have inferred from the fluidity and transparency of water, that it would suffocate him, or from the light and warmth

warmth of fire that it would confume him. No object ever difcovers, by the qualities which appear to the fenfes, either the caufes which produced it, or the effects which will arife from it; nor can our reafon, unaffifted by experience, ever draw any inferences concerning real exiftence and matter of fact. Prefent two fmooth pieces of marble to a man who has no tincture of natural philofophy: he will never difcover, that they will adhere together in fuch a manner as to require great force to feparate them in a direct line, while they make fo fmall a refiftance to a lateral preffure. No man imagines that the explofion of gunpowder, or the attraction of the loadftone, could ever be difcovered by arguments *à priori*. Who will affert, that he can give the ultimate reafons why milk or bread is proper nourifhment for a man, not for a lion or a tyger?—Were any object prefented to us, and were we required to pronounce concerning the effect which will refult from it, without confulting paft obfervation, after what manner muft the mind proceed in this operation? It muft invent or imagine fome event, which it afcribes to the object as its effect; and it is plain that this invention muft be arbitrary. The mind can never poffibly find the effect in the fuppofed caufe by the moft accurate fcrutiny and examination: For the effect is totally different from the caufe; and confequently can never be discovered in it. A stone raised into the air, and left without any support, immediately falls; but to consider the matter *à priori*, is there any thing we discover in this situation which can beget the idea of a downward, rather than an upward, or any other motion, in the stone?—In a word, then, every effect is a distinct event from its cause. It could not, therefore, be discovered in the cause; and the first invention or conception of it *à priori* must be entirely arbitrary. And even after it is suggested, the conjunction of it with the cause must appear equally arbitrary; since there are always many other effects which, to reason, must seem fully as consistent and natural. In vain, therefore, should we pretend to determine any single event, or infer any cause or effect, without the assistance of observation and experience. The utmost effect of human reason is, to reduce the principles productive of natural phenomena to a greater simplicity, and to resolve the many particular effects into a few general causes, by means of reasoning from analogy, experience, and observation. But the causes of these general causes, the ultimate springs and principles of nature, are totally shut up from human curiosity and inquiry.

HUME.

The Foundation of all Conclusions from EXPERIENCE.

NATURE has kept us at a great distance from all her secrets, and has afforded us only the knowledge of a few superficial qualities of objects; while she conceals from us those powers and principles on which the influence of these objects entirely depends. Our senses inform us of the colour, weight, and consistence of bread; but neither sense nor reason ever can inform us of those qualities which fit it for the nourishment and support of a human body. Sight, or feeling, conveys an idea of the actual motion of bodies: but as to that wonderful force or power, which would carry on a moving body for ever in a continued change of place, and which bodies never lose but by communicating it to others; of this we cannot form the most distant conception. But notwithstanding this ignorance of natural powers and principles, we always presume, where we see like sensible qualities, that they have like secret powers, and expect, that effects, similar to those which we have experienced, will follow from them. If a body of like colour and consistence with that of bread, which we have formerly eat, be presented to us, we make no scruple of repeating the experiment; and foresee, with certainty, like nourishment and support. But it is allowed on all hands, that there is no known connection between the sensible qualities and the secret powers; and consequently, that the mind is not led to form such a conclusion concerning their constant and regular conjunction, by any thing which it knows of their nature. As to past *experience*, it can be allowed to give *direct* and *certain* information only of those precise objects, and that precise period of time, which fell under its cognizance. The bread, which I formerly eat, nourished me; that is, a body of such sensible qualities was at that time endued with such secret powers: But does it follow, that other bread must also nourish me at another time; and that like sensible qualities must always be attended with like secret powers? The consequence seems nowise necessary. These two propositions are far from being the same, *I have found such an object has always been attended with such an effect;* and, *I foresee, that other objects, which are in appearance similar, will be attended with similar effects.* The one proposition is, in fact, always inferred from the other: But this inference is not made by a chain of reasoning. If this conclusion were formed by reason, it would be as perfect at first; and upon one instance, as after ever so long a course of experience. But the case is far otherwise. Nothing is so like as eggs; yet no one, on account of this apparent similarity,

rity, expects the same taste and relish in all of them. It is only after a long course of uniform experiments in any kind that we attain a firm reliance and security with regard to a particular event. This inference is not intuitive; neither is it demonstrative. That there are no demonstrative arguments in the case, seems evident; since it implies no contradiction, that the course of nature may change, and that an object, seemingly like those we have experienced, may be attended with different and contrary effects. Is it not clearly and distinctly to be conceived, that a body falling from the clouds, and which, in all other respects resembles snow, has yet the taste of salt, or feeling of fire? Is there any more intelligible proposition, than to affirm, that all the trees will flourish in *December* and *January*, and decay in *May* and *June*? Now, whatever is intelligible, and can be distinctly conceived, implies no contradiction, and can never be proved false by any demonstrative arguments or abstract reasoning *à priori*.

If we be therefore engaged by arguments to put trust in past experience, and make it the standard of our future judgment, these arguments must be probable only, or such as regard matter of fact and real existence: but all arguments concerning existence are founded on the relation of cause and effect; and our knowledge of that relation

lation is derived entirely from experience; and all our experimental conclusions proceed upon the suppofition, that the future will be conformable to the paſt. To endeavour, therefore, the proof of this laſt fuppofition by probable arguments, or arguments regarding exiſtence, is begging the queſtion.

All arguments or inferences from experience fuppofe, as their foundation, that the future will refemble the paſt; and that fimilar powers will be conjoined with fimilar fenfible qualities. If there be any fufpicion that the courfe of nature may change, and that the paſt may be no rule for the future, all experience becomes ufelefs, and can give rife to no inference or conclufion. It is impoffible, therefore, that any arguments from experience can prove this refemblance of the paſt to the future; fince all thefe arguments are founded on a fuppofition of this refemblance. Let the courfe of things be allowed hitherto ever fo regular; that alone, without fome new argument or inference, proves not, that for the future it will continue fo. In vain do we pretend to have learned the nature of bodies from our paſt experience. Their fecret nature, and confequently all their effects and influence, may change, without any change in their fenfible qualities. This happens fometimes, and with regard to fome objects: why may it not happen always, and with regard

to

to all objects? There is no logic, or procefs of argument, which can fecure us againft this fuppofition.

In all reafoning, therefore, from experience, there is a ftep taken by the mind, which is not eftablifhed by any argument or procefs of the underftanding. But if the mind be not engaged by argument to make this ftep, it muft be induced by fome other principle of equal weight and authority; and that principle will preferve its influence as long as human nature remains the fame. Suppofe a perfon, though endowed with the ftrongeft faculties of reafon and reflection, to be brought on a fudden into this world: he would, indeed, immediately obferve a continual fucceffion of objects, and one event following another; but he would not be able to difcover any thing further. He would not be able by any reafoning to reach the idea of caufe and effect; fince the particular powers, by which all natural operations are performed, never appear to the fenfes; nor is it reafonable to conclude, merely becaufe one event, in one inftance precedes another, that therefore the one is the caufe, the other the effect. Their conjunction may be arbitrary and cafual. There may be no reafon to infer the exiftence of the one from the appearance of the other. And, in a word, fuch a perfon without more experience, could never employ his conjecture or reafoning concerning

ing any matter of fact, or be assured of any thing beyond what was immediately present to his memory or senses.

Suppose again, that he has acquired more experience, and has lived so long in the world as to have observed similar objects or events to be constantly conjoined together; what is the consequence of this experience?—He immediately infers the existence of the one object from the appearance of the other. Yet he has not, by all his experience, acquired any idea or knowledge of the secret power by which the one object produces the other; nor is it by any process of reasoning he is engaged to draw this inference. But still he finds himself determined to it: and though he should be convinced that his understanding has no part in the operation, he would nevertheless continue in the same course of thinking. To this he is determined by *custom* or *habit*. For wherever the repetition of any particular act or operation produces a propensity to renew the same act or operation, without being impelled by any reasoning or process of the understanding, we always say, that this propensity is the effect of custom. *Custom*, then, is the great guide of human life. It is that principle alone which renders our experience useful to us; and makes us expect for the future a similar train of events with those which have appeared in the past. Having found, in many instances, that any two kinds of objects, flame and heat, snow and cold, have always been conjoined together; if flame or snow be presented anew to our senses, the mind is carried by custom to expect heat or cold; and to *believe* that such a quality does exist, and will discover itself upon a nearer approach. This belief is the necessary consequence of placing the mind in such circumstances. It is an operation of the soul, when we are so situated as unavoidably to feel the passion of love when we receive benefits; or hatred, when we meet with injuries. All these operations are a species of natural instincts, which no reasoning or process of the thought and understanding is able either to produce or to prevent!

HUME.

The Existence of EXTERNAL Objects only Probable.

WHOEVER will be satisfied with evidence only, can hardly be sure of any thing except his own existence. How could he, for example, be convinced of that of other bodies? For cannot God, by his omnipotence, make the same impressions on our senses as the presence of the objects would excite? And if we grant, that the Deity can do this, how can it be affirmed, that he does not employ his power in this manner; and that the whole universe

universe is nothing more than a mere phenomenon? Besides, as we are affected in our dreams by the same sensation we should feel were the object present, how can it be proved, that our life is not one continued dream? I would not be understood from hence to deny the existence of bodies, but only to show that we have less assurance of it than of our own existence. And as truth is an indivisible point, we cannot say of a certain fact, that it is more or less true: It is therefore evident, that if we are more certain of our own existence than that of other bodies, the existence of the latter is no more than a probability. It is, indeed, a very great probability; and with regard to the conduct of life, equivalent to evidence; notwithstanding which, it is only a probability.

HELVETIUS.

F.

DIFFICULTY OF DETECTING FABULOUS STORIES.

THE difficulty of detecting falsehood in any private, or even public history, at the time and place where it is said to happen, is very great; but much more so where the scene is removed to ever so small a distance. Even a court of judicature, with all the authority, accuracy, and judgement which they can employ, find themselves often at a loss to distinguish between truth and falsehood in the most recent actions. But the matter never comes to any issue, if trusted to the common method of altercation, and debate, and flying rumours; especially when mens passions have taken party on either side.

In the infancy of new religions, the wise and learned

learned commonly esteem the matter too inconsiderable to deserve their attention and regard: And when afterwards they would willingly detect the cheat, in order to undeceive the deluded multitude, the season is now past, and the records and witnesses, which might clear up the matter, have perished beyond recovery. No means of detection remain but those which must be drawn from the very testimony itself of the reporters: and these, though always sufficient with the judicious and knowing, are commonly too fine to fall under the comprehension of the vulgar.

* *

MATTERS OF FACT NOT DEMONSTRATIVELY CERTAIN.

ALL the objects of human reason and inquiry may be naturally divided into two kinds, viz. *Relations of ideas*, and *matters of fact*. Of the first kind are the sciences of geometry, algebra, and arithmetic; and, in short, every affirmation which is either intuitively or demonstratively certain. Propositions of this kind are discoverable by the mere operation of thought, without dependence on what is any where existent in the universe. Matters of fact, which are the second objects of human reason, are not ascertained in the same manner; nor is our evidence of their truth, however great, of a like nature with the foregoing. The contrary of every matter of fact is still possible, because it can never imply a contradiction; and is conceived by the mind with equal facility and distinctness, as if ever so conformable to reality. *That the sun will not rise to-morrow*, is no less intelligible a proposition, and implies no more contradiction, than the affirmation *that it will rise*. We should in vain, therefore, attempt to demonstrate its falsehood. Were it demonstratively false, it would imply a contradiction; and could never be distinctly conceived by the mind. HUME.

The Nature of our Reasonings concerning Matters of FACT.

ALL reasonings concerning matters of fact, seem to be founded in the relation of cause and effect. By means of that relation alone, we can go beyond the evidence of our memory and senses. If you were to ask a man, why he believes any matter of fact which is absent; for instance, that his friend is in the country, or in France? he would give you a reason: and this reason would be some other fact; as a letter received from him, or the knowledge of his former resolutions and promises. A man finding a watch, or any other machine, in a desert island, would conclude that there had once been men in that ifland. All our reafonings concerning fact are of the fame nature. And here it is conftantly fuppofed, that there is a relation between the prefent fact and that inferred from it. Were there nothing to bind them together, the inference would be entirely precarious. The hearing of an articulate voice and rational difcourfe in the dark, affures us of the prefence of fome perfon. Why? Becaufe thefe are the effects of the human fhape and fabric, and clofely connected with it. If we anatomize all the other reafonings of this nature, we fhall find, that they are founded on caufe and effect; and that this relation is either near or remote, direct or collateral. Heat and light are collateral effects of fire; and the one effect may juftly be inferred from the other. HUME.

FAITH.

THERE being many things wherein we have very imperfect notions, or none at all; and other things, of whofe paft, prefent, or future exiftence, by the natural ufe of our faculties, we can have no knowledge at all; thefe, as being beyond the difcovery of our natural faculties, and above reafon, are, when revealed, the proper matter of faith. Thus, that part of the angels rebelled againft God, and thereby loft their firft happy

happy state; and that the dead shall rise, and live again: these, and the like, being beyond the discovery of our reason, are purely matters of faith; with which reason has directly nothing to do.

But since God, in giving us the light of reason, has not thereby tied up his hands from affording us, when he thinks fit, the light of revelation in any of those matters, wherein our natural faculties are able to give a probable determination; revelation, where God has been pleased to give it, must carry it against the probable conjectures of reason: Because the mind, not being certain of the truth of what it does not evidently know, but only yielding to the probability that appears in it, is bound to give up its assent to such a testimony; which, it is satisfied, comes from one who cannot err, and will not deceive. But yet it still belongs to reason to judge of the truth of its being a revelation, and of the signification of the words wherein it is delivered. Indeed, if any thing shall be thought revelation which is contrary to the plain principles of reason, and the evident knowledge the mind has of its own clear and distinct ideas; there reason must be hearkened to, as to a matter within its province: since a man can never have so certain a knowledge, that a proposition which contradicts the clear principles and evidence of his own knowledge, was divinely revealed, or that he understands the words rightly wherein it is delivered, as he has that the contrary is true; and so is bound to consider and judge of it as a matter of reason, and not swallow it, without examination, as a matter of faith.

First, Whatever proposition is revealed, of whose truth our mind, by its natural faculties and notions, cannot judge; that is purely matter of faith, and above reason.

Secondly, All propositions, whereof the mind, by the use of its natural faculties, can come to determine and judge from naturally acquired ideas, are matter of reason; with this difference still, that in those concerning which it has but an uncertain evidence, and so is persuaded of their truth only upon probable grounds, which still admit a possibility of the contrary to be true, without doing violence to the certain evidence of its own knowledge, and overturning the principles of all reason; in such probable propositions, I say, an evident revelation ought to determine our assent even against probability. For where the principles of reason have not evidenced a proposition to be certainly true or false, there clear revelation, as another principle of truth, and ground of assent, may determine; and so it may be matter of faith, and be also above reason. Because reason, in that particular matter, being able to reach no higher than probability, faith gave the determination where reason came short;

and

and revelation discovered on which side the truth lay.

Thus far the dominion of faith reaches, and that without any violence or hinderance to reason; which is not injured or disturbed, but assisted and improved, by new discoveries of truth coming from the eternal fountain of all knowledge. Whatever God hath revealed, is certainly true; no doubt can be made of it. This is the proper object of faith: but whether it be a divine revelation or no, reason must judge; which can never permit the mind to reject a greater evidence to embrace what is less evident, nor allow it to entertain probability in opposition to knowledge and certainty. There can be no evidence, that any traditional revelation is of divine original, in the words we receive it, and in the sense we understand it, so clear and so certain, as that of the principles of reason: and therefore nothing that is contrary to, and inconsistent with the clear and self-evident dictates of reason, has a right to be urged or assented to as a matter of faith; wherein reason hath nothing to do. Whatsoever is divine revelation, ought to over-rule all our opinions, prejudices, and interest, and hath a right to be received with full assent. Such a submission as this, of our reason to faith, takes not away the land-marks of knowledge; this shakes not the foundations of reason, but leaves us that use of our faculties for which they were given us.   LOCKE.

On the same Subject.

Belief or disbelief can neither be a virtue or a crime in any one who used the best means in his power of being informed. If a proposition is evident, we cannot avoid believing it; and where is the merit or piety of a necessary assent? If it is not evident, we cannot help rejecting it, or doubting of it; and where is the crime of not performing impossibilities, or not believing what does not appear to us to be true?
                                         WHITBY.

FAITH and REASON.

IF the provinces of faith and reason are not kept distinct by these boundaries, there will, in matters of religion, be no room for reason at all; and those extravagant opinions and ceremonies that are to be found in the several religions of the world, will not deserve to be blamed. For to this crying up of faith, in opposition to reason, we may, I think, in good measure, ascribe those absurdities that fill almost all the religions which possess and divide mankind. For men having been principled with an opinion, that they must not

not consult reason in the things of religion, however apparently contradictory to common sense, and the very principles of all their knowledge, have let loose their fancies and natural superstition; and have been by them led into so strange opinions and extravagant practices in religion, that a considerate man cannot but stand amazed at their follies, and judge them, so far from being acceptable to the great and wise God, that he cannot avoid thinking them ridiculous and offensive to a sober good man. So that in effect religion, which should most distinguish us from beasts; and ought most peculiarly to elevate us, as rational creatures, above brutes; is that wherein men often appear most irrational and more senseless than beasts themselves. *Credo, quia impossibile est,* " I believe, because it is impossible," might in a good man pass for a sally of zeal; but would prove a very ill rule for men to choose their opinions or religion by.

* *

FAME.

A MAN, whose talents and genius give him the consciousness of deserving reputation, may let the public voice alone. He need not trouble himself in dictating what it shall determine; but wait, if I may say so, for future fame to come

come and take his orders. He will soon put to silence every inferior voice, as the force of the fundamental sound in a concord destroys every dissonance which tends to alter the harmony.— We must act in fame as cautiously as in sickness; impatience is fatal in either of them. How many men are there distinguished for their rare endowments, to whom we may apply the rebuke formerly made to a Carthaginian general: " The " gods do not give all talents to one; you have " that of obtaining a victory, but not that of " using it." Renown is a kind of game at commerce, where chance sometimes gets a fortune; but where merit acquires, in general, more certain gains; provided, that while it uses the tricks of gamesters, it does not expose itself to be betrayed by them. But it is too frequently considered as a mere lottery, where persons imagine they make their fortunes by inventing false tickets. D'ALEMBERT.

Origin of the love of FAME.

Our opinions of all kinds are strongly affected by society and sympathy; and it is almost impossible for us to support any principle or sentiment against the universal consent of every one with whom we have any friendship or correspondence. But of all our opinions, those, which we form in our own favour, however lofty or presuming, are at bottom the frailest, and the most easily shaken by the contradiction and opposition of others. Our great concern, in this case, makes us soon alarmed, and keeps our passions upon the watch; our consciousness of partiality still makes us dread a mistake. And the very difficulty of judging concerning an object, which is never set at a due distance from us, nor is seen in a proper point of view, makes us hearken anxiously to the opinions of others, who are better qualified to form just opinions concerning us. Hence that strong *love of fame* with which all mankind are possessed. It is in order to fix and confirm their favourable opinion of themselves, not from any original passion, that they seek the applauses of others. And when a man desires to be praised, it is for the same reason that a beauty is pleased with surveying herself in a favourable looking-glass, and seeing the reflection of her own charms.

HUME.

FANATICISM.

FANATICISM is to superstition what a delirium is to a fever, and fury to anger: He who has ecstasies and visions, who takes dreams for realities, and his imagination for prophecies, is an enthusiast;

fiaft; and he who sticks not at supporting his folly by murder, is a fanatic.

The only remedy for this infectious disease is a philosophical temper, which spreading through society, at length softens manners, and obviates the excesses of the distemper; for whenever it gets ground, the best way is to fly from it, and stay till the air is purified. The laws and religion are no preservative against this mental pestilence. Religion, so far from being a salutary aliment in these cases, in infected brains becomes poison.

The laws likewise have proved very ineffectual against this spiritual rage; it is indeed like reading an order of council to a lunatic. The creatures are firmly persuaded that the spirit by which they are actuated is above all laws, and that their enthusiasm is the only law they are to regard.

What can be answered to a person who tells you, that he had rather obey God than men; and who, in consequence of that choice, is certain of gaining heaven by cutting your throat?

The leaders of fanatics, and who put the dagger into their hands, are usually designing knaves; they are like the old man of the mountain, who, according to history, gave weak persons a foretaste of the joys of paradise, promising them an eternity of such enjoyments, provided they would go and murder all those whom he should name to them.

In the whole world, there has been but one religion

ligion clear of fanaticism, which is that of the Chinese literati. As to the sects of philosophers, instead of being infected with this pestilence, they were a ready and sure preservative against it: for the effect of philosophy is to compose the soul, and fanaticism is incompatible with tranquillity.

VOLTAIRE.

The Punishment of FANATICISM.

PAINFUL and corporal punishments should never be applied to fanaticism; for, being founded on pride, it glories in persecution. Infamy and ridicule only should be employed against fanatics: if the first, their pride will be overbalanced by the pride of the people; and we may judge of the power of the second, if we consider that even truth is obliged to summon all her force when attacked by error armed by ridicule. Thus by opposing one passion to another, and opinion to opinion, a wise legislator puts an end to the admiration of the populace, occasioned by a false principle, the original absurdity of which is veiled by some well-deduced consequences.

This is the method to avoid confounding the immutable relations of things, or opposing nature; whose actions not being limited by time, but operating incessantly, overturn and destroy all those vain regulations which contradict her laws. It is is not only in the fine arts that the imitation of nature is the fundamental principle; it is the same in sound policy, which is no other than the art of uniting and directing to the same end the natural and immutable sentiments of mankind.

BECCARIA.

FILIAL AFFECTION.

THE bond that ties children to their parents is less strong than commonly imagined. Nothing is more common in Europe than to see children desert their parents, when they become old, infirm, incapable of labour, and forced to subsist by beggary. We see, in the country, one father nourish seven or eight children; but seven or eight children are not sufficient to nourish one father. If all children be not so unnatural, if some of them have affection and humanity, it is to education and example they owe that humanity. Nature, no doubt, designed that gratitude and habit should form in man a sort of gravitation, by which they should be impelled to a love of their parents; but it has also designed that man should have, in the natural desire of independence, a repulsive power, which should diminish the too great force of that gravitation. From hence perhaps comes the proverb, founded on common and constant observation, *That the love of parents descends, and does not remount.*

HELVETIUS.

FINAL CAUSES.

A MAN must be (it seems) stark mad to deny that the stomach is made for digestion, the eye to see, and the ear to hear.—On the other hand, he must be strangely attached to final causes to affirm, that stone was made to build houses, and that China breeds silk worms to furnish Europe with sattin.—But it is said, if God has manifestly made one thing with design, he had a design in every thing. To allow a Providence in one case, and deny it in another, is ridiculous. Whatever is made, was foreseen and arranged; now every arrangement has its object, every effect its cause: therefore every thing is equally the result or the product of a final cause: therefore it is equally true to say, that noses were made to wear spectacles, and fingers to be decorated with diamonds, as it is true to say, that the ears have been made to hear sounds, and the eyes to receive light.

This difficulty, I apprehend, may be easily cleared up, when the effects are invariably the same in all times and places; when such uniform effects are independent of the beings they appertain to, there then is evidently a final cause.—All animals have eyes, and they see; all have ears,

and they hear; all a mouth, with which they
eat; a ſtomach, or ſomething ſimilar, by which
they digeſt; all an orifice, which voids the excre-
ments; all an inſtrument of generation; and
theſe natural gifts operate in them without the
intervention of any art. Here are clear demon-
ſtrations of final cauſes; and to contradict ſo univerſal a truth, would be to pervert our faculty of
thinking.—But it is not in all places, nor at all
times, that ſtones form edifices; all noſes do not
wear ſpectacles; all fingers have not a ring; nor
are all legs covered with ſilk ſtockings: therefore a ſilk-worm is not made to cover my legs, as
your mouth is made to eat, &c. Thus there are
effects produced by final cauſes; but withal many
which cannot come within that appellation. But
both one and the other are equally agreeable to
the plan of a general providence; for certainly
nothing comes to paſs in oppoſition to it, or ſo
much as without it. Every particular within the
compaſs of nature is uniform, immutable, and
the immediate work of their Author. Men were
not eſſentially created to butcher one another;
but the compoſition we are made of is frequently
productive of maſſacres, as it produces calum-
nies, vanities, perſecutions, and impertinences:
not that the formation of man is preciſely the
final cauſe of our follies and brutalities; a final
cauſe being univerſal and invariable, in all places,

and

and at all times. The crimes and absurdities of the human mind are, nevertheless, in the eternal order of things. In threshing corn, the flail is the final cause of the grain's separation; but if the flail, threshing the corn, destroys a thousand insects, this is not from any determinate will of mine, neither is it mere chance: these insects were at that time under my flail; and it was determined they were to be there, that is, it was consequential to the nature of things.

The instruments given to us by nature cannot be final causes, ever in motion, and infallible in their effect. The eyes, given us for sight, are not always open; every sense has its intervals of rest, and its exertion is frequently prevented by extraneous causes; nevertheless the final cause subsists, and as soon as it is free will act.

VOLTAIRE.

FLATTERY.

EVERY body hates praise when he believes it to be false; people then love flatterers only in the quality of sincere admirers. Under this it is impossible not to love them; because every one believes that his actions are laudable and worthy of praise. Whoever disdains elogiums, suffers at least people to praise him on this account. When they detest a flatterer, it is because they know him to be such. In flattery, it is not the praise, but

but the falsehood, which shocks us. If the man of sense appears little sensible of elogiums, it is because he more frequently perceives the falsehood: but let an artful flatterer praise, persist in praising him, and sometimes seem to censure with the elogiums he bestows; and even the man of the greatest sense and penetration will, sooner or later, be his dupe. This taste derives its source from a vanity common to all men. Every man, therefore, would be praised and flattered; but all would not have it done in the same manner; and it is only in this particular that the difference between them consists. Of all praises the most flattering and delicate is, without dispute, that which most evidently proves our own excellence. What gratitude do we owe to those who discover to us defects that, without being prejudicial to us, assure us of our superiority? Of all flattery this is the most artful. HELVETIUS.

FRIENDSHIP.

FRIENDSHIP is a tacit contract between two sensible and virtuous souls: I say sensible; for a monk, a hermit, may not be wicked, yet live a stranger to friendship. I add virtuous; for the wicked have only accomplices, the voluptuous have companions, the designing have associates, the men of business have partners, the politicians

form

form a factious band, the bulk of idle men have connections, princes have courtiers; but virtuous men alone have friends. Cethegus was Catiline's accomplice, and Mæcenas was Octavius's courtier; but Cicero was Atticus's friend.——What is implied in this contract between two tender and ingenuous souls? Its obligations are stronger and weaker, according to their degree of sensibility, and the number of good offices performed.

VOLTAIRE.

ON THE SAME SUBJECT.

LOVE implies want, and there is no friendship without it; for this would be an effect without a cause. All men have not the same wants; and therefore the friendship that subsists between them is founded on different motives: some want pleasure or money, others credit; those conversation, and these a confident to whom they may disburthen their hearts. There are consequently friends of money, of intrigue, of the mind, and of misfortune. In friendship, as in love, people form the the most romantic ideas; they always search for the hero, and every instant think they have found him. We are never so violently affected with the virtues of a man as when we first see him; for as custom renders us insensible to personal beauties, a good understanding, and even the qualities of the soul, we are never so strongly agitated as by the pleasure of surprise. We generally love a man while we know little of him, and are desirous of knowing him better; but no sooner is this curiosity satisfied, than we are disgusted. In considering friendship as a reciprocal want, it cannot but be acknowledged, that it is very difficult for the same wants, and consequently for the same friendship, to subsist between two men for a long course of time; and therefore nothing is more uncommon than friendship of a long standing. The circumstances in which two friends ought to be found being once given, and their characters known; if they are ever to quarrel, there is no doubt but that a man of penetration, by foreseeing the time when these two men would cease to be reciprocally of use to each other, might calculate the moment when their rupture would happen, as an astronomer calculates the time of an eclipse. We ought not, however, to confound with friendship the chains of habit, the respectful esteem felt for an acknowledged friend, or that happy point of honour, so useful to society, that makes us keep an acquaintance with those whom we call our friends. We perform the same services for them as we did when they filled us with the warmest sensations, though in reality we do not want their company.—Friendship supposes a want; and the more this want is felt,

felt, the more lively will be the friendſhip; the want is then the meaſure of the ſenſation. A man and woman eſcaping ſhipwreck, ſave themſelves on a deſert iſland; where, having no hope of ever ſeeing their native country, they are forced to bend their mutual aſſiſtance, to defend themſelves from the wild beaſts, to enjoy life, and to eſcape deſpair: no friendſhip can be more warm than that between this man and woman, who perhaps would have hated each other had they remained at Paris. If one of them happens to periſh, the other has really loſt the half of himſelf: no grief can equal his; a perſon muſt dwell alone on a deſert iſland, who can be ſenſible of all its violence. The unfortunate are in general the moſt tender friends; united by their reciprocal diſtreſſes, they enjoy, while condoling the misfortune of a friend, the pleaſure of being affected with their own. What is true of circumſtances, is alſo true of characters; there are ſome who cannot live without a friend. The firſt are, thoſe of a weak and timid diſpoſition, who, in their whole conduct, never conclude on any thing without the advice and aſſiſtance of others. The ſecond are, the perſons of a gloomy, ſevere, and tyrannical diſpoſition, who are warm friends of thoſe over whom they vent their ſpleen: theſe are like one of the wives of Socrates, who, at the news of the death of that great man, became more inconſolable folable than the fecond, who being of a mild and amiable temper, loft in Socrates only an hufband; while the other loft in him the martyr of her capricious temper, and the only man who could bear with it. If we loved a friend only for himfelf, we fhould never confider any thing but his happinefs; we fhould not reproach him for being fo long without feeing or writing to us; we fhould fay that he had probably fpent his time more agreeably, and fhould rejoice in his happinefs.

Men have taken great pains to repeat after each other, that thofe ought not to be reckoned in the lift of friends whofe interefted views make them love us only for our ability to ferve them. This kind of friendfhip is certainly not the moft flattering; but it is neverthelefs a real friendfhip. Men, for inftance, love in a minifter of ftate the power he has of obliging them; and in moft of them the love of the perfon is incorporated with the love of the preferment. Why is the name of friendfhip refufed to this fenfation? Men do not love us for ourfelves, but always on fome other account; and the above-mentioned is as good as any other. A man is in love with a woman; can it be faid he does not love her becaufe he only admires the beauties of her eyes or complexion? But, it is faid, the rich man reduced to poverty is no longer beloved. This is not denied; but when the fmall-pox robs a woman of

her

her beauty, all addresses to her commonly cease; though this is no proof she was not beloved while she was beautiful. Suppose a friend in whom we had the greatest confidence, and for whose mind, disposition, and character, we had the greatest esteem, was suddenly become blind, deaf, and dumb; we should regret in him the loss of a friend; we should still respect his memory; but, in fact, we should no longer love him, because he would have no resemblance to the man who was the object of our friendship. If a minister of state fall into disgrace, we no longer love him; for this reason, because he is the friend who is suddenly become blind, deaf, and dumb. It is nevertheless true, that the man, anxious for preferment, has great tenderness for him who can procure it for him. Whoever has this want of promotion is born the friend of the minister of state. It is, then, our vanity that makes us refuse giving the name to so selfish and necessary a passion. It may, however, be observed, that the most solid and durable friendships are commonly those of virtuous men, however villains themselves are susceptible of it. If, as we are forced to confess, friendship is only the sensation by which two men are united, we cannot deny but that friendships subsist between the wicked, without contradicting the most authentic facts. Can we, for instance, doubt that two conspirators may be united by the
warmest

warmest friendship? That Jaffier did not love James Piero? That Octavius, who was certainly not a virtuous man, did not love Mecænas, who was at best but a weak man? The power of friendship is not in proportion to the virtue of two friends, but to the force of the interest by which they are united. HELVETIUS.

FUTURE PUNISHMENTS.

IF Supreme Justice avenges itself on the wicked, it avenges itself here below. It is you and your errors, ye nations! that are its ministers of vengeance. It employs the evils you bring on each other, to punish the crimes for which you deserve them. It is in the insatiable hearts of mankind, corroding with envy, avarice, and ambition, that their avenging passions punish them for their vices amidst all the false appearances of prosperity. Where is the necessity of seeking a hell in another life, when it is to be found even in this, in the hearts of the wicked?

Where our momentary necessities or senseless desires have an end, there ought our passions and our vices to end also. Of what perversity can pure spirits be susceptible? As they stand in need of nothing, to what end should they be vicious? If destitute of our grosser senses, all their happiness consists in the contemplation of things, they
cannot

cannot be defirous of any thing but good; and whoever ceafes to be wicked, is it poffible he fhould be eternally miferable?   ROUSSEAU.

FUTURE REWARDS AND PUNISHMENTS.

MAN is confidered as a moral, becaufe he is regarded as an accountable, being: But an accountable being, as the word expreffes, is a being that muft give an account of its actions to fome other; and that confequently muft regulate them according to the good liking of this other. Man is accountable to God and his fellow-creatures. But though he is, no doubt, principally accountable to God, in the order of time he muft neceffarily conceive himfelf as accountable to his fellow-creatures, before he can form any idea of the Deity, or of the rules by which that Divine Being will judge of his conduct. A child furely conceives itfelf as accountable to its parents, and is elevated or caft down by the thought of their merited approbation or difapprobation, long before it forms any idea of its accountablenefs to the Deity, or of the rules by which that Divine Being will judge of its conduct. The great Judge of the world has, for the wifeft reafons, thought proper to interpofe between the weak eye of human reafon and the throne of his eternal juftice a degree of obfcurity scurity and darkness, which, though it does not entirely cover that great tribunal from the view of mankind, yet renders the impression of it faint and feeble, in comparison of what might be expected from the grandeur and importance of so mighty an object. If those infinite rewards and punishments, which the Almighty has prepared for those who obey or resist his will, were perceived as distinctly as we foresee the frivolous and temporary retaliations which we may expect from one another, the weakness of human nature, astonished at the immensity of objects so little fitted to its comprehension, could no longer attend to the little affairs of this world: and it is absolutely impossible that the business of society could have been carried on, if, in this respect, there had been a fuller revelation of the intentions of Providence than that which has already been made. A. SMITH.

FUTURE STATE.

CICERO, in his speech for Cluentius, says to a full senate, What hurt does death to him? All the idle tales about hell none of us give the least credit to; then what has death deprived him of? Nothing but the feeling of pain.—Does not Cæsar, Catiline's friend, in order to save that wretch from an indictment brought against him by the same Cicero, object, that to put a criminal to death is not punishing him; that death is nothing; that it is only the end of our sufferings; and that it is rather a happy than a fatal moment? And did not Cicero and the whole senate yield to these arguments?

VOLTAIRE.

G.

GALLANTRY.

Nature has implanted in all living creatures an affection between the sexes, which even in the fiercest and most rapacious animals is not merely confined to the satisfaction of the bodily appetite, but begets a friendship and mutual sympathy, which runs through the whole tenor of their lives; nay, even in those species where nature limits the indulgence of this appetite to one season and to one object, and forms a kind of marriage or association between a single male and female, there is yet a visible complacency and benevolence, which extends farther, and mutually softens the affections of the sexes towards each other. How much more must this have place in man, where the confinement of the appetite is not natural; but either is derived accidentally from some strong charm of love, or arises from reflections on duty and convenience? Nothing, therefore, can proceed less from affectation than the passion of gallantry. It is natural in the highest degree. Art and education, in the most elegant courts, make no more alteration on it, than on all the other laudable passions. They only turn the mind more towards it; they refine it; they polish it; and give it a proper grace and expression.—But gallantry is as generous as it is natural. Nature has given man the superiority above woman, by endowing him with greater strength both of mind and body: it is his part to alleviate that superiority as much as possible by the generosity of his behaviour, and by a studied deference and complaisance for all her inclinations and opinions. Barbarous nations display this superiority, by reducing their females to the most abject slavery; by confining them, by beating them, by selling them, by killing them: But the male sex among a polite people, discover their superiority in a more generous, though not less evident manner; by civility, by respect, by complaisance, and in a word by gallantry.——— Gallantry is not less consistent with wisdom and prudence, than with nature and generosity; and, when under proper regulations, contributes more than any other invention to the entertainment and improvement of the youth of both sexes. Among every species of animals, Nature has founded on the love between the sexes their sweetest and best enjoyment. But the satisfaction of the bodily appetite is not alone sufficient to gratify the mind; and even among brute creatures, we find that their play and dalliance, and other expressions of fondness, form the greatest part of the entertainment. In rational beings, we must certainly admit the mind for a considerable share. Were we to rob the feast of all its garniture of reason, discourse, sympathy, friendship, and gaiety, what remains would scarcely be worth acceptance in the judgment of the truly elegant and luxurious. —What better school for manners than the company of virtuous women; where the mutual endeavour to please must insensibly polish the mind; where the example of female softness and modesty must communicate itself to their admirers; and where the delicacy of that sex puts every one on his guard, lest he give offence by any breach of decency? HUME.

GENIUS.

GENIUS is properly the faculty of invention, by means of which a man is qualified for making new discoveries in science, or for producing original works of art. We may ascribe taste, judgement,

ment, or knowledge, to a man who is incapable of invention; but we cannot reckon him a man of genius. In order to determine how far he merits that character, we must inquire, whether he has discovered any new principle in science, or invented any new art, or carried those arts, which are already practised, to a higher degree of perfection than former masters? Or, whether, at least, in matters of science, he has improved on the discoveries of his predecessors, and reduced principles formerly known to a greater degree of simplicity and consistence, or traced them through a train of consequences hitherto unknown? or, in the arts, designed some new work, different from those of his predecessors, though perhaps not excelling them? Whatever falls short of this is servile imitation, or a dull effort of plodding industry, which, as not implying invention, can be deemed no proof of genius, whatever capacity, skill, or diligence it may evidence. But if a man shows invention, no intellectual defects which his performance may betray can forfeit his claim to genius. His invention may be irregular, wild, undisciplined; but still it is regarded as an infallible mark of real natural genius: and the degree of this faculty that we ascribe to him, is always in proportion to our estimate of the novelty, the difficulty, or the dignity of his invention.

GERARD.

GOD.

GOD.

NEWTON was fully perfuaded of the exiftence of a GOD; and by that term underftood, not only an infinite, almighty, eternal, creative Being, but a mafter, who had eftablifhed a relation between himfelf and his creatures; as, without this relation, the knowledge of a God is only a barren idea, which would feem to invite every reafoner of a perverfe nature to the practice of vice by the hopes of impunity.

Accordingly, that great Philofopher, at the end of his *Principia*, makes a fingular remark, namely, That we do not fay, My eternal, my infinite, becaufe thefe attributes do not at all relate to our nature; but we fay, My God: and are thereby to underftand the mafter and preferver of our life, the object of our thoughts. Newton's philofophy leads to the knowledge of a Supreme Being, who freely created and arranged all things. For if the world be finite; if there be a vacuum, the exiftence of matter is not neceffary; and therefore has received exiftence from a free caufe. If matter gravitates, it does not appear to gravitate from its nature, as it is extended by its nature; it has therefore received its gravitation from God. If the planets, in a fpace void of refiftance, revolve one way rather than another, the hand of their Creator

Creator must have directed their course that way with an absolute freedom.

It may, perhaps, appear strange to many, that among all the proofs of the existence of a God, the strongest in Newton's opinion is that of final causes. The design, or rather the designs, various *ad infinitum*, displayed in the most enormous and most minute parts of the universe, form a demonstration, which, from its being so manifestly sensible, is little regarded by some philosophers; but Newton thought that these infinite relations could only be the work of an artist infinitely wise. He made little account of the proof from the succession of beings. It is commonly said, that if men, animals, vegetables, and whatever compose this world, were eternal, a series of generations without cause must of consequence be admitted. The existence of these beings, it is said, would have no origin; no eternal can be supposed to rise again from generation to generation without a beginning; no eternal, because no one can exist of itself. Thus every thing would be effect, and nothing cause. This argument appeared to him founded only on the ambiguity of *generations*, and of beings *formed one by the other*. For Atheists, who admit a plenum, answer, that there are, properly speaking, no generations: there are not several substancès: the universe is a whole, necessarily existing, incessantly displaying itself.

itself. It is one and the same being, whose nature is immutable in its substance, and eternally varied in its modifications. Thus the argument drawn from the succession of beings would, perhaps, prove very little against an Atheist who should deny the plurality of beings. He would have recourse to those ancient axioms, That nothing is produced by nothing; that one substance cannot produce another; that every thing is eternal and necessary.

Matter, says the Atheist, is necessary, because it exists; motion is necessary, because nothing is at rest; and motion is so necessary, that in nature never any motive forces are lost.

What is to-day was yesterday; therefore it was before yesterday, and thus recurring without end. No person will dare to say, that things shall return to nothing; how then dare to say, that they came from nothing? In a word, I know not if there be a metaphysical proof more striking, and which speaks more strongly to man, than the admirable order in the world; and whether there has ever been a finer argument than the following, *The heavens declare the glory of God.* Accordingly, you see that Newton, at the end of his Optics and Principia, uses no other. No reasoning appeared to him more grand and convincing in favour of a Deity than that of Plato, who makes one of his interlocutors say, You think I have

have an intelligent foul, becaufe you perceive order in my words and actions; furely, then, from the order you fee in this world, there muft be in it a fpirit fupremely intelligent.

But if the exiftence of an eternally almighty Being be proved, it is not equally proved that this Being is infinitely good in the general fenfe of the word.

This is the grand refuge of the Atheift. If I admit a God, fays he, this God muft be goodnefs itfelf. He who has given me a being, fhould alfo give me happinefs: but I fee only diforder and calamity among mankind. The neceffity of an eternal matter offends me lefs, than a Creator dealing fo harfhly with his creatures. My doubts are not to be removed by being told, that a firft man, compofed of a body and foul, offended his Creator, and that mankind fuffers for his offence. For if our bodies are derived from the firft man, our fouls are not; and even if they are, it feems the moft horrid injuftice, for the punifhment to defcend from the father to the children.

It is evident, that the Americans, and the people of the old world, the Negroes and the Laplanders, are not at all defcended from that firft man. The interior conftitution of the organs of the Negroes is a palpable demonftration of this. ——I had, therefore, rather admit the neceffity of matter, generations, and eternal viciffitudes,

than

than a God, the free author of miserable creatures.

To this, it is answered, The words, *good, comfort,* and *happiness,* are equivocal: what is evil with regard to you, is good in the general plan. Will you deny a God, because you have been afflicted with a fever? You say he owed you happiness: but what reason have you to think so? Why did he owe you this happiness? Was you in any treaty with him? Therefore to be only happy in this life, you need only acknowledge a God. You who cannot pretend to be perfect in any one thing, how can you expect to be perfectly happy? But suppose that in a continual happiness for one hundred years, you may have a fit of the headach, shall this short interval induce you to deny a Creator? Surely no. If, therefore, you do not startle at a quarter of an hour's suffering, why at two hours; why at a day? Why should a year of torment prevail on you to reject the belief of a supreme universal Artisan?

It is proved, that there is in this world more good than evil; for, after all, few men are to be found who really wish for death.

Men are fond of murmuring; there is a pleasure in complaining, but more in living. We delight in viewing only evil, and exaggerating it. Read history, it is replied; what is it more than a continual series of crimes and misfortunes? Agreed;

greed; but histories are only the repositories of great events: tempests only are recorded; calms are overlooked.

After examining the relations between the springs and organs of an animal, and the designs which display themselves in every part, the manner by which this animal receives life, by which he sustains it, and by which he gives it; you readily acknowledge the supreme Artist. Will you then change your opinion, because wolves eat the sheep, and spiders catch flies? Do not you, on the contrary, perceive, that these continual generations, ever devoured, and ever reproduced, are a part of the plan of the universe? Wisdom and power, you say, are perceivable in them, but goodness is still wanting.

In fine, if you may be happy to all eternity, can any pains and afflictions in this life be worth mentioning?

You cannot think the Creator *good*, because there is some evil in this world. But if necessity supply the place of a Supreme Being, will affairs be mended? In the system which admits a God, some difficulties only are to be removed; in all the other systems, we must encounter absurdities.

Philosophy, indeed, plainly shows us, that there is a God; but it cannot teach us what he is, what he is doing, how and wherefore he does it; whether he exists in time or in space; whether he
has

has commanded once, or whether he is always acting; whether he be in matter, or whether he be not there, &c. To himself only these things are known. VOLTAIRE.

On the same Subject.

Though God has given us no innate *ideas* of himself; though he has stampt no original characters on our minds, wherein we may read his being; yet having furnished us with those faculties our minds are endowed with, he hath not left himself without witness; since we have sense, perception, and reason, and cannot want a clear proof of him, as long as we carry ourselves about us. Nor can we justly complain of our ignorance in this great point, since he has so plentifully provided us with the means to discover and know him, so far as is necessary to the end of our being, and the great concernment of our happiness. But though this be the most obvious truth that reason discovers; and though its evidence be (if I mistake not) equal to mathematical certainty; yet it requires thought and attention, and the mind must apply itself to a regular deduction of it from some part of our intuitive knowledge, or else we shall be as uncertain and ignorant of this as of other propositions, which are in themselves capable of clear demonstration. To show, therefore,

fore, that we are capable of knowing, i. e. being certain that there is a God; and how we may come by this certainty, I think we need go no further than ourselves, and that undoubted knowledge we have of our own existence.

Man knows by an intuitive certainty, that bare nothing can no more produce any real being, than it can be equal to two right angles. If a man knows not that non-entity, or the absence of all being, cannot be equal to two right angles, it is impossible he should know any demonstration in Euclid. If, therefore, we know there is some real being, and that non-entity cannot produce any real being, it is an evident demonstration, that from eternity there has been something; since what was not from eternity had a beginning, and what had a beginning must be produced by something else.

Next, it is evident, that what had its being and beginning from another, must also have all that which is in, and belongs to its being, from anoother too. All the powers it has must be owing to, and received from, the same source. This eternal source, then, of all being, must also be the source and original of all power; and so this eternal Being must be also the most powerful.

Again, a man finds in himself perception and knowledge: we have then got one step further; and we are certain now, that there is not only some being, but some knowing intelligent being in the world.

There was a time, then, when there was no knowing being, and when knowledge began to be; or else there has been also a knowing being from eternity. If it be said, there was a time when no being had any knowledge, when that eternal being was void of all understanding; I reply, that then it was impossible there should ever have been any knowledge: it being as impossible that things wholly void of knowledge, and operating blindly, and without any perception, should produce a knowing being, as it is impossible that a triangle should make itself three angles bigger than two right ones. For it is as repugnant to the idea of senseless matter, that it should put into itself sense, perception, and knowledge, as it is repugnant to the idea of a triangle, that it should put into itself greater angles than two right ones.

Thus from the consideration of ourselves, and what we infallibly find in our own constitution, our reason leads us to the knowledge of this certain and evident truth, That there is an eternal, most powerful, and most knowing Being; which, whether any one will please to call God, it matters not. The thing is evident; and from this idea duly considered, will easily be deduced all those other attributes which we ought to ascribe to this eternal Being. If, nevertheless, any one should

be

be found so senselessly arrogant, as to suppose man alone knowing and wise, but yet the product of mere ignorance and chance, and that all the rest of the universe acted only by that blind haphazard; I shall leave with him that very rational and emphatical rebuke of Tully l. ii. *De Leg.* to be considered at his leisure. "What can be more "sillily arrogant and misbecoming, than for a man "to think that he has a mind and understanding "in him, but yet in all the universe beside there "is no such thing? Or that those things, which "with the utmost stretch of his reason he can "scarce comprehend, should be moved and ma- "naged without any reason at all?" *Quid est enim verius, quam neminem esse oportere tam stulte arrogantem, ut in se mentem et rationem putet inesse, in cælo mundoque non putet?*

From what has been said, it is plain to me, we have a more certain knowledge of the existence of a God, than of any thing our senses have not immediately discovered to us. Nay, I presume I may say, that we more certainly know that there is a God, than that there is any thing else without us. When I say we know, I mean there is such a knowledge within our reach which we cannot miss, if we will but apply our minds to that as we do to several other inquiries.

LOCKE.

The Prevalence of GOOD over Evil.

That the good overbalances the evil in the phyſical and moral world, is clear from their ſubſiſting with regularity and order. If evil preponderated in the former, nature would ſoon deſtroy herſelf; if in the latter, rational beings would put an end to their own exiſtence. The preference of life to death in one, and the prevalence of order over diſorder in the other, lead us to the ſame deſirable concluſion. From the oppoſition of the different elements in the phyſical world ariſes all phyſical evil; ſuch as ſtorms and earthquakes: but from this ſame oppoſition ariſes all the phyſical good; ſuch as the regularity of the whole, the viciſſitude of ſeaſons, generation, vegetation, and an endleſs variety of other beneficial effects.—From the contrariety of intereſts in the moral world, ariſe wars, devaſtations, and murders; but from the ſame contrariety proceed peace, order, harmony, commerce, art, and ſcience, with every advantage of cultivated ſcience.—To complain that there is pain in the moral world, is as unreaſonable, and as abſurd, as to complain that there is darkneſs in the phyſical; as all cannot be light in the one, ſo neither can all be pleaſure in the other.—It is enough if pleaſure preponderate; and that point has been already eſtabliſhed.

The Difference between a Free and a Despotic Government.

The difference between a free and a despotic state, consists in the manner in which that whole mass of power, which, taken together, is supreme, is, in a free state, distributed among the several ranks of persons that are sharers in it:—in the source from whence their titles to it are successively derived:—in the frequent and easy changes of condition between the governors and governed; whereby the interests of one class are more or less indistinguishably blended with those of the other:—in the responsibility of the governors; or the right which a subject has of having the reasons publicly assigned and canvassed of every act of power that is exerted over him:—in the liberty of the press; or the security with which every man, be he of the one class or the other, may make known his complaints and remonstrances to the whole community:—in the liberty of public associations; or the security with which malcontents may communicate their sentiments, concert their plans, and practise every mode of opposition short of actual revolt, before the executive power can be justified in disturbing them.

Jer. Bentham.

Resistance to GOVERNMENT.

It is then, and not till then, allowable to, if not incumbent on every man, as well on the score of duty as of interest, to enter into measures of resistance; when, according to the best calculation he can make, the probable mischiefs of resistance (speaking with respect to the community in general), appear less to him than the probable mischiefs of submission. This then is to him, that is, to each man in particular, the juncture of resistance. A natural question here is,—By what sign shall this juncture be known? By what common signal alike conspicuous to all? A common sign there is none. Every man must be determined by his own internal persuasion of a balance of utility on the side of resistance; for utility is the test and measure of loyalty.—It may be said, that the letter of the *law* is the measure of government in free states; and not that other loose and general rule, To govern in subservience to the happiness of the people. True it is, that the governing in opposition to the law is one way of governing in opposition to the happiness of the people: the natural effect of such a contempt of the law being, if not actually to destroy, at least to threaten with destruction, all those rights and privileges that are founded on it; rights and privileges, on the enjoyment,

joyment of which that happiness depends. But still this is not sufficient; and that for several reasons. *First*, Because the most mischievous, and under some constitutions the most feasible, method of governing in opposition to the happiness of the people, is, by setting the law itself in opposition to their happiness.—*Secondly*, Because it is a case very conceivable, that a king may, to a great degree, impair the happiness of his people without violating the letter of any single law. *Thirdly*, Because extraordinary occasions may now and then occur, in which the happiness of the people may be better promoted by acting, for the moment, in opposition to the law, than in subservience to it. *Fourthly*, Because it is not any single violation of the law, as such, that can release the people from allegiance; for it is scarce ever any single violation of the law that, by being submitted to, can produce so much mischief as shall surpass the probable mischief of resisting it. If every single instance whatever of such violation were to be deemed an entire release from allegiance, a man, who reflects at all, would scarce find anywhere under the sun, that government which he could allow to subsist for twenty years together. Utility then is the test and measure of all government; and the obligation of governors of every denomination to minister to general happiness, is an obligation superior to, and inclusive of every other.

other. This is the reason why kings, on the one hand, should in general keep within established laws; and, to speak universally, abstain from all such measures as tend to the unhappiness of their subjects: and, on the other hand, why subjects should obey kings as long as they so conduct themselves, and no longer; why they should obey, in short, so long as the probable mischiefs of obedience are less than the probable mischiefs of resistence: why, in a word, taking the whole body together, it is their duty to obey just so long as it is their interest, and no longer—where a state is limited by express convention, as the German Empire, Dutch Provinces, Swiss Cantons, and the ancient Achæan league. There we may be furnished with a common signal of resistance. A certain act is in the instrument of convention specified, with respect to which, the government is therein precluded from issuing a law to a certain effect. A law is issued to that effect notwithstanding. The issuing then of such a law (the sense of it, and likewise the sense of that part of the convention which provides against it, being supposed clear) is a fact notorious and visible to all: in the issuing then of such a law we have a fact which is capable of being taken for that common signal of resistance. These bounds the supreme body has marked out to its authority: of such a demarcation, then, what is the effect? Either

ther none at all; or this, that the difposition to obedience confines itfelf within thefe bounds. Beyond them the difposition is ftopped from extending: beyond them the fubject is no more prepared to obey the governing body of his own ftate, than that of any other. No convention, however, fhould prevent what the parties affected fhall deem a reformation: no difeafe in a ftate fhould be without its remedy. Such might by fome be thought the cafe, where that fupreme body, which in fuch a convention was one of the contracting parties, having incorporated itfelf with that which was the other, no longer fubfifts to give any new modification to the engagement. Although that body itfelf which contracted the engagement be no more, a larger body, from whence the firft is underftood to have derived its title, may ftill fubfift. Let this larger body be confulted. Various are the ways that might be conceived of doing this; and that without any difparagement to the dignity of the fubfifting legiflature: of doing it to fuch effect, as that, fhould the fenfe of fuch larger body be favourable to the alteration, it may be made by a law; which, in this cafe, neither ought to be, nor probably would be, regarded by the people as a breach of the convention.

JER. BENTHAM.

On the same Subject.

RANK, privileges, and prerogatives in a state, are constituted for the good of the state; and those who enjoy them, whether they be called kings, senators, or nobles, or by whatever names or titles they be distinguished, are, to all intents and purposes, the servants of the public, and accountable to the people for the discharge of their respective offices. If such magistrates abuse their trust, in the people lies the right of *deposing*, and consequently of punishing them. And the only reason why abuses which have crept into offices have been connived at, is, that the correcting them, by having recourse to first principles, is far from being easy, except in small states; so that the remedy would often be worse than the disease. But, in the largest states, if the abuses of government should at any time be great and manifest; if the servants of the people, forgetting their masters, and their masters interest, should pursue a separate one of their own; if, instead of considering that they are made for the people, they should consider the people as made for them; if the oppressions and violations of right should be great, flagrant, and universally resented; if, in consequence of these circumstances, it should become manifest, that the risk which would be run in attempting a revolution would be trifling, and the evils which might be apprehended from it, were far lefs than thofe which were actually fuffered, and which were daily increafing; what principles are thofe which ought to reftrain an injured and infulted people from afferting their natural rights, and from changing, or even punifhing their governors, that is, their fervants, who had abufed their truft; or from altering the whole form of their government, if it appeared to be of a ftructure fo liable to abufe? It will be faid, that it is opening a door to rebellion, to affert that magiftrates abufing their power may be fet afide by the people, who are of courfe their own judges when their power is abufed. May not the people, it is faid, abufe their power as well as their governors? I anfwer, It is very poffible they may abufe their power: it is poffible they may imagine themfelves oppreffed when they are not: it is poffible their animofity may be artfully and unreafonably inflamed by ambitious and enterprifing men, whofe views are often beft anfwered by popular tumults and infurrections; and the people may fuffer in confequence of their folly and precipitancy: But what man is there, or what body of men (whofe right to direct their own conduct was never called in queftion) but are liable to be impofed upon, and to fuffer in confequence of their miftaken apprehenfions and precipitate conduct?

With

With respect to large societies, it is very improbable that the people should be too soon alarmed, so as to be driven to these extremities. In such cases, the power of the government, that is, of the governors, must be very extensive and arbitrary; and the power of the people scattered and difficult to be united; so that if a man have common sense, he will see it to be madness to propose, or to lay any measures against the government, except in case of very general and great oppression. Even patriots, in such circumstances, will consider that present evils always appear greater in consequence of their being present; but that the future evils of a revolt, and a temporary anarchy, may be much greater than are apprehended at a distance. They will also consider, that unless their measures be perfectly well laid, and their success decisive, ending in a change, not of men, but of things; not of governors, but of the rules and administration of government, they will only rivet their chains the faster, and bring upon themselves and their country tenfold ruin.

So obvious are these difficulties that lie in the way of procuring redress of grievances by force of arms, that I think we may say, without exception, that in all cases of hostile opposition to government, the people must have been in the right; and that nothing but very great oppression could drive them to such desperate measures. The bulk of a people seldom so much as complain without reason, because they never think of complaining till they feel; so that in all cases of dissatisfaction with government, it is most probable that the people are injured. The case, I own, may be otherwise in states of small extent, where the power of the governors is comparatively small, and the power of the people great and soon united. If it be asked, how far a people may lawfully go in punishing their chief magistrates? I answer, that if the enormity of the offence (which is of the same extent as the injury done to the public) be considered, any punishment is justifiable that a man can incur in human society. It may be said, there are no laws to punish those governors, and we must not condemn persons by laws made *ex post facto;* for this conduct will vindicate the most obnoxious measures of the most tyrannical administration. But I answer, that this is a case, in its own nature, prior to the establishment of any laws whatever; as it affects the very being of society, and defeats the principal ends for which recourse was originally had to it. There may be no fixed law against an open invader who should attempt to seize upon a country, with a view to enslave all its inhabitants; but must not the invader be apprehended, and even put to death, though he hath broken no express law then in being, or none of which he was properly apprised? And why should a man, who takes the advantage of being king, or governor, to subvert the laws and liberties of his country, be considered in any other light than that of a foreign invader? Nay, his crime is much more atrocious; as he was appointed the guardian of the laws and liberties which he subverts, and which he was therefore under the strongest obligation to maintain. In a case, therefore, of this highly criminal nature, *Salus populi suprema est lex;* " That " must be done which the good of the whole re" quires:" and generally kings deposed, banished, or imprisoned, are highly dangerous to a nation; because, let them have governed ever so ill, it will be the interest of some to be their partisans, and to attach themselves to their cause. So plain are these first principles of all government, that they must overcome the meanest prejudices, and carry conviction to every man. Whatever be the form of any government, whoever be the supreme magistrates, or whatever be their number; that is, to whomsoever the power of the society is delegated, their authority is in its own nature reversible. No man can be supposed to resign his natural liberty, but on conditions. These conditions, whether they be expressed or not, must be violated, whenever the plain and obvious ends of government are not answered; and a delegated power, perverted from the intention for which it

was

was bestowed, expires of course. Magistrates, therefore, who consult not the good of the public, and who employ their power to oppress the people, are a public nuisance; and their power is abrogated *ipso facto*. This, however, can only be the case in extreme oppression, when the blessings of society and civil government, great and important as they are, are bought too dear; when it is better not to be governed at all, than to be governed in such a manner; or, at least, when the hazard of a change of government would be apparently the less evil of the two; and, therefore, these occasions rarely occur in the course of human affairs: but where they do occur, resistance is a duty; and a regard to the good of society will certainly justify this conduct of the people.

PRIESTLEY.

Civil GOVERNMENT.

WHETHER government be the appointment of a pretended religion; whether originating with the Patriarchs; or owing to a social compact?—are not matters worthy of inquiry. If it produce happiness at home, and be just and beneficent to all the world; it is good, it is valuable, and should be supported: If it be otherwise; if it render people corrupt, depraved, and miserable; if it be unjust and oppressive to its dependants and neighbours; its origin is not worth investigating: for, be its descent what it may, it is an injury, and an evil, and a curse; and mankind may and ought to treat it as such.

WILLIAMS.

GOVERNMENT.

HAD every man sufficient sagacity to perceive, at all times, the strong interest which binds him to the observance of justice and equity, and strength of mind sufficient to persevere in a steady adherence to a general and a distinct interest, in opposition to the allurements of present pleasure and advantage; there had never, in that case, been any such thing as government or political society; but each man, following his natural liberty, had lived in entire peace with all others. What need of positive laws, where natural justice is of itself a sufficient restraint? Why create magistrates, where there never arises any disorder or iniquity? Why abridge our native freedom, when, in every instance, the utmost exertion of it is found innocent and beneficial? It is evident, that if government were totally useless, it never could have place; and that the sole foundation of the duty of allegiance is the advantage which it procures to society, by preserving peace and order among mankind. As the obligation to justice is
founded

founded entirely on the interests of society, which require mutual abstinence from property, in order to preserve peace among mankind; it is evident, that when the execution of justice would be attended with very pernicious consequences, that virtue must be suspended, and give place to public utility, in such extraordinary and pressing emergencies. The maxim, *Fiat justitia et ruat cælum*, " Let justice be performed, though the universe be destroyed," is apparently false; and by sacrificing the end to the means, shows a preposterous idea of the subordination of duties. What governor of a town makes any scruple of burning the suburbs, when they facilitate the advances of the enemy? Or what general abstains from plundering a neutral country, when the necessities of war require it, and he cannot otherwise maintain his army? The case is the same with the duty of allegiance; and common sense teaches us, that as government binds us to obedience only on account of its tendency to public utility, that duty must always, in extraordinary cases, when public ruin would evidently attend obedience, yield to the primary and original obligation. *Salus populi suprema lex;* " The safety of the people is the supreme law." This maxim is agreeable to the sentiments of mankind in all ages. Accordingly we may observe, that no nation, that could find any remedy, ever yet suffered the cruel ravages of a tyrant, or were blamed for their refiftance. Thofe who took up arms againft Dionyfius or Nero, or Philip II. have the favour of every reader in the perufal of their hiftory; and nothing but the moft violent perverfion of common fenfe can ever lead us to condemn them. Government is a mere human invention for the intereft of fociety; and where the tyranny of the governor removes this intereft, it alfo removes the obligation to obedience. Refiftance, therefore, being admitted in extraordinary cafes, the queftion can only be with regard to the degree of neceffity which can juftify refiftance, and render it lawful and commendable; which can only be in defperate cafes, when the public is in the higheft danger from violence and tyranny. For befides the mifchiefs of a civil war, which commonly attend infurrections, it is certain that, where a difpofition to rebellion appears among any people, it is one chief caufe of tyranny in the rulers. Thus the tyrannicide or affaffination approved of by ancient maxims, inftead of keeping tyrants and ufurpers in awe, made them ten times more fierce and unrelenting; and is now juftly, on that account, abolifhed by the laws of nations. HUME.

On the same Subject.

THE general good is the end of all juſt government; and all the rules of conduct agreed upon, all the ſtatutes, laws, and precepts enacted and promulgated, are made with a view to promote and ſecure the public good: and therefore the very nature and deſign of government requires new laws to be made, whenever it is found that the old ones are not ſufficient; and old ones to be repealed, whenever they are found to be miſchievous in their operation. If the eſſential parts of any ſyſtem of civil government are found to be inconſiſtent with the general good, the end of government requires that ſuch bad ſyſtem ſhould be demoliſhed, and a new one formed, by which the public weal ſhall be more effectually ſecured. And further, if, under any conſtitution of government, the adminiſtration ſhould vary from the fundamental deſign of promoting and ſecuring the common good; in ſuch caſe the ſubjects are in duty bound to join all their ſtrength to reduce matters to their *original good order.*

LAYTHROP's *Sermon at Boſton.*

Principles of GOVERNMENT.

TO begin with firſt principles, we muſt, for the ſake of gaining clear ideas on the ſubject, do what

what almost all political writers have done before us; that is, we must suppose a number of people existing, who experience the inconvenience of living independent and unconnected; who are exposed without redress to insults and wrongs of various kinds, and are too weak to procure themselves many of the advantages which they are sensible might easily be compassed by united strength. These people, if they would engage the protection of the whole body, and join their force in enterprises and undertakings calculated for the common good, must voluntarily resign some part of their natural liberty, and submit their conduct to the direction of the community: for without these conceptions, such an alliance, attended with such advantages, could not be formed. Were these people few in number, and living within small distances of one another, it might be easy for them to assemble upon every occasion, in which the whole body was concerned; and every thing might be determined by the votes of the majority, provided they had previously agreed the votes of the majority to be decisive. But were the society numerous, their habitations remote, and the occasions on which the whole body must interpose frequent, it would be absolutely impossible that all the members of the state should assemble, or give their attention to public business. In this case, though, with Rousseau, it

be

be giving up their liberty, there muſt be deputies or public officers appointed to act in name of the whole body; and, in a ſtate of very great extent, where all the people could never be aſſembled, the whole power of the community muſt neceſſarily, and almoſt irreverſibly, be lodged in the hands of theſe deputies. It may be ſaid, no ſociety on earth was ever formed in the manner repreſented above. I anſwer, it is true; becauſe all governments whatever have been in ſome meaſure compulſory, tyrannical, and oppreſſive in their origin; but the method I have deſcribed muſt be allowed to be the only equitable and fair method of forming a ſociety. And ſince every man retains, and can never be deprived of his natural right (founded on a regard to the general good) of relieving himſelf from all oppreſſion, that is, from every thing that has been impoſed upon him without his own conſent; this muſt be the only true and proper foundation of all the governments ſubſiſting in the world, and that to which the people who compoſe them have an unalienable right to bring them back. It muſt neceſſarily be underſtood, then, whether it be expreſſed or not, that all people live in ſociety for their mutual advantage; ſo that the good and happineſs of the members, that is, the majority of the members, of any ſtate, is the great ſtandard by which every thing relating to that ſtate muſt finally be
deter-

determined. And though it may be supposed, that a body of people may be bound by a voluntary resignation of all their interests to a single person, or to a few, it can never be supposed that the resignation is obligatory on their posterity; because it is manifestly *contrary to the good of the whole that it should be so.* In treating of particular regulations in states, this principle must necessarily obtrude itself; all arguments in favour of any law being always drawn from a consideration of its tendency to promote the public good. Virtue and right conduct consist in those affections and actions which terminate in general utility; justice and veracity, for instance, having nothing intrinsically excellent in them, separate from their relation to the happiness of mankind; and the whole system of right to power, property, and every thing else in society, must be regulated by the same consideration: the decisive question, when any of these subjects are examined, being, What is it that the good of the community requires?

PRIESTLEY.

END OF THE FIRST VOLUME.

CHARLES ELLIOT, Bookseller in Edinburgh, begs leave to inform the Public, that he has just purchased from the Proprietors the whole remaining COPIES of the following extensive and valuable Work, which reflects honour upon the Editors, and that part of the country which produced it.

JUST PUBLISHED,
Now completed in Ten very large Volumes in Quarto, containing above 10,000 pages of close print, illustrated with about 400 Copperplates,
(Price TWELVE POUNDS in Boards),

ENCYCLOPÆDIA BRITANNICA;
OR, A
DICTIONARY OF ARTS, SCIENCES, &c.
ON A PLAN ENTIRELY NEW:
By which
The different Sciences and Arts are digested into the Form of distinct
TREATISES OR SYSTEMS,
Comprehending the History, Theory, and Practice of each, according to the latest discoveries and improvements;
And
Full Explanations are given of the various detached Parts of Knowledge, whether relating to natural and artificial objects, or to matters ecclesiastical, civil, military, &c.

Together with
A Description of all the Countries, Cities, principal Mountains, Seas, Rivers, &c. throughout the World;
A general History, ancient and modern, of the different Empires, Kingdoms, and States;
And an Account of the Lives of the most eminent Persons in every nation, from the earliest Ages down to the present Times.

The whole compiled from
The writings of the best Authors in several languages; the most approved Dictionaries, as well of general science as of particular branches; the transactions, journals, and memoirs of learned societies, both at home and abroad; the manuscript lectures of eminent professors on different sciences; and a variety of original materials, furnished by an extensive correspondence.

Sold in London by G. G. J. and J. Robinson, N° 25. Paternoster-Row.

Of whom and C. ELLIOT *may be had,*
1. The Independent, a novel, by the author of Velina, 2 vols 12mo, 6s.

2. Velina,

Books printed for C. ELLIOT, *Edinburgh.*

2. Velina, a poetical fragment, by the author of the Independent, 8vo, 1s. 6d. sewed.
3. Maria, or the generous ruſtic, 2s. 6d.
4. Mrs Mackiver's cookery and paſtry, a new edition. This book upon trial will be found the moſt uſeful of any, it being eaſy and plain, and adapted to the middling ranks of life, 12mo, 2s. 6d.
5. Dalrymple's cookery, upon the moſt elegant and neweſt taſte, 8vo, 6s.
6. Donaldſon's elements of beauty, and reflections on the harmony of ſenſibility and reaſon, 8vo, 2s. boards.
7. Michael Bruce's poems on different ſubjects, 2s. 6d.
8. Callendar of Craigforth's two Scottiſh ballads, viz. the Gauberlunzie man, and Chriſt's kirk on the green, with many curious notes, 8vo, 2s. 6d. boards.
9. Charmer, a moſt excellent collection of the neweſt and beſt ſongs, 2 vols, 12mo, 6s.
10. Lindeſay's (Sir D. of the Mount, Lyon King at Arms), whole poetical works, 12mo, 1s. 6d.
11. Lindeſay of Pitſcottie's hiſtory of Scotland from 1436 to 1604, very curious, with index, 12mo, 3s. 6d.
12. Crawford's memoirs of the affairs of Scotland from 1567 to 1581, 12mo, 3s.
13. Farces, a collection of the moſt eſteemed, performed on the Britiſh ſtage, 4 vols, containing 57 pieces. Price only 12s. bound, or 2s. 6d. each vol. in boards.
14. Hume's dialogues on natural religion, 8vo, 5s.
15. Taylor and Shinner's roads through Scotland, from an actual ſurvey, on 67 very large copperplates. The diſtances are exactly marked in Engliſh miles; and every gentleman's houſe, river, rivulet, ruins, or public buildings, for ſeveral miles on each ſide of the road, exactly laid down, neatly bound for the pocket, only 10s. 6d.
16. Scott's (Will. of Edin.) ſpelling-book, third edition, with his grammar, &c. price only 1s.
17. ―― leſſons on elocution, third edition, much enlarged and improved, 2s 6d.
18. ―― eſſay on elocution, 1s. 6d. ſewed.
19. ―― arithmetic, 2s. 6d. bound.
20. ―― new ſpelling and pronouncing dictionary in the preſs.
21. ―― elements of geometry, 12mo, 3s.
22. Perry's oratory, an Engliſh collection for ſchools, 12mo, 2s. 6d.

www.ingramcontent.com/pod-product-compliance
Lightning Source LLC
Chambersburg PA
CBHW020307240426
43673CB00039B/734